Extending
Knowledge in Practice
Primary Science

Extending

Knowledge in Practice

Primary Science

Judith Roden
Hellen Ward
Hugh Ritchie

Acknowledgements

The authors and publisher would like to thank the following for permission to reproduce copyright material.

'The Sound Collector' by Roger McGough from *Pillow Talk* (Roger McGough 1990) is reproduced by kind permission of PFD (*www.pfd.co.uk*) on behalf of Roger McGough.

Jacket illustrations by Derek Whitely for INSECTS by Gwen Allen and Joan Denslow (The Clue Books, OUP, 1969), reproduced by permission of Oxford University Press.

Covers from MINI BEASTS FIRST HAND SCIENCE published in 2003 by Franklin Watts, a division of The Watts Publishing Group Ltd., 338 Euston Road, London NW1 3BH.

The cover of Insects of Britain and Northern Europe 1999, Bob Gibbons, reproduced by permission of HarperCollins Publishers Ltd., London. Copyright in the customised version vests in Canterbury Christ Church University.

Every effort has been made to trace the copyright holders and to obtain their permission for the use of copyright material. The publisher and authors will gladly receive any information enabling them to rectify any error or omission in subsequent editions.

First published in 2007 by Learning Matters Ltd.

British Library Cataloguing in Publication Data
A CIP record for this book is available from the British Library.

ISBN: 978 1 84445 106 7

Cover design by Topics – The Creative Partnership
Text design by Code 5 Design Associates Ltd
Project management by Deer Park Productions, Tavistock
Typeset by PDQ Typesetting Ltd, Newcastle under Lyme
Printed and bound in Great Britain by Cromwell Press Ltd, Trowbridge, Wiltshire

Learning Matters
33 Southernhay East
Exeter EX1 1NX
Tel: 01392 215560
info@learningmatters.co.uk
www.learningmatters.co.uk

Contents

Introduction

This book provides an opportunity for readers to develop a deeper understanding of science through exposure to and consideration of scientific ideas and theory. These are linked to and translated into practice at the Foundation and Key Stages 1 and 2 of the science National Curriculum. The aim is to identify activities for use in the classroom by readers to help extend their understanding of science and teaching of science whilst supporting reflection on aspects of science in the primary classroom.

The target audience for this book includes primary trainee teachers, Newly Qualified Teachers and others wishing to extend their knowledge, understanding and teaching of science who work with children aged three to eleven. Despite the need for trainees to hold minimal qualifications in English, mathematics and science for entry into programmes of initial teacher training, it could be stated that this requirement is inadequate in terms of the subject knowledge needed to teach science effectively in the primary classroom. This demand has often affected the quality of provision for science in the classroom, but also the confidence of some teachers. This sometimes leads to a reluctance to teach science following training, particularly if science does not have a high profile in their school.

Each chapter in this book will explore aspects of science in relevant and meaningful contexts that aims to extend trainees' understanding. Some suggested classroom activities will be drawn from and will provide opportunities to extend good practice in science. However, the approach will be, of necessity, indicative rather than exhaustive. Activities will include 'hands-on' as well as those designed to develop thinking skills. Readers will be encouraged to try out tasks in the classroom and to reflect on their own and others' practice. This book draws from and complements other publications in the Learning Matters Achieving QTS series, notably Peacock, G., et al. (2007) *Primary Science: Knowledge and Understanding* (3rd edition); Sharp, J., et al. (2007) *Primary Science: Teaching Theory and Practice* (3rd edition); and Roden, J. (2005) *Primary Science Reflective Reader*.

Since the late 1960s, there has been an underlying problem related to a lack of understanding of science amongst those who favoured primary teaching. Although the situation is changing slowly, many trainees in primary schools are still women and there have been many contributory factors influencing the negative attitudes of women to science in the United Kingdom. Factors such as females rejecting science at an early age through choice of subjects at secondary school, their own education with a lack of a 'hands-on' investigative approach and too much emphasis on dry 'facts to be learned', which contribute to making science unappealing. This has led to few teachers being willing to teach science and teachers often lacking the confidence to do so. School-based factors such as a real or perceived lack of easily accessible resources, lack of time, and the potential noise and mess in the classroom have limited the type of science carried out. For some the fear of behaviour problems when pupils are allowed freedom to move around the room to select materials for practical work rather than sitting at a desk has prevented child-centred learning. For others the fear of 'not knowing the answer' when pupils asked questions, has led to a delivery of a predominantly facts-based model of science teaching. There is also a lack of recognition that classroom practice and schemes of work require attention. This is in part due to a lack of leadership or support for science coupled with a limited view of success in science being related to Key Stage 2 national test outcomes rather than pupil motivation and participation.

The prevalent view amongst the Department for Education and Skills (DfES) and Her Majesty's Inspectors has been that raising the knowledge base of trainee teachers would improve the teaching of science in schools. In 1998 the ITT National Curriculum for primary science was set out in detail in Annex E of the Department for Education and Employment (DfEE) (1998) *Teaching: High Status, High Standards* Circular Number 4/98. This specified the subject knowledge trainees were expected to know and understand. In reality this led to many courses of initial teacher training focusing on and monitoring trainees developing subject knowledge, sometimes at the expense of analysis and reflection on how the knowledge could be used in primary schools. Whilst there was recognition that trainees needed frequent opportunities to develop their own understanding through 'hands-on' activities and discussion, the overt focus on the systematic development of science subject knowledge did not provide a very effective model. The focus on content rather than process reduces the learners' ability to make links. It is generally accepted that effective learning occurs when learners can relate the science to their current understanding and have a reason to develop this. Therefore much of the subject knowledge disseminated did not embed and trainee confidence was not increased.

The changes to science at Key Stage 4 and the likely impact of the strategy on teaching at Key Stage 3 may change the historical emphasis on content and 'stuff' that is taught. It could also alter the perceived relevance of science as a subject worthy of study at A level. The focus on how science works with the reduction in the content of the programme of study seriously signals that changes are needed. Early responses from pupils suggest the new GCSE courses including twenty-first-century science have relevance and are enjoyable to study.

Qualifying to Teach (DfES/TTA, 2002, 2005) has continued to emphasise the need for sound subject knowledge but unlike Circular 4/98 does not specify any subject matter content. Indeed Standard 2.1 merely stated that 'those awarded Qualified Teacher Status must demonstrate that they have a secure knowledge and understanding of the subject(s) they are trained to teach'. Whilst some science educators heaved a sigh of relief at the change, there is still an uncertainty about the **level** of subject knowledge emphasised in science within programmes of ITT. There is also a requirement for training institutions to monitor trainees developing subject knowledge throughout their training. This can lead to a separation of the acquisition and development of subject knowledge from its application in the classroom. The most recent standards to come into effect in September 2007 continue this trend.

Therefore, this book is intended to make explicit links between the necessary subject knowledge and how this underpinning knowledge translates into practice in the classroom. It will do so by:

- **providing an opportunity to develop a deeper understanding of specific aspects of science related to the science aspects of the Curriculum Guidance for the Foundation Stage (CGFS) and the Science National Curriculum at Key Stages 1 and 2;**
- **making some connections between the various aspects of science located in a cross-curricular context;**
- **applying this knowledge to practice in the Early Years and the primary science curriculum;**
- **helping trainees translate this into more effective teaching by providing pointers for their reflection on their own practice.**

Format of chapters

Essentially, each of the following chapters has a common format. The starting point for each will be an exploration of your own understanding of the topic and the essential vocabulary associated with it. The first reason for this is simply that at whatever level we are teaching, we should always 'start where the learners are' and we believe that it is important to model good practice. Secondly, you will be aware that some scientific words often mean different things in everyday life to the accepted definition in science, for example, 'force' or 'amphibian'. In science, each scientific word has its own very precise, specific definition and it is important that you clarify your own understanding of terms at an early stage before you begin to teach a science topic. Otherwise, it is likely that you may, inadvertently, reinforce incorrect understanding. Indeed, a general lack of science vocabulary is currently a major concern in science education. Recently, Ofsted (QCA, 2005) reported that pupils were still not developing sufficient scientific vocabulary as part of their science learning. Teachers are concerned that this lack of familiarity with scientific words will impact on pupils' later understanding of science and, as QCA (2005) suggests, this may have an impact on children's science learning well beyond the primary years.

You will be aware that science learning is hindered by the holding of misconceptions. Learners of all ages often do not realise they hold misconceptions and, unfortunately, will cling to their misunderstandings even when their ideas are challenged by discussion. The practice of exploring children's ideas before teaching has been long advocated, but, it may well be more important for you to know, beforehand, the misconceptions you are likely to meet within a topic and to plan flexibly to be able to provide appropriate activities to challenge these misconceptions when met in the classroom (Roden, 2005). Therefore, in each chapter, common misconceptions will be revealed and explained. Research summaries, will be presented, but to ensure relevance to the primary age range, only those misconceptions that are most relevant to the primary years will be considered.

Early in each chapter you will be asked to think about the background information, i.e. the 'basic key ideas' related to the topic. These will then be revisited later when more 'in-depth subject knowledge' underpinning the topic will be presented.

Each chapter will then provide a number of activities specifically chosen to extend pupils' learning and to challenge identified misconceptions. However, these are only examples of what might be provided. It is not intended to provide specific activities for a specific year group, as we believe that because all pupils have different needs, within different schools and even within different classes, you, as the professional, should tailor activities to meet the needs of your pupils. Indeed it is possible, by increasing or decreasing the demands you make on specific pupils, to use the same starting point for different ages and abilities and in doing so differentiating and reinforcing ideas throughout the primary years.

Reflective tasks within each chapter will be of two types, i.e. those relating to:

1. your own knowledge and understanding;
2. an interactive classroom activity, i.e. related to your pupils rather than yourself.

There are also practical tasks for you to undertake.

In all chapters there will be three layers of tasks presented at the Foundation Stage, Key Stage 1 and Key Stage 2. These are likely to include:

- **a sorting or basic skill type task suitable for an individual or a group;**
- **an illustrative task suitable for groups of children; and**
- **some investigative opportunities.**

Additionally, each chapter will have a practical focus e.g. how learning might be assessed as well as providing an explanation of the principles that underpin the activities.

REFERENCES REFERENCES REFERENCES REFERENCES REFERENCES REFERENCES

Peacock, G., Sharp, J., Johnsey, R., and Wright, D. (2007) *Primary Science: Knowledge and Understanding*, 3rd edition. Exeter: Learning Matters

Sharp J., Peacock, G., Johnsey, R., Simon, S. and Smith, R. (2007) *Primary Science: Teaching Theory and Practice*, 3rd edition. Exeter: Learning Matters

QCA (2005) *Science 2004/5 annual report on curriculum and assessment* December 2005. London: QCA

National Assessment Agency (NAA) (2006) Implications for teaching and learning from the 2006 Science National Curriculum tests. London: QCA

Roden, J. (2005) *Primary Science Reflective Reader*. Exeter: Learning Matters

PART 1
SCIENTIFIC ENQUIRY

1
Introduction to scientific enquiry

Scientific enquiry encompasses a whole range of aspects of both 'hands-on' and 'minds-on' activities that includes ideas and evidence as well as investigative skills, obtaining and considering and presenting data. In some ways, ideas and evidence are the most exciting aspect of science and are what science really is all about. Over the course of history scientists often had ideas about how the world worked and tested these out. The fun part of science was when their ideas did not work because they had to find another way to explain things. Ideas and evidence about the world started with the ancients who thought that the world was flat and was supported in space in a big bowl of water. It had to be held up by something and they knew things floated! When sailors did not fall off the edge and when only the top of a sail was seen at the horizon, rather than a smaller whole boat, the flat world idea had to be changed.

As with scientists in real life, investigative skills are fundamental to children's learning in scientific enquiry. These encompass a range of skills, often termed science 'process' skills that help pupils to explore, make sense of the world and to develop their knowledge and understanding of things scientific. Young children's instinctive exploration of the world, from birth, forms the basis for more exploration including opportunities to extend learning during the Foundation Stage and more formal work, both structured and unstructured, throughout Key Stages 1 and 2.

In the Foundation Stage, science is part of the 'Knowledge and understanding of the world' where there is a need for teachers to provide opportunities for exploration. Scientific enquiry (Sc1) is the first programme of study within the National Curriculum where it is a statutory requirement that should be taught through contexts located within the other three programmes of study, i.e. life processes and living things, materials and their properties and physical processes. This means that scientific enquiry should not be taught separately from other aspects of the National Curriculum, but that it should be woven into schools' schemes of work. Included in this approach is the whole range of aspects including ideas and evidence, observation, asking questions, planning and presenting evidence, and considering evidence and evaluating. All these aspects are linked so that it is difficult to separate them out and although from time to time specific skills will be focused on but to do so all the time would be artificial.

Teachers often find investigative learning challenging and yet it is the aspect of learning most enjoyed by pupils in schools. Mirroring previous reports, Ofsted inspectors (QCA, 2005) found that many teachers spend little time on Sc1. Alarmingly, some teachers even suggested that with class sizes over 26 it was difficult to teach practical lessons. The reasons that investigative elements of the Sc1 programme of study are found very challenging are that pupils need to be given freedom to plan, to ask questions and to decide how and what data to collect. In practice, teachers often fail to provide these opportunities. This may be because it is considered easier and more time-effective to tell pupils what to use and what data to collect. This denies pupils the challenge of observing effects and commenting on the outcomes, and also their full entitlement for optimum learning.

Teaching about ideas and evidence can be hard but if links are made between the initial ideas held and how they have changed as new things have been developed, children will see that science is an active process and one that continues today.

In this book an attempt has been made to link the nature of scientific ideas into a range of chapters and introduced the changing ideas where possible. It would have been easy to start each chapter in such a way but science is made up of many other aspects so each chapter has been linked to a theme. Because of the importance of ideas and evidence it occurs as a thread rather than as one theme in one chapter. Similarly, considering evidence and evaluating and presenting evidence have not been treated in individual chapters.

Throughout the book we have tried to encourage a range of recording and communicating strategies. The use of worksheets is mentioned from time to time. Often these are commercially produced materials that are tempting to use because they offer to save time, but frequently do not promote children's skills and offer effective learning. Children do not learn to write wonderful stories by filling the missing words on a sheet provided by the teacher. Shared writing, where all the class copies the same thing into their books does little to develop creative expression. This approach might promote handwriting but few other literacy skills as children's literacy is an emerging process. In the same way, children will not develop their ideas and understanding of science unless they are encouraged to also undertake emergent science writing. Supporting this process requires the teacher to understand the child's literacy level and make choices about what should be recorded and how.

The myth that science is about doing not writing is a dangerous one. This myth damages children's opportunities. In fact there are times when pure practical tasks can add little to the learning of the child. We believe that the recording method should fit the need of the child and the task and should include diagrams, drawings, annotations, photographs, cartoons, floor books and poems. Creative teachers who know their children will promote different recording strategies with different ability groups, thus helping all from the less literate to the gifted and talented to develop their science knowledge and understanding by explaining their ideas. We hope these points will be borne in mind as you read through the rest of the book.

2
Investigative skills

By the end of this chapter you should:

- **be aware of some of the significant subject knowledge that underpins the range of activities that comprise investigations and the understanding of planning as part of the investigative process;**
- **recognise some of the common problems associated with planning investigative work;**
- **understand the importance of progression within this aspect of learning and be able to use some examples of learning activities from 3–11 years;**
- **identify opportunities for specific basic skill acquisitions, illustrative and investigative approaches within this area;**
- **recognise how pupils can record their findings from the activities in this area, in a variety of ways;**
- **have reflected upon the importance of progression within this aspect.**

Professional Standards for QTS

Q1, Q4, Q7a, Q8, Q10, Q12, Q14, Q15, Q22, Q25b, Q25c, Q25d, Q26b, Q27, Q29, Q30, Q31

Curriculum Guidance for the Foundation Stage and the National Curriculum

In the Foundation Stage pupils should:

- **investigate objects and materials by using all of their senses as appropriate (QCA, p86);**
- **explore objects;**
- **notice and comment on patterns;**
- **look closely at similarities and differences, patterns and change;**
- **ask questions about why things happen and why things work (QCA, p88).**

At Key Stage 1 pupils should be taught to:

- **ask questions, for example, 'How?, 'Why', 'What will happen if . . . ?' and decide how they might find answers to them;**
- **use first-hand experience and simple information sources to answer questions;**
- **think about what might happen before deciding what to do;**
- **recognise when a test or comparison is unfair (DfEE, 1999 p.78).**

At Key Stage 2 pupils should be taught to:

- **ask questions that can be investigated scientifically and decide how to find answers;**
- **consider what sources of information, including first-hand experience and a range of other sources, will they use to answer questions;**
- **think about what might happen or try things out when deciding what to do, what kinds of evidence to collect, and what equipment to use;**
- **make a fair test or comparison by changing one factor and observing or measuring the effect while keeping other factors the same (DfEE, 1999, p83).**

Introduction

This chapter will focus on specific investigative skills, how these might be planned into your teaching and the importance of providing continuity and progression in this crucial aspect of science.

Check your understanding

What do you understand by the following terms? Make a note of your ideas.

Experiment	Basic skills	Control
Fair test	Dependent variable	Independent variable
Investigation	Illustrative activity	Survey

What do you think is the difference between the terms experiment and investigation?

Check your understanding with the Glossary.

PRACTICAL TASK PRACTICAL TASK PRACTICAL TASK PRACTICAL TASK PRACTICAL TASK

This task comes from research by the AKSIS project (see Appendix 1 for the research summary), where teachers at Key Stage 2 and Key Stage 3 were asked whether, in their view, the pupil statements below were scientifically acceptable.

Below are some examples of how pupils have used these words.
Work with a colleague. Talk about how the highlighted words are used in each sentence. Decide for yourself. What do you think?
Indicate whether you think the use of these words is scientifically acceptable in each case.

To make it a **fair test**, I will make sure the force meter is in working order.

To make a **fair test** of how good our pressure-pads are, at detecting burglars, we must make the same person tread on each pad that we test.

When we were testing whether light affected germination of seeds we made it **fair** by watering the seeds equally and putting them all on blotting paper to grow.

We rolled a toy car down a ramp from different heights. We made it a **fair test** by always measuring from the bottom of the ramp to the nearest point of the car.

We repeated the measures three times to make it more **fair.**

What do you think?
How do your responses compare with those of a colleague?
Compare your thoughts with those of the teachers involved in the research (see Appendix 1).
What conclusions do you come to about the understanding of teachers' use of the terms '**fair**' and '**fair test**'?
Why might there be a difference in the teachers' responses to this task? What are the implications for **your** practice?

Investigative skills: some basic ideas

A common misconception about science and scientists is a stereotypical one where men in white coats undertake 'experiments' to 'prove' a theory. In reality, scientists of both genders undertake a wide range of activities that singly or in combination find answers to a whole range of questions that push forward the combined knowledge and understanding of the natural and physical world and beyond.

The specific skills and procedures that are adopted by different scientists in their work depend upon the subject of their study. For example, zoologists researching into the behaviour of gorillas in the jungle, or of life in the oceans, investigate largely through observation, looking for patterns in behaviour and coming to conclusions based on their close observations. On the other hand, chemists working in the pharmaceutical industry may well use fair test type investigations in the development of specific drugs for the treatment of specific medical conditions, however they will also use observations and measurements to note the effects of a new drug on patients. Whether they are working in a recognisable 'laboratory' or in a range of different environments, scientists choose from a range of methods appropriate to their specific area of study. They do not set out to 'prove' theories; instead they set out to test questions and to gather substantial evidence to support existing theories.

Investigative skills, include a whole range of different procedures and are the very ones used by children in school science. The range of skills that form part of 'investigative skills' includes questioning, the use of secondary sources, first-hand observations as well as the understanding of all aspects of planning investigative work. The success of scientific investigation at any level depends on how well the professional scientist or young scientist in school engage with these skills singly or together.

The youngest children explore through trial-and-error investigation all the time so it is not expected that they should approach investigative work systematically. Older children, however, will need your help to structure their own questions and their ideas to enable them to undertake parts of investigations, or simple 'whole' investigations. Children at Key Stage 2 should be able to take far more control over what and how they work and to undertake whole investigations regularly and with little support.

Basic skills and equipment use

Procedural understanding is different from process (or basic) skills of observation, questioning, interpreting data and concluding. Procedural understanding is an understanding of how to carry out the process of finding out. Pupils also need to be taught the basic skills associated with scientific enquiry. Some basic skills relate to measurement, for example when using a ruler or a stop watch. The reliability of the findings may well depend on an individual's ability firstly to select and then to use a piece of equipment appropriately and accurately. The National Curriculum requires pupils to be able to make choices within their scientific enquiry.

You might think that specialised equipment could make science a distant and isolated subject (Harlen, 1993). It is true that science in the primary school has long been seen as needing only yogurt pots, string and film canisters. However, without simple scientific equipment this investigative approach can reduce children's ability both to work as scientists and to find out about the world through investigation in its widest sense.

In order to be able to choose and to use equipment properly, children have to be familiar with items and their uses. You might find it surprising to learn that there are large numbers of children who do not know what a measuring cylinder, a thermometer or a Newton meter is called or who get confused with how to use a stopwatch, but evidence from a variety of sources suggests that this is true. Pupils need to be introduced to these resources and to learn their names. They need to be allowed to explore what they do, find out what they are for and be taught how to use them accurately. If not, pupils cannot be expected to be able to choose items appropriately and measure with them accurately. Too often adults take such things for granted and assume that all children will automatically have the knowledge, understanding, sufficient motor control and observational skills required for investigative work without the need for teaching. Sometimes, adults do not know how to use equipment correctly themselves. Recently when trainees were undertaking a practical activity investigating forces, one group wanted to measure how much force was needed to push a block of wood. The demonstration given used a traditional Newton meter. The end opposite the hook was placed against the object and used to exert a force on the block rather like a snooker cue. This is innovative – however, attaching string to the block and using the Newton meter in a more conventional way would be recommended.

In the early years, pupils need the opportunity to use equipment with simple displays, for example large measuring jugs, whilst older pupils, in order to investigate effectively, require more sophisticated observations and accurate equipment. Newton meters, data-logging equipment and digital microscopes have brought immense opportunities to primary science, and it is pity if they remain unused in the cupboard.

Observation

Observation is an important skill in science, but this too needs to be taught. Observation is important in many ways; for example, making measurements, noticing similarities and differences between living things and materials. Scientific questions often arise from observation of objects and events and therefore lead to further observation, exploration and investigation.

PRACTICAL TASK PRACTICAL TASK **PRACTICAL TASK** PRACTICAL TASK **PRACTICAL TASK**

A great deal has been written about how to help pupils develop individual process skills. Dip into the books suggested at the end of the chapter to fine tune your knowledge and understanding of how to provide opportunities for your pupils to become better scientists.

RESEARCH SUMMARY RESEARCH SUMMARY **RESEARCH SUMMARY** RESEARCH SUMMARY

Planning investigative work and investigative skills

The AKSIS Project (**A**SE–**K**ing's College, London, **S**cience **I**nvestigations in **S**chools) was a three-year project funded by the Wellcome Trust and focused on Key Stages 2 and 3. It set out to identify current practice in schools and to make recommendations to inform future reviews of the curriculum. The project team defined the term 'investigation' as one where children make choices, either as individuals or groups, and are given some autonomy in how the investigative process is carried out. They also suggested that an investigation must involve pupils in using investigational procedures, for example, planning, measuring and observing. However, it was recognised that not all investigative work needs to include all the processes together and in addition the amount of autonomy given to children could vary at different stages of the investigative process. In the context of this chapter there are two factors that are important to bear in mind:

> *Both whole investigations and part investigations should continue to be encouraged by the statutory orders. Part investigations allow for teaching to focus on parts of investigational processes.* (Watson et al., 1998, p2)

Earlier in the chapter, it was suggested that the National Curriculum level descriptions provide guidance on the progression in children's questions. The QCA (2005) review of the curriculum noted that teachers do not make enough use of the level descriptions when planning work and this is limiting teachers' ability to plan appropriative activities at the right level.

Teaching example 2.1: Basic skills
Using equipment at all ages

Ensuring children are taught to use the equipment through basic skills lessons is vital if later they are to use them effectively to gather their own data. Planning what equipment is required to complete the investigation is also important. In the early years teachers sometimes ask children what equipment they think they would like to use. This will help children to think about appropriate equipment and to give choice. Frequently, however, teachers in the early years will often provide a small range of equipment for children to choose from, but as children get older they should be taught to select their own from a greater range.

At the planning stage in investigative work children can be asked to draw a sketch of the equipment they intend to use. This not only helps to visualise what they will need but will also provide insight into the thought processes involved. It is important to increase the demands and the type of equipment used as pupils get older. For example, when Year 2 children carry out an investigation on how far away it is possible to hear a sound, they can have their backs to the source of a sound and then count footsteps to measure the distance the sound travelled until they can no longer hear it. At Key Stage 2 a hand-held decimetre or a data-logger will enable the children to see the effect of distance on the loudness of sound. As the children develop in age and experience the quality of their measurements should also develop.

Organising practical work

Organising equipment is an area where teachers have problems, 'Where should it be placed?' and 'How can you stop children fiddling with it?' are two of the most common questions asked. Equipment should be available for children and they should be able to collect it themselves from an area in the classroom. This is not to say all of it needs to be in the same place or that everyone should be on the move at once. Thinking about flow around the classroom, health and safety and the promotion of independence, usually results in strategies that will work for you. If you put equipment in front of children they will touch it, but placing it in a tray on the floor out of sight may enable you to get through the instruction or demonstration of its use without having to stop to reinforce your authority.

Teaching example 2.2: Foundation Stage

Learning intention: To learn science through child-initiated activity
There is a requirement in the Foundation Stage that practitioners need to plan for all children to participate in the activities provided in the Foundation Stage curriculum. Resources and equipment need to be readily available to children. They need to be wide ranging to challenge children to make real choices. It is very easy to plan for child-initiated activity in the nursery, playgroup, Reception class or other early years settings. Give children items to look at and they explore, often using all their senses. Learning through play in this way comes naturally to children and you need to capitalise on this in your work. It is important, however, not to provide too much 'equipment' or too many items to explore at once.

Task
Set up a water tray or sand pit for child exploration. Observe children at play firstly with a large number of items in the tray then with a small selected number.

What similarities and differences do you notice?

What are the implications for productive child-initiated learning in science in your practice?

Learning intention: To explore bouncing and rolling balls
One specific suggestion for teachers of young children is to provide a range of equipment, e.g. balls, and to let the children explore for themselves. Following free exploration, intervention in their learning can develop specific tasks and ideas. Teachers can ask 'predictive' type questions such as, 'Will they all bounce?', 'Can they bounce the same number of times?', 'Which ball would win the ball-bouncing world cup?' Here, teachers are instrumental in planning the work with the children if it is considered acceptable to focus the children towards a comparison. On the other hand, the exploration, development of language and experience might be considered more important and children might be left to explore for themselves with the adults posing questions such as 'What have you noticed?', so enquiring about observations, thoughts and feelings.

Teaching example 2.3: Key Stage 1

At Key Stage 1, children need to be encouraged to take a more systematic approach to finding out in science. Starting with exploration it is your role to select appropriate child-friendly contexts and to encourage children's own questions. This involves helping to refine and turn their questions into those that can lead to further observation or investigation and to help your children to work in a less trial-and-error fashion.

Exploring marbles
Developing children's ability to ask questions is a crucial teaching skill. For example, if a child asks, 'Why does a marble stop rolling?' it is possible to think of a range of further reflective questions that relate to this aspect such as, 'Do all marbles stop at the same place?', 'Will the amount of push to start the marble moving, affect the distance it will travel?', 'Will the surface make a difference?' These questions are identifying the variables that might be investigated.

It is also important to note that the answer to the original question is not given because giving children the answer is not always the most effective learning strategy.

Identifying further but related questions that can be developed from the original question in this way, is called, a 'variable scan' (Jelly, 1985). This term has been used by many writers since, and is useful because this strategy supports the understanding, and identification, of the independent variable (something that could be changed). Adopting such approaches will support you in developing investigative work, and especially the planning aspect in the classroom.

Learning intention: To make comparisons and talk about what is found
Context: Teddy down ramp, answering the question: what will give teddy the longest ride?

Success criteria:

To be able to ask a question that can be answered.
To change only one thing.
This activity can help children identify the things that can be changed as well as develop a question. Using a set of matchbox bottoms of different sizes, a range of materials and bears, children can plan how to give teddy the longest ride.

The bottom of each matchbox needs to have a different material glued to it, so that children can change the surface without having to have large samples of materials on the slope.

The independent variables are:

- the size of the matchbox (sledge);
- the type of materials on the base of the sledge (foil, cotton wool, sandpaper, no material);
- the size of the bear; small, medium or large;
- the height of the slope;
- the number of bears placed in the sledge.

When undertaking the popular 'cars down the ramp' investigation, children often want to change the height of the slope. With this alternative activity children seem happy to change the type of sledge or the number of bears, which extends their experience. Children are often helped with this work if they can see the different variables pictorially. It is also important to ensure children know that for this activity they can only change one thing at once.

Older Year 2 children could use their developing understanding of the variables in this activity to help them pose their own question for investigating. For example, if they change the material on the bottom of the sledge and measure the distance travelled, their question might be, 'Which material will give Teddy the longest ride?' However, if they change the size of the matchbox the question might be, 'Will the biggest matchbox give teddy the longest ride?' Question generation is a skill developed in the literacy strategy and can be extended and developed in the science curriculum.

Currently, there is an emphasis on schools presenting a creative curriculum. Planning focused on cross-curricular learning with a flexible, open-ended starting point is increasingly being adopted in schools. It is important for you to provide an environment in your classroom where children are active in their learning. This approach is also necessary to help develop children's questioning skills. Using a question board or the question of the week are strategies used by many teachers to promote independence and questioning. 'What happens if...?' type questions will develop work that promotes the ability to seek patterns.

CASE STUDY CASE STUDY **CASE STUDY** CASE STUDY **CASE STUDY** CASE STUDY

Recently some pupils were looking at pine cones as part of an investigative session, when one asked whether pine cones could predict the weather. One child had been told by her grandmother that she used to have a pine cone hanging in her porch at home. Seeing an opportunity for a simple investigation, the teacher asked whether this could be investigated. When probed, the children decided that the pine cone must open and close to predict the weather. Then one asked, 'What will happen if it is put in water?' This question arose because her friend had told her that the pine cones would close up in water, but she wanted proof. They tested the theory and after an initial disappointment when nothing happened, they decided that it was probably because the cone was too old. After a while the pine cone closed. This was a surprise to some as they had thought the pine cone would open further. The wet closed-up pine cone was then taken from the water and left in the classroom. As it dried up, the scales began to open and the seeds were revealed. This led to further research in books to find out about seed dispersal in conifers. Questions were then posed about other fruits and seeds and what would happen to them, if they were put into water.

This supports the work of Elstgeest (1985), who suggested that 'what if' questions should be followed by 'can you find a way?' type questions. This is a simple but helpful suggestion to remember.

Teaching example 2.4: Key Stage 2

Investigation: Variable selection and planning investigations

Children need to be able to identify variables and to be able to plan and carry out a whole investigation for themselves. However, this is not something they can do without being taught the procedures that will enable them to carry out a fair test. There is, however, a way of developing children's work systematically (Feasey and Goldsworthy, 1998). This strategy can be applied to many fair test investigations. Look at the following diagram:

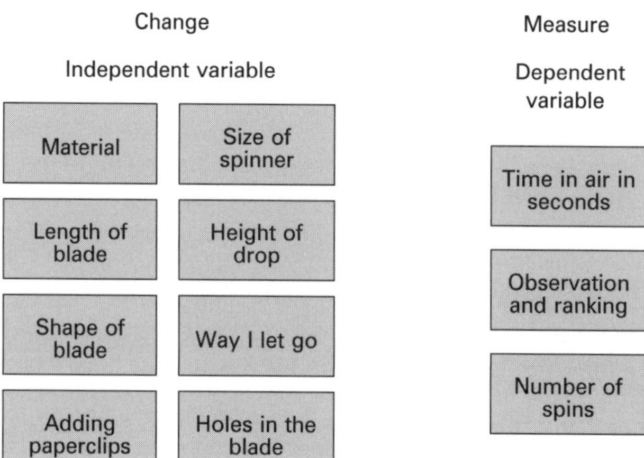

What is the question?
The diagram shows the children the variables that can be changed and those that can be measured in relation to investigating spinners. Discussion can be introduced to decide what this investigation is about and what we already know about it. The children can then be asked to select one variable to change and one to be measured and as a result of these choices, to then decide on the question they will be answering as well as the equipment they will need. The assessment focus in this lesson is on planning investigations. At a later stage the children will implement their planning and attempt to find the answer to their questions.

Another related activity might involve the children in being shown a set of independent variables and then being asked to identify appropriate dependent variables and the possible questions for investigation. It is important to teach the children to identify the variables to be changed (independent ones) and those to be measured (outcomes – dependent variables). Sometimes using different coloured sticky notes helps children with this.

Starting with a question about a possible investigation will help children practise identifying variables. For example, what would or could be changed if the global question is:

- What factors affect the time a spinner is in the air?
- What could be changed to make sugar dissolve quickly?
- Will all shoes have the same amount of grip?

Teaching example 2.5: Key Stage 2

Learning intention: To explore the viscosity of liquids
Context: running liquids

- To be able to identify equipment needed.
- To identify a variable to change.
- To identify a variable to measure.

For this activity the global question would be: 'Will all liquids travel the same distance?'

The independent variables would be:
- the height of slope, (angle);
- the type of material the liquids run down (newspaper, foil, clingfilm, sandpaper, etc.);
- the type of liquids (water, oil, honey, etc);
- the amount of liquid.

The dependent variables are:
- time taken to run a set distance; or
- the distance travelled in a set time.

This activity is fun and easy to carry out. Use cardboard squares as the surface and cover them with different types of material. These squares can be thrown away in the bin at the end of the lesson. Syringes are easy to use, as long as the liquids are not too thick. This activity enables children to select equipment and plan their work.

PRACTICAL TASK PRACTICAL TASK PRACTICAL TASK PRACTICAL TASK PRACTICAL TASK

Progression in learning

Investigations and parts of investigations should increase in difficulty as the children progress through the key stages. Identify the variables for each of the following investigative questions and then place the investigations in an order of difficulty. All investigations selected are explained at some point within the book and the relevant key stage is identified. A more complex investigation may have more variables, need sophisticated measuring equipment and the necessary methodology or understanding of the underpinning science is more complex.

- **'How can we keep teddy dry?'**
- **'Are all types of milk and cream good for making butter?'**
- **'What makes the bounciest material?'**

PRACTICAL TASK PRACTICAL TASK PRACTICAL TASK PRACTICAL TASK PRACTICAL TASK

Web activity

The Improving Science Education website has some activities related to teaching skills. Look at how to plan a fair test and evaluate the activities given.

www.ise5-14.org.uk/Prim3/New_Guidelines/Investigations/Fair_test.htm

Key questions

What examples of progression are evident?

How are scaffolding and modelling used here?

Try one suggested activity with your class and evaluate its success.

Subject knowledge that underpins the activities in this chapter

Questioning and question generation

Questions are fundamental to scientific enquiry. The most useful questions are those that arise from observation or can be answered by exploration involving practical enquiry where a simple investigation is planned and carried out. However, some young children's questions are often limited to 'why' questions. Whilst 'why' questions are important in finding out about the world, your role is to extend the range of questions asked and to encourage your children to ask a wider range of questions.

Within the Curriculum Guidance for the Foundation Stage, children are expected to learn to investigate, be curious and pose questions. Anyone observing very young children at play can be in no doubt that questions are being asked, but of course these are rarely verbalised. As a teacher of young children, your role is to help them gain the vocabulary to enable them to verbalise their questions and actions. In the National Curriculum Sc1 programme of study there is an expectation that children will become more proficient at each science skill as they proceed through the key stages. The level descriptions for science in the National Curriculum reflect this progression, but for example at level 1, there is no mention of children's questions so there is no requirement that the quality of these should be assessed. At level 2, however, children should be able to respond to your question and make their own suggestions. By level 5 this has developed into learners deciding on an appropriate approach to posing and answering questions themselves. (DfES National Curriculum Attainment Targets 1998, p17). Clearly, an ability to ask questions is a skill that can be developed and improved and is essential in investigative work.

Jelly (1985) discusses a useful classification of suitable questions. She suggests that there are 'productive' questions, which stimulate productive activity, and 'unproductive' questions, which although useful in encouraging conversation, tend to promote science as information gathering. In order for children to develop the skill of asking productive questions you need to think whether the question can be turned into a practical task. This process can be applied at any level. Children ask questions based on their previous knowledge; these indicate the things they are interested in finding out. The difference relates to the level of sophistication of the questions asked initially by the children and the complexity of the resulting investigation. In fact, many questions asked by pupils at whatever age can be turned into productive questions at a level to suit the age and ability of the pupils. This is one way that investigations can be differentiated to meet the needs of the different groups in your class.

Illustrative activities

Some kinds of practical work are called illustrative activities. Illustrative activities often start with a question provided by the teacher, and unlike investigations, usually have a known, predictable outcome. Illustrative activities are used to illustrate a concept and are useful for teaching basic skills. However, they should not be confused with investigations, for although they do not have to be totally structured by the teacher, the teacher often decides what equipment will be used and how pupils will record. Illustrative work allows no choice for the children.

Investigations

Although many teachers equate investigation with a fair test, it is important to understand that the term 'investigation' actually includes other types of enquiry. The AKSIS project (1998) asked teachers to identify the kinds of enquiry they undertook with their pupils. Six different types of enquiry were identified including the fair test investigation. These were:

- **exploring;**
- **classifying and identifying;**
- **pattern seeking;**
- **making things;**
- **fair test;**
- **using and applying models (not usually found in primary science).**

A balanced scheme of work should include the whole range of types of investigation over a period of time.

Exploring

Play will form the basis for much exploring in the early years, but being given the opportunity to explore, particularly when meeting a situation for the first time, is important for older pupils too. You may have already noticed when equipment is put on the table how pupils find it hard not to fiddle with it. This sometimes leads teachers to associate practical work with misbehaviour. However, if this is turned from a threat to an opportunity, pupils can be asked to explore (observe) the equipment and to find out as much about it as they can and report back on what they notice, thereby harnessing their curiosity. In exploring, pupils make observations and measurements over time and choose what to observe and what and how often to measure, helped along by teacher questions that direct pupils to focus on important aspects. Examples include:

- **How does the seed change over time?**
- **What happens to teddy's temperature over time?**
- **Which sound travels the furthest?**

Pattern finding

This sort of investigation asks pupils to look for relationships between two characteristics. These are not fair test investigations because although the task can involve pupil choice and measurement, variables are not controlled. Examples of pattern finding activities include:

- **Does the person with the biggest hand span have the biggest grasp?**
- **Where do we find the biggest woodlice?**
- **Does the tallest plant have the longest roots?**

Classifying and identifying

Classifying and identifying involves children in sorting things, both living and never alive, into groups and identifying the criteria used for grouping. This kind of investigation is important in science and throughout the primary years. For example:

- **What is the name of this tree?**
- **Which materials are good conductors of electricity and which are good insulators?**
- **To which group of animals does a bat belong?**
- **Is this a chemical change?**

Problem solving

Linking with design technology, making things requires pupils to apply their knowledge of the properties of materials, or their understanding of a concept to a problem-solving activity. Examples include:

- **Can you make a machine (mangonel) to fire a piece of plasticine 50cm across a table?**
- **Can you light the dolls' house using a simple electrical circuit?**
- **Can you make an ear trumpet?**

Fair testing

Even young children in the Foundation Stage are capable of deciding what to play and in addition can think up interesting and imaginative outcomes. However, they are often not aware of the concept of the fair test or scientifically acceptable ways of working; rather they explore by trial and error. The method of trying out things systematically in a set way, is not as established an approach as it might seem and only came into being in the late 1700s. Prior to this ideas were suggested and some things discovered but the testing of ideas and discoveries by gathering supportive data to confirm them was not the accepted way to work.

Fair test investigations start with a question and children are given a wide choice in planning the investigation, choosing the materials, deciding what to measure and how to record. They involve the children in identifying variables, choosing what to change, what to keep the same and what to measure. Many children find fair test investigations confusing because the variable that is measured is often confused with the variable that is to be changed. It is important to be clear about this before you begin fair testing with your children.

Variable selection

A variable scan is relatively easy to undertake. For example, if you were investigating kites, the variables that could be changed include the size of the kite, the material the kite is made from, the length of the tail, the length of the string, etc. If children were to undertake an investigation to find out which kite stays in the air the longest, following the variable scan, they could decide which variable they would change, which to keep the same (control) and which to measure.

The independent variable is the variable that is changed. So if the investigation is more about dissolving sugar, the global question might be, 'Can sugars be made to dissolve quicker?' The independent variables could be:

- **the amount of water;**
- **the temperature of the water;**
- **the amount of solute (sugar);**
- **the type of solute (sugar);**
- **whether or not to stir.**

In order to measure the quickest way to dissolve sugar, it is possible to measure the time taken for the solute to dissolve, or the number of stirs needed. This is the outcome, or the dependent variable, and therefore what is actually being measured or observed.

It is important for you to appreciate that there is a potential problem with just talking about what is being measured. This is because children think about everything they measure: how much water, how much sugar, the temperature, etc., and this becomes confusing for them. For each of these variables they will be using a mathematical measurement when setting up the investigation and, important though each is, they are not the outcome or answer to the question. So measuring the amount of sugar will not give the answer to the question 'which sugar dissolved the quickest?'

REFLECTIVE TASK

Look back at the different categories of investigative work. Either choose one of the examples from each category or structure a context of your own and then consider what equipment you would need to provide for your children to undertake the activity for themselves.
Reflect upon progression issues:
What equipment would not be easy to find in your school?
What other equipment could be used instead?

A SUMMARY OF **KEY POINTS**

- **Children need to undertake a range of practical work, not just fair tests.**
- **Children should be helped to raise their own questions.**
- **Investigations require the teacher to give children choice.**
- **Questions of all kinds will develop children's learning.**
- **Equipment choice can help or hinder children's learning.**

Moving on

What investigations have you undertaken with children? This chapter suggests that the skills of planning need to be taught. Think about how you might teach children to plan an investigation the next time you teach science. Read the outcome of the AKSIS work in the Appendix.

REFERENCES REFERENCES REFERENCES REFERENCES REFERENCES REFERENCES

Jelly, S. (1985) Helping children raise questions and answering them, Ch 5, in W. Harlen (ed.) *Primary Science: Taking the Plunge*. Oxford: Oliver and Boyd

Elstgeest, J. (1985) *The right question at the right time,* Ch 4 in W. Harlen (ed.) *Primary Science: Taking the Plunge*. Oxford: Oliver and Boyd

Watson, J.R., Goldsworthy, A. and Wood-Robinson, V. (1998) *ASE-King's Science Investigations in Schools (AKSIS) Project: Second Interim Report to the QCA.* London: King's College

Watson, J. R. Goldsworthy, A. and Wood-Robinson, V. (2000) 'Science: beyond the fair test', Ch 8 in J. Sears and P. Sorensen, *Issues in Science Education*. Abingdon: RoutledgeFalmer

FURTHER READING FURTHER READING FURTHER READING FURTHER READING

Goldsworthy, A. (2004) Acquiring scientific skills, Ch 3 in J. Sharp (ed.) *Developing Primary Science*. Exeter: Learning Matters

QCA (2006) 2004/5 Report on curriculum and assessment. London: QCA

Harlen, W. (ed.) (1985) *Primary Science: Taking the Plunge*. Oxford: Oliver and Boyd

Roden, J. (2005) Scientific enquiry, Chapter 4 in *Primary Science Reflective Reader*. Exeter: Learning Matters

3
Obtaining and presenting evidence

By the end of this chapter you should:

- **be aware of some of the significant subject knowledge that underpins obtaining and considering evidence as part of scientific enquiry;**
- **recognise some of the common problems associated with undertaking practical work;**
- **understand the continuity issues related to this topic using some examples of learning activities from 3 to 11 years;**
- **identify opportunities for the development of basic skills;**
- **understand health and safety in scientific enquiry;**
- **recognise how pupils can record activities in different ways;**
- **have reflected upon the use of ICT in science.**

Professional Standards for QTS

Q1, Q2, Q3b, Q4, Q6, Q7a, Q8, Q9, Q10, Q11, Q14, Q15, Q17, Q19, Q21a, Q21b, Q22, Q25a, Q25b, Q25c, Q25d, Q26b, Q27, Q28, Q29, Q30, Q31

Curriculum Guidance for the Foundation Stage and National Curriculum

In the Foundation Stage pupils are encouraged to:

- **investigate objects and materials in their environment but there are no specific requirements related to obtaining and presenting evidence at this stage;**
- **explore the world naturally in a trial-and-error, largely unsystematic manner where formal recording is largely inappropriate.**

At Key Stage 1 pupils should be taught to:

- **follow simple instructions to control the risks to themselves and to others;**
- **explore, using the senses of sight, hearing, smell;**
- **communicate what happened in a variety of ways, including using ICT (for example, in speech and writing, by drawings, tables, block graphs and pictograms) (DfEE, 1999, p78).**

At Key Stage 2 pupils should be taught to:

- **use simple equipment and materials appropriately and take action to control risks;**
- **make systematic observations and measurements, including the use of ICT for data-logging;**
- **check observations and measurements by repeating them where appropriate;**
- **use a wide range of methods, including diagrams, drawings, tables, bar charts, line graphs and ICT, to communicate data in an appropriate and systematic manner. (DfEE, 1999, p.83)**

Additionally, in the breadth of study at Key Stage 2, pupils are required to:

- **use appropriate scientific language and terms, including SI units of measurement (for example, metre, Newton), to communicate ideas and explain the behaviour of living things, materials, phenomena and processes.**

Introduction

Obtaining and presenting evidence is the part of the scientific enquiry (Sc1) element of the programme of study where children are required to undertake different types of practical work, collect evidence, record and interpret data in order to facilitate the process of making valid conclusions based on the collected data. This requirement is important, but often under-represented in the curriculum presented to primary children. Even when children are given regular 'hands-on' experience the following 'minds-on' or reflective activity is sometimes totally lacking or undemanding. Your own experience might suggest that some teachers tend to rely heavily on the same, traditional, repetitive methods of recording. This predictable procedure may be comforting in some respects, but may become tedious and boring for the children.

When children undertake illustrative activities, the teacher provides a pre-planned practical enquiry, with predetermined methods and recording strategy. In these activities learning intentions should focus on and relate to the process of collecting, presenting and analysing evidence, rather than on the knowledge and understanding that might result from the activity. Importantly, as children become more skilled at presenting evidence in a variety of ways, they will become more skilled at choosing appropriate ones for themselves. So, when they carry out true investigations the pupils will have tried and tested ways of presenting evidence from which to choose.

Like many teachers, you may well be worried about the health and safety aspects of practical work. You may be reluctant to allow children to undertake some practical activities that, given careful planning, should not cause any real problems provided that common-sense, but realistic approaches are taken. To help you to plan safe but worthwhile activities, in this chapter, the notion of risk assessment will be explored and the need to refer to relevant safety literature will be stressed throughout. You may be unsure about how children should be recording their work and be reluctant to experiment with different ways of recording in science. This is an area ripe for the introduction of more creativity, so this chapter will also consider a range of alternative ways of presenting evidence, incorporating the use of ICT where appropriate to optimise pupil understanding of science. In particular, it will look at ways of developing communication strategies.

Check your understanding

What do you understand by the following terms? Make a note of your ideas.

Risk	Hazard
Control	Systematic
Reliability	Data-logging
Simulation	Chart
Graph	Table

Check your understanding with the Glossary.

Make a list of the ways in which you have:

- used ICT in your teaching of science;
- asked pupils to record data in practical work;
- asked pupils to record their scientific experiences.

Obtaining and presenting evidence: some basic ideas

A consideration of the health and safety aspects of the activities you wish to provide for your pupils is crucial before you put them into practice.

PRACTICAL TASK PRACTICAL TASK PRACTICAL TASK PRACTICAL TASK PRACTICAL TASK

This task is based upon an idea developed by the ASE (Association of Science Education, 2002) to help experienced and inexperienced teachers to evaluate common activities in the classroom. Look at the following statements and decide if the statement is true or not from a health and safety viewpoint:

1. It is safe to cut up fireworks to show children what is inside.
2. Rechargeable batteries can be used in the classroom for electrical circuit work.
3. Copper sulphate is great for making crystals and can be used in primary schools.
4. Animals can be kept in school just like at home.
5. All plants can be grown and used with children.
6. There are no problems with looking at blood with a digital microscope.
7. Growing bacteria to show what happens when you do not wash your hands is a great activity.
8. Kettles are fine in the classroom as long as you supervise children.
9. Having foxes living under the classroom provides a first-hand experience to learn about animals and their young.
10. African land snails carry diseases and should not be kept.

See the Appendix 2 for the answers.

The first steps in planning safe activities

One of the most important things to do when deciding what activities to carry out in your school is to consult the school's science planning and policy. However, if you want to change any of the activities outlined in the scheme, it is imperative that you consult with the science co-ordinator or a member of the senior management team because the responsibility for health and safety in the school remains with the individual school and its governors at all times. Even if you think their viewpoint is overcautious, you **must** follow their advice, as it is they who are ultimately responsible if things go wrong, not you. If something does go wrong, provided that you have followed guidance, you can only be prosecuted if it is shown that you did something reckless, that children were put at risk and the school had not agreed to changes you were making.

Some issues of health and safety differ between schools even within the same local authority. You may think there is no real risk to health, e.g. typically in the use of tubes from toilet paper, or egg boxes, but if your school has stated that they may not be used, they must not be used. Despite it being more important to ensure that children wash hands after going to the toilet than using toilet roll tubes in the classroom, if they are banned they must stay banned.

Health and safety: risk assessment

When planning to provide safe activities, the important things to ask yourself are: 'What are the hazards?', 'What are the risks?', 'Is this activity safe to undertake in my classroom?' A hazard is the thing that might happen, e.g. in the use of scissors the hazard is the opportunity to get cut, stabbed or to cause potential damage to hair or clothing. However, most school scissors are not sharp enough for these eventualities to occur so, in reality, the hazards with most safety scissors are much lower. In fact, most teachers would consider it ridiculous to think that harm might come through the use of school scissors. Even so, the risks are made less likely to occur by training children how to use scissors and by ensuring adequate supervision when they are used. This is what happens in most classrooms. Decisions of this kind are termed 'risk assessment'. However, if the types of scissors were changed and/or children were not able to use scissors in a safe way, then changes would be made to the way in which they were used.

Risk assessment helps teachers and children to be safe, and is not designed to prevent children from enjoying good science activities. Indeed, the National Curriculum requires children, as they get older, to think about their own safety and that of others. Children can only do this if they have previously been introduced to, and trained to deal with, potentially risky situations. However, even though you might encourage children of all ages to consider risks and make joint decisions with you about what and how activities will be carried out, in the Foundation Stage and at Key Stage 1, you will largely control the activities children carry out. Here your role is mainly to point out the potential dangers, encouraging children to be aware of these as they work and follow instructions to ensure that they and others are safe. At Key Stage 2, however, the onus must be on enabling the children to begin to identify the risks and hazards and to start to look after themselves whilst they carry out practical work.

Expecting children to take responsibility and make decisions about what types of investigations they will carry out is part of the progression in scientific enquiry. If children are not able to identify the risks themselves their investigative work will always be subject to censure. When older children are asked to identify the variables to change and measure or when identifying the question to follow, at the same time they should also be asked to identify the things that could be hazardous. This facilitates a shared agreement on the acceptable ways of working to ensure the safety of all, rather than merely assuming that children will work safely. For example when children are going to test paper spinners to see which float more slowly to the ground, you will need to discuss with them the potential problems associated with standing on chairs, standing off the ground on other furniture, the use of scissors. What would happen if they fell? How could this be prevented? Will it be safe to throw a parachute into the air with a plastic man attached; could it hit other people and cause damage? Notably, recent national test papers in science at the end of Key Stage 2 have asked children to identify the risks and think about ways to make sure they are limited in some given scenarios.

Observation and measurement

The National Curriculum level descriptions for science reveal progression in these essential skills:

Level	Observation	Measurement
1	Simple observations	Non-standard
2	Observations related to tasks and compared	Related to tasks and comparison with non-standard (and cm)
3	Relevant	Length or mass
4	Series of adequate observations for the task	Series of adequate observations for the task
5	Make a series of observations with precision, begin to repeat	Make a series with precision, begin to repeat

You will notice that children working at lower levels are not expected to make measurements. Only at level 2 might some measurement be expected and it is level 3 before SI units are introduced.

SI units stand for Système International d'Unités. This is an internationally agreed system of units used by the international science community. There are seven units:

- **mass – kilograms (kg)**
- **length – metres (m)**
- **time – seconds (s)**
- **electrical current – ampere (A)**
- **temperature – Kelvin (K)**
- **amount of substance – mole (mol)**
- **amount of light – candela (cd)**

The Treaty of the Metre was signed in Paris in 1875 and even the USA is a charter member, having signed in the original document. All the units are worked out in relation to scientific equations so, for example. The only measure which is still compared is the kilogram. The International Bureau of Weights and Measures (BIPM) keeps the world's standard kilogram in Paris and all other kilograms are measured against this standard kilogram.

So, although in mathematics it is possible to measure mass in grams, ounces, pounds, kilograms and tonnes, the units in science are only kilograms. The unit of measure of volume in science is the cubic centimetre (cm^3) and is used to measure gases, liquids and solids. You need to remember that one millilitre is the same volume as one cubic centimetre. Although the National Curriculum has adopted most SI units, there are some exceptions. For example, for temperature the Celsius scale is used and not the SI unit of the Kelvin scale, because the Kelvin would not be understood in a classroom context.

There are some areas of science where fine measurements are not appropriate even at Key Stage 2 so that children should instead continue to make observations of the effects. This is because the equipment to measure the effect, for example for current in electricity, is not normally available in primary schools. Generally, the number and type of measurements taken by children within practical work should increase as they progress through school. If you are working with Years 5 or 6 children you should therefore ensure that a series of measurements are made and that time is allowed for the children to repeat readings and talk about their results. This means extra equipment and time devoted to thinking about and making sense of collected data.

The use of ICT

Information communication technology (ICT) can make a contribution to science education even in the Foundation Stage. In fact in recent consultation on a single quality framework for services from birth to five, the Early Years Foundation Stage (DfES, 2006), the expectation is that by the end of the Foundation Stage most children will be able to use ICT to support their learning. The important point is that at all stages, ICT should be used to support science learning and not merely as a context for ICT skill development. In order for children to be able to use their ICT skills effectively they need to practise essential skills prior to their use within an investigation. This means you need to plan to teach the skill before its application in science.

There are three principles that you should remember whenever ICT is used in science:

1. ICT should support what is known as good practice in science;
2. ICT should enable the learning intention to be achieved;
3. The use of ICT in the science lesson should add something to the learning process that could not be achieved if ICT was not being used (Becta).

These are important points but need to be coupled with aspects of good practice in science, namely learning that:

- **stimulates children's curiosity;**
- **provides 'hands-on' experience;**
- **allows children to question their world.**

If ICT is used merely as a research, fact-finding comprehension activity then 'good' science is lost. Furthermore, if children spend valuable science time typing, showing their ICT skills when a quick sticky note would have been more effective, then the ICT keyboard activity hinders rather than enhances the science. On the other hand, using a digital microscope to look at fabrics at a magnification of up to 200 times provides children with opportunities to explain and explore why some materials are absorbent. This is something that could not be achieved as effectively without ICT and is therefore an excellent application of ICT in science.

ICT provides a range of opportunities in science, and communication by email is an excellent way to share practice and to provide authentic learning opportunities. Again this is good science as it provides real audiences for children's work, and is better than not using it because 'snail mail' is slower and email can have instantaneous results, particularly if you share ideas with a colleague in another school. Science across the world links children in schools in England with those in other continents. You and your class could email children in Africa and share information on healthy diets and growing foods, or any of the other topics available. Nearer to home, there are valuable links to be made with pupils in schools in Europe.

PRACTICAL TASK PRACTICAL TASK **PRACTICAL TASK** PRACTICAL TASK **PRACTICAL TASK**

ICT in science

Task 1

The British Education Communication and Technology Agency (Becta) is a useful organisation that provides supportive materials in science and ICT. Look at its website, **www.becta.org.uk**

- **Critically evaluate an aspect of the site of interest to you. Share your findings with a colleague.**

Task 2

Look at the ASE website, **www.ase.org.uk** ('Science across the world' for links with other countries.)

- **How might you incorporate these opportunities into your teaching? What could your children share with children abroad?**
- **Make links with your colleagues who will spend some of their school experience during their training away from the UK. How could such links be developed for the benefit of your pupils?**

Data-logging

Data-logging is a powerful tool that can be used with the youngest children, e.g. where they can see that when they make a sound it registers as either a raised bar or a line on the computer screen. By the end of Key Stage 2 children can use data-logging to record temperature, light and sound perhaps over a 24-hour period or to compare data from different times of the year. This can be useful if trends over time are needed, for example changing day length with seasonal change. It is also possible to use data-logging to record light levels and temperature in different environments. Today, many systems allow children to record data in the environment without having to have the sensors attached to a computer. In the QCA (2006) review of the curriculum, data-logging was one aspect of ICT most used by teachers in science.

You may have met teachers who believe that ICT has no place in science and could deskill children, e.g. by drawing graphs for children rather than making the children construct them in a traditional way. Most teachers however, now see the advantages that ICT can bring to teaching. Usefully, there are also graph tools available that can help children to construct graphs and can teach children basic skills, such as how to label axes, what goes where and what scales are useful.

PRACTICAL TASK PRACTICAL TASK **PRACTICAL TASK** PRACTICAL TASK **PRACTICAL TASK**

"Getting to Grips with Graphs" is a programme that can teach your pupils about graph construction.

- **What does it offer to your teaching? Could you incorporate its use with your children?**
- **Identify any issues related to the use of this sort of package in the classroom**

Simulation software

Simulation software is becoming more widely available than in the past and can provide contexts where children can change variables and see the outcomes without having to set up the equipment or wait for things to happen. The 'virtual classroom' series provides many everyday activities such as absorbency, for children to undertake on the screen. There are issues with this if it is used to replace the children's real-life practical activity. Once again, when planning for the use of simulations you should revisit and reflect on the three principles of good ICT above.

Classroom management

The QCA (2006) review of the curriculum found that although teachers valued ICT in science they encountered difficulties when asked to work in computer suites, where timetabling along with organisational issues become problematic.

REFLECTIVE TASK

Look at the Becta research summary into ICT at **www.becta.org.uk**
Reflect on how you currently use ICT in science.
Make a list of your own issues related to management of ICT in your setting.

PRACTICAL TASK PRACTICAL TASK **PRACTICAL TASK** PRACTICAL TASK **PRACTICAL TASK**

Look at the equipment available for ICT and science in the equipment catalogues available in your school.

- **What is available?**
- **How does it work?**
- **What age-range is it intended for?**

Find out if colleagues are familiar with the available equipment. Ask colleagues if the school owns some of the items – sometimes equipment can be found lurking hidden in cupboards!

Recording and communicating findings

There is a myth that science is about doing and not writing anything down: that it is more important to undertake science work than to make a record. Conversely, that practical work should be followed by a traditional 'write-up' of aim, apparatus, method, etc., to provide evidence of learning. Both ideas lead to poor practice. Importantly, children need to apply a range of language skills across the curriculum and to be encouraged to develop communication strategies in many contexts. Science should be stimulating and fun and recording and interpreting data are important skills in science.

Pollard and Triggs (2000) found that children disliked science as a subject because of the need to write, preferring art as a favourite subject not only because there was no writing, but there was also more choice. How science is recorded might be significant here. Many writers introduce alternative ways to record children's work.

PRACTICAL TASK PRACTICAL TASK **PRACTICAL TASK** PRACTICAL TASK **PRACTICAL TASK**

Recording science
Look at the National Curriculum in action site, **www.ncaction.org.uk**

Here you will find, amongst others, an excellent example of a floor book produced by Key Stage 1 children to record an investigation to keep an apple from going brown. This shows not only an easy way to record children's conversations but provides a record of what happened and what was found out for children and interested others.

- **Make a list of the ways science has been recorded.**
- **Add more from your experience or your own ideas.**

Different ways of recording science

The science National Curriculum suggests that children should demonstrate their understanding and communication of science through a wide range of methods. Therefore the range and type of recording are important. However, whatever recording style is selected, it should suit the activity and develop children's scientific vocabulary as well as their communication strategies. Fitness for purpose should be the most important feature.

Electronic scrapbooks, where children keep an ICT class-based record of the science that occurs during the year, can also provide a resource for learners to use to remind them of their previous learning. This can contain digital photographs of their work with some typed sentences or scanned material becoming a record of what science is happening, as well as providing teachers with another method of assessing progress during the year. Alternatively, older pupils can use a PowerPoint presentation to record and communicate what was done and what was found out for sharing with others in a more formal way.

Traditional science writing is a genre which is easily recognisable; however, a 'method, apparatus, result, conclusion' format is not suited to all work in primary schools across all the ability range, neither is the practice of requiring pupils to copy from the board. The former is as unrealistic as expecting the average primary children to write a novel and the latter undemanding and lacking in both creativity and challenge. Focusing on such limited and inappropriate approaches to communication does not help children to express their ideas and understanding and does not reflect scientists' practice.

Whilst developing their ideas, scientists have always worked using a number of communication strategies. For example, Darwin began recording his observations as a diary containing notes and drawings where he identified similarities and differences between species and, as a result, made hypotheses about how adaptation had occurred in animals and plants. Leonardo da Vinci's work was diagrammatic with notes and annotations. Unfortunately, the opportunities offered to some primary children have been more limited.

Different recording strategies available to children include:

- **cartoon strips, letters, e.g. to manufacturers of washing-up liquid to report on which type of liquid made the best bubbles (they often get letters back, which helps children see the relevance of their work);**
- **annotated diagrams;**
- **diagrams;**
- **drawings;**
- **tables;**
- **bar charts;**
- **block graphs;**
- **pictograms;**
- **line graphs;**
- **ICT;**
- **speech;**
- **writing.**

REFLECTIVE TASK

What types of recording in science have you used?
What types of recording happen in your school?
What does this say about science and the use of language across the curriculum?

RESEARCH SUMMARY RESEARCH SUMMARY **RESEARCH SUMMARY** RESEARCH SUMMARY

Look at **www.ttrb.ac.uk**, which provides a useful summary of the Becta report (2003) which links its own findings to research of others. This can be found on the Teacher Training Resource Bank site along with other useful science research summaries.

The key findings from the report:

- **Data-loggers are the most important tool for supporting practical work.**
- **Simulations can improve scientific understanding particularly if they are interactive.**
- **Girls benefit from simulations due to the non-competitive environment provided.**
- **ICT can provide pupils with greater control over their learning.**
- **Effective ICT places considerable pedagogical demands on teachers.**
- **ICT is more effective in secondary rather than primary settings.**
- **More research is needed.**

REFLECTIVE TASK

- **Reflect on your experience of the use of ICT in science.**
- **Do any of the above findings surprise you? How do the findings relate to your experience?**
- **Do girls really benefit from the use of simulations because of the lack of a competitive environment?**
- **How could you go about investigating this aspect of science teaching?**
- **Carry out research in your own classroom and compare your findings to those presented above.**

Teaching example 3.1: Foundation Stage

Developing recording in the early years

Scenario

Learning intentions:

To know that there are many sources of sounds.
To be able to identify sounds and where they come from.
To know sounds can be loud or soft.

Success criteria

To compare sounds at a distance from the source.
To be able to talk about sounds.

Children formed a large circle. The class teacher and teaching assistant (TA) handed out a collection of musical instruments. One child who was selected to stand in the circle wore a blindfold. The other children then took turns to make a noise with their instrument when quietly indicated by their teacher. The child in the middle of the circle then indicated the direction of the sound by pointing and naming the instrument. During the activity the TA took digital photographs that were later shared with children by use of the interactive whiteboard.

The most interesting aspect of this activity was that the learning did not end with the practical task. Later, the class were asked to record the experience in a number of ways, thus developing their scientific vocabulary and understanding. The teacher then used arrows and added words suggested by children to the photographs on the whiteboard. Pictures of the instruments had already been printed out on sticky labels. Next the children were encouraged to select and record their ideas about instruments that make quieter sounds and louder sounds by sticking pictures in their books. Sticky word labels were also provided so that all children could record their work in a meaningful way. Pictures of each of the children undertaking the activity were printed and left in the writing corner for the children to use during the week. Many children added arrows to show where the sound came from mimicking what their teacher had done.

Adopting this approach enabled children to demonstrate their learning at different levels. Children were introduced to relevant science words and encouraged to sort sounds by loudness. Whilst this approach took time in planning and preparation, the pictures of the instruments, once prepared, could be used on other occasions, in a number of ways. Sticky labels are no more expensive than photocopied worksheets and can provide much more interesting and challenging learning experiences. Here children were learning relevant vocabulary whilst immersed in science and, even if unable to write, sufficient support enabled each to communicate effectively at their own level.

Further examples

It is common practice for children to use worksheets to record information, e.g. parts of plants, on a picture of a stereotypical plant. It would be much more meaningful to record by going round the school grounds with labels of root, stem, leaf and flower to stick to parts of real plants. Sticky labels, e.g. of different colours, can help children to show their understanding of types of materials. Here a child may have yellow stickers for sticking or placing on materials that are made of wood, or perhaps blue for plastic objects. All this approach needs is a little thought and imagination, but it may well significantly transform the activity in a very practical way.

Teaching example 3.2: Key Stage 1

Learning intention: To find out about the different kinds of plants and animals in the local environment

If children are introduced to plant care labels in literacy and have been given opportunities to look at the details they contain, they can use this in science. Plant labels often have a picture of the plant and some simple information such as *shade-loving, will grow to 20 cm.* Children can then be encouraged to walk around the school grounds to identify two plants, very different from each other, that they want to study.

The choice should be their own, and if possible the plants should come from different places in the school grounds, or be different sizes or shapes. Next, provide the children with blank card care labels and ask them to create a label for their chosen plants. Differentiation is also possible here: the most able children can use measurement, detailed observational drawings along with information about location whilst other children could use digital cameras to take images of their plants and select pre-prepared words from a word bank, which includes a range of suitable, and unsuitable vocabulary.

Teaching example 3.3: Key Stage 2

Learning intention: The use of a story genre to develop understanding

Scenario

Some Year 5 children were asked to imagine what adventures an ice cube could have after being taken out of the freezer and then to write a story about 'Icky the Ice Cube'. The only requirements were to use scientific words and that Icky must end up as he started, as a solid lump of ice. The task was taken up with enthusiasm. Those whose literacy skills were less strong were encouraged to use drawings as well as writing, almost like a storyboard.

Whilst deciding what would happen in the story, the children talked to each other about the stages the ice cube would go through, how they would get the water to be return to ice, and what stages would need to be included. Some children gave 'Icky' some interesting adventures, but at the same time, all children demonstrated their understanding of the melting process. The most adventurous story had the ice cube eaten by a dog, excreted, washed away into the drains by rain, evaporated (without the nasty bits, as they would not evaporate) turned into a cloud, back to earth, into the river and out of the tap and back into the ice tray ready to be used by the child of the houses at their birthday. Icky almost got into a glass of water when he fell to the floor to be eyed by the same dog!

Teaching example 3.4: Key Stage 2

Learning intention: To be able to identify common observable features of rocks

Provide your children with a set of rocks of different kinds and some 'guess what I am cards'. For example:

- I contain crystals, I am pink, white, grey and brown. I am hard and will not break easily.
- I am white in colour, I have no crystals, I can be broken easily and will leave white powder on your hands.

Let the children match each card to individual rocks by observation, then introduced new cards with testable properties such as:

- I am permeable; I scratch easily and will bubble if you put a drop of vinegar on me.

Complete the activity by asking the children to make their own 'guess-who' cards for others rocks, stones or another aspect of science.

PRACTICAL TASK PRACTICAL TASK PRACTICAL TASK PRACTICAL TASK PRACTICAL TASK

Continuity in learning

Collect together some examples of children's science work from each key stage in your school. Compare and contrast the work as follows:

- **What methods of recording have been used?**
- **Is there a progression in what is being required of pupils in terms of ways of recording and use of ICT?**
- **What language and mathematical skills are being used?**
- **Do you think that greater demands could be made on children to record work in their own ways? If so, what might you advise?**
- **What good ideas have you found as a result of looking at other teachers methods?**

Using ideas from colleagues can enrich your pupils' diet of science. Charles Deforges (2006) calls this 'academic theft'.

PRACTICAL TASK PRACTICAL TASK PRACTICAL TASK PRACTICAL TASK PRACTICAL TASK

Web activity

Look at the following website selecting Key Stage 1:

www.ncaction.org.uk/subjects/science/index.htm

Look at the ways in which the children have recorded their work. Make a note of the different approaches.

- **Analyse how the ways of communicating enable children to demonstrate what they know.**
- **How might you improve on these methods in your own classroom to meet the needs of different abilities?**

Subject knowledge that underpins the activities in this chapter

Essentially, the activities in this chapter are concerned with obtaining and considering scientific evidence and doing so safely. The ideas of hazards and risks were examined: a hazard is the agent of harm and the risk is the likelihood of that harm occurring. In order to undertake a risk assessment the severity of the harm needs to be judged as high, medium or low, along with the likelihood of that harm occurring, which is also ranked as high, medium and low. Obviously if you assess an activity as a high harm with a high risk of the harm occurring then the risk assessment would be that this activity had some considerable dangers. It is at this point that you would think about how you could minimise the dangers. This might be by changing the equipment, the organisation or the layout so that the risk was reduced, e.g. candles in classrooms could be dangerous – the harm could be fire, burnt hair or clothing. It is more likely to happen if the candles fall over, if the children are not supervised and if the candles are not in sand trays. If night-lights are used then the candle cannot fall over but a source of heat is provided. Hair should be tied back, supervision increased and sand trays used. You will never reduce all risks but life is a hazardous activity and being aware of risks and working to minimise these should become an automatic part of children's thought process.

Using a computer suite for science provides an opportunity to teach some basic skills to all the children at the same time. However, the layout of some suites makes visibility for the teacher and pupils problematic. Pupils frequently have to share computers as few schools have rooms equipped for simultaneous whole-class individual use. Team tutoring by pupils can provide benefits, but this also can slow down the rate of learning of the more able whilst also making less computer-literate children feel inadequate. You must remember that the pedagogy of using computers for learning is still in its infancy.

According to the DfES/Becta survey, more than six schools in ten now have an interactive whiteboard (IWB) and the average number per school is two (HMI, 2006) which will support teachers in science delivery. Advantages include children's vocabulary being stored after each lesson, making for more effective links to previous learning than in the past. However, the report highlights some pitfalls in using IWBs, e.g the:

- **over-use of the resource, resulting in insufficient variety of approach;**
- **planning for the use of ICT across subjects to shift from learning to teaching.**

Increasingly, the use of ICT not just in education but in life is being debated. What might be the long-term effects on learning and the way the brain functions? Has there been enough research into this aspect of education? Greenfield (2006) stated that:

> We must surely choose to adopt technology that will ensure that the classroom will fit the child, and buck the growing trend for technology to be used to make the 21st-century child fit the classroom.
>
> Education, science and technology. House of Lords (2006)

As long ago as the 1990, Pollard stated that the way children use the computer is different from the process involved in accessing information from books. Books are generally linear and have a start and finish and one clear way through. However, using the computer is non-linear and children can have many screens open, accessing information in a number of formats at the same time. Although there are no answers to the concerns raised by these issues it is perhaps worthwhile to acknowledge that there are issues to be addressed and, as someone highly skilled and knowledgeable in ICT, you need to reflect on these issues and be prepared to voice your views.

The ways children are asked to record information collected can significantly influence the level of motivation, interest and the resultant outcome in terms of learning. You need to use your creative skills at the planning stage to fully capitalise on the effort you put into your work. You should also ensure that you include a range of different types of recording over a period of time to sustain interest. The way science is introduced and the methods used will also provide children with a model of appropriate recoding strategies and opportunities.

REFLECTIVE TASK

Look at the following list of activities.

- **Understanding the role of the skeleton.**
- **The results of an experiment in sending cars down ramps.**
- **How to show a balanced diet is important.**

How could you present these parts of the national curriculum programme of study in an interesting and varied way to children?
Remember to think about the way you present the information.
Using a different strategy for each, how could you ask your children to communicate their findings?

A SUMMARY OF **KEY POINTS**

> **Health and safety should not be used as a reason for boring science, but risks should be assessed.**
> **A range of recording strategies should be used and the focus should be on developing children's communication skills.**
> **Children in Key Stage 2 should assess risks in their own work.**
> **ICT has possibilities but the pedagogy must be developed.**

Moving On

Reflect on your current use of ICT in science in your classroom:

How many different ways of recording in science do you favour?

Could you ensure a progressive approach to using literacy and numeracy skills to develop science?

Make a note of the main points of your learning from this chapter for later reference.

REFERENCES REFERENCES REFERENCES REFERENCES REFERENCES REFERENCES

ASE (2002) Be Safe. Inset Pack, 2nd edition. Hatfield: Association for Science Education

Goldsworthy, A., Watson, J.R. and Wood-Robinson, V. (1999) *Investigations: Getting to Grips with Graphs*. Hatfield: Association for Science Education

Pollard, A (1990) *Learning in Primary Schools: An Introduction for Parents, Governors and Teachers*. London: Cassell

Rowlett (2002) **www.unc.edu/~rowlett/units/sifundam.html**

http://www.publications.parliament.uk/pa/ld199900/ldhansrd/pdvn/lds06/text/60420-18.htm for the full text of Baroness Greenfield's report to Parliament.

Watson, J.R., Goldsworthy, A. and Wood-Robinson, V. (1998) *The Practices and Perceptions of 1000 Teachers about Science Investigations – A National Questionnaire Survey.* London: King's College

FURTHER READING FURTHER READING FURTHER READING FURTHER READING

Byrne, J. and Sharp, J. (2002) *Using ICT in Primary Science Teaching*. Exeter: Learning Matters

Duffty, J. (2006) *Achieving QTS Extending Knowledge in Practice: Primary ICT*. 3rd edition. Exeter: Learning Matters

Sharp, J., Peacock, G., Johnsey, R., Simon, S. and Smith R., (2007) Using ICT in Science, Chapter 9, and Health and Safety, Chapter 10 in *Primary Science: Teaching Theory and Practice*. 3rd edition. Exeter: Learning Matters

PART 2
LIFE PROCESSES AND LIVING THINGS

4
Humans and other animals

By the end of this chapter you should:

- **be aware of significant subject knowledge that underpins the understanding of humans and other animals;**
- **recognise common misconceptions associated with humans and other animals;**
- **understand the progression of this topic using some examples of learning activities from 3 to 11 years;**
- **identify specific basic skills, illustrative and investigative opportunities within this topic;**
- **have reflected upon how to present this aspect of science using ICT.**

Professional Standards for QTS

Q1, Q2, Q4, Q7a, Q8, Q9, Q10, Q14, Q15, Q17, Q18, Q19, Q21a, Q21b, Q22, Q23, Q25a, Q25b, Q25c, Q25d, Q26b, Q27, Q28, Q29, Q30, Q31

Curriculum Guidance for the Foundation Stage and National Curriculum

In the Foundation Stage pupils should:

- **find out about, and identify, some features of living things (QCA, 2000, p86);**
- **show an interest in why things happen and how things work;**
- **talk about what is seen and what is happening (QCA, 2000, p88);**
- **show an interest in the lives of people familiar to them (QCA, 2000, p94).**

At Key Stage 1 pupils should be taught:

- **to recognise and compare the main external parts of the bodies of humans and other animals;**
- **that humans and other animals need food and water to stay alive;**
- **that taking exercise and eating the right types and amounts of food help humans to keep healthy;**
- **about the role of drugs as medicines;**
- **how to treat animals with care and sensitivity;**
- **that humans and other animals can produce offspring and that these offspring grow into adults;**

- **about the senses that enable humans and other animals to be aware of the world around them (DfEE, 1999, p79).**

At Key Stage 2 pupils should be taught:

Nutrition

- **about the functions and care of teeth;**
- **about the need for food for activity and growth, and about the importance of an adequate and varied diet for health.**

Circulation

- **that the heart acts as a pump to circulate the blood through vessels around the body, including through the lungs;**
- **about the effect of exercise and rest on pulse rate.**

Movement

- **that humans and some other animals have skeletons and muscles to support and protect their bodies and to help them to move.**

Growth and reproduction

- **about the main stages of the human life cycle.**

Health

- **about the effects on the human body of tobacco, alcohol and other drugs, and how these relate to their personal health;**
- **about the importance of exercise for good health (DfEE, 1999, p85).**

Introduction

Young children are naturally interested in, and fascinated by, their own bodies and those of others. Remarkably, the structures and systems that enable the human animal to function are similar to those found in other animals, particularly vertebrates. Surprisingly, even less complex but equally fascinating animals like worms, snails, millipedes and insects have systems that children can recognise and relate to.

A jigsaw book aimed at primary age children describes the human body as a human machine:

> . . . more amazing than any machine ever invented. It is made up of microscopic units called cells. Each cell contains complex information about who we are, called DNA which makes up our genes and within our genes is contained the chemical instructions for our body's entire life. (Clarke, 2006, p1)

Clarke's book not only feeds curiosity but explains complex ideas that many find difficult to understand, by using simple terms. The material is presented in a colourful, creative way and provides an excellent model for you to adopt in your teaching as you extend your children's understanding of this topic. There is no doubt that many have been put off this fascinating topic by the dry, uninspired way it was presented to them in school. This topic, almost more than any other, requires a creative, imaginative approach if you are to communicate with enthusiasm the potentially fascinating ideas to your children.

The complexity of the organisation of cells within systems that ensure the smooth running of the human body, and the bodies of other animals, is truly amazing. It may be tempting to provide children with worksheets that they can complete to reinforce aspects of this topic. However, with a little creative thought you can introduce your pupils to significant ideas and attitudes that will help them to understand themselves and their bodies better and also the bodies of other animals. This might fundamentally affect their future well-being but also their quality and enjoyment of life.

Check your understanding

What do you understand by the following terms? Make a note of your ideas.

Plant cell	Animal cell
Tissue	Organ
Sensitivity	Excretion
Growth	Respiration
Food	Movement
Reproduction	Vitamin
Mineral	Fat
Protein	Skeleton
Carbohydrate	Tendon
Muscle	Diet
Digestion	

Check your understanding with the Glossary.

Humans and other animals: some basic ideas

Humans are animals. Like plants, all animals exhibit the seven processes of living things: they move, feed, respire, grow, reproduce, excrete and are sensitive to things that happen around them. Unlike plants, however, animals move their bodies, in different ways, in order to feed and to escape from danger. All organisms feed and this is necessary to provide the energy for their life processes. Animals that eat plants are called herbivores, whilst omnivorous animals eat plants and animals and those that eat only other animals are called carnivores. Respiration is an important process of living because it releases the energy from the food to fuel the chemical reactions involved in supporting movement, growth and to repair damaged parts of the organism. All living things grow and many animals grow quickly in the early stages of their lives, but stop growing when they reach adulthood. All organisms produce waste, and excretion is the process of removing unwanted and potentially toxic substances from the organism. All organisms are sensitive and react to the world around them and some animals have sense organs. The number and type of senses used depends on how the organism has become adapted to its environment. Reproduction, the process of making of new individuals, ensures that the organism does not become extinct. Some plants and simple animals like amoeba and hydra reproduce asexually but most animals reproduce sexually.

Cells are the building blocks of living things and all organisms contain them. Animals and plants cells have basic differences that reflect their function, e.g. plants have a tough cellulose cell wall to allow pressure to build up inside them and give structure, but animals have skeletons. Animals also have specialised cells, which perform different and highly complex functions, e.g. nerve cells, bone cells, red blood cells, white blood cells, muscle cells, sperm and egg cells. Under the microscope it can be seen that as well as performing different functions these cells also look different. Chemical reactions take place within cells. You can find out more about cells and their function in Chapters 2 and 3 of Peacock et al. (2007).

A group of identical cells, together performing the same function in an animal's body is called a tissue, e.g. muscle cells in muscle tissue. Different tissues working together to perform a bodily function make up an organ. The heart, lungs, kidneys, stomach, liver and brain are all organs. Different organs work together within systems, e.g. digestive system, excretory system, or the nervous system. An important system for you to understand well is the circulatory system, where the heart and blood vessels make up the blood system that carries blood around the body to perform various functions essential to life at an individual level.

The bodies of organisms are made up of chemicals (materials). Organisms gain their energy either from photosynthesis if they are green plants, or by eating other organisms if they are not able to manufacture their own food. Some organisms gain their nutrition from other organisms without providing any benefit to that organism; these are called parasites. Others carry out a symbiotic relationship, which has some benefit to both parties. Parasites such as tapeworms do not provide any benefit to their hosts, whilst the plover will eat the leeches from a Nile crocodile's gums, a mutually useful arrangement for both animals. Nutrition provides the energy to fuel all aspects of life. Without energy organisms would die. There are basic, different materials in the foods that humans eat, i.e. proteins, carbohydrates and fats. Healthy eating means eating a balanced diet, i.e. not too little or too much of each type of food material.

Food energy, like all forms of energy, can be measured in joules (J), but in everyday life the term 'calorie' is more commonly used. Organisms require different quantities of food energy at different stages of their lives, because different amounts of energy are required to carry out the various life processes of the organism. The more an organism moves, grows, reproduces, etc. the more energy is needed. Animals that eat more food than they use become fat. More exercise requires more energy.

In addition to food, humans and other animals need small amounts of vitamins and minerals that are essential to good health. Lack of these can cause illness. Water is essential to life and it makes up two-thirds of the body weight of humans. The human body needs water because it is essential for many of the chemical reactions that occur within cells, it carries waste materials out of our bodies, and in sweat it helps to maintain a constant body temperature. Humans are warm-blooded; this means that the body maintains a constant temperature and uses large amounts of energy to do so. Reptiles and other simpler organisms are cold-blooded; they take on the temperature of their surroundings. When it is hot, cold-blooded animals have hotter body temperatures than warm-blooded animals. Cold-blooded animals are able to use most of the food they eat to put on body weight, as they do not have to use food energy to maintain their body temperature.

Teeth play an important part in digestion by breaking food down into smaller pieces. This makes the food easier to swallow and provides larger surface areas for enzymes to continue the breakdown during digestion. Human adults normally have 32 teeth of different types: incisors, canines, premolars and molars, which are different shapes. Humans generally have two sets of teeth: the first set, milk teeth, are gradually lost throughout childhood and replaced by permanent teeth.

In vertebrates, animals with backbones, the skeletal system provides the support for the body and the protection for the essential organs like the brain, heart, lungs and liver. The skeleton is not just a movable frame, it is an efficient factory that produces red blood cells from the bone marrow of certain bones, and white cells, to destroy harmful bacteria, from the marrow of other bones. Babies are born with 270 soft bones; this is about 64 more than an adult and many of these will fuse together by the age of 20 or 25 into the 206 hard, permanent bones that make up an adult skeleton. The muscular system keeps the body moving. Muscles cover the skeleton and are connected to bones or tendons, thus allowing and controlling movement. Muscles need food to provide the energy for movement. However, they also need to be used regularly to continue to function properly and therefore exercise is important to keep muscles strong and healthy. The more they are used, the stronger they become.

The health of humans can be affected by a number of factors including the amount of exercise taken. Drugs are chemicals that can be good for the body in the case of medicines or harmful as in the case of tobacco, alcohol or other 'social drugs' that can cause illness and disease.

Children's ideas about humans and other animals

Children often do not believe that humans are animals, because the term 'animal' in everyday conversations usually relates to pets or to animals in the wild, on farms and in zoos. In turn, their ideas are linked with the notion that animals have four, not two, legs, have fur and make animal noises and do not talk. This misconception is potentially reinforced if teachers or others describe children as 'behaving like animals' or ask children to 'stop making animal noises'.

The ideas children have about 'the things they think to be alive' are similarly problematic. Piaget (1929, cited in Peacock et al. 2007), found that children thought bicycles, clocks, the sun, the moon, clouds and fire were alive. Young children, perhaps encouraged through popular media, often treat their teddies and dolls as if they were alive and even think cars are alive 'because they move'. The SPACE (Science Process and Concept Exploration 1990 onwards) project found that drawings of what children thought were inside their body revealed strange ideas about the location of organs, even where older children could list the names of those same organs. Bones and muscles were often not connected to each other and ideas about reproduction were highly imaginative. Of course, much research evidence is now dated, but commonly, trainees and teachers report that similar misconceptions persist even in our more openly liberal society where children are exposed to far more explicit information about living things and bodily functions than ever before.

Children might associate the term 'diet' with its everyday usage of losing weight rather than the type and amount of food that is consumed everyday. In some cases they also think that high-fat diets are good and carbohydrates are bad, an effect of the Atkins diet. Many children believe that chocolate is bad for you and fruit is good, rather than realising that a diet composed only of fruits would be as unhealthy as one composed of only chocolate.

Teaching Example 4.1: Foundation Stage

Children at the Foundation Stage are more likely than others to have been around younger children and babies, either within their own homes, those of their peers or in the nursery, playgroup or mother and toddler group. They will be familiar with how babies grow rapidly and become bigger over a short time and will know and recognise a range of older people within and outside their families, including parents or carers and possibly grandparents and great grandparents. Change over time is there to be observed and can be easily discussed in the classroom context. This is also the time, more than any other that photographs of their own development may be available to share in the classroom with others. Foundation Stage children are likely to also be familiar, if not at first hand, with baby and adult animals, particularly pets, farm and zoo animals, through pictures and simple factual books. Here then, are many opportunities to develop children's ideas of maturation and growth over time.

Action rhymes such as 'heads, shoulders knees and toes' help to reinforce simple external parts of the body. Early exploration of different materials, e.g. fur, hair, skin, and asking pupils to describe them in words will help develop scientific vocabulary as well as familiarising them with body coverings.

Collections are always useful in the Early Years and collections of shoes and clothes can be used to help children realise that they grow. If a collection of vests is used, those from babies of less than 3 months can be compared with those of children of 1, 3, 5, 7 years of age. If too many are used it can become confusing for very young children; however, a greater sample could be used with more able and older children. Socks for different ages (and sizes of feet) can be placed in order on a washing line. Even simple clothes like pyjamas will make it clear to children that they grow and grow quickly.

CASE STUDY CASE STUDY CASE STUDY CASE STUDY CASE STUDY CASE STUDY

In many classes children from a number of backgrounds and nationalities will mix together. Humans are not all the same: the colour of our eyes, our hair and even our skin can differ. However, there are many ways in which we are the same. Ignoring differences does not help children to see that there is a continuum and using colour matching can help children to gain a wider understanding. In an Early Years class, which had a range of children from many ethnic backgrounds the children were following a topic of 'themselves'. The teacher decided that colour matching would be a good activity to show that basically people are all the same and that skin colour was like having different eye colour and was a feature that had been adapted according to the environment. Using good quality paint in white, pink, yellow, brown, red and black the children were asked to mix the paint to match their skin colour. When they decided they had produced the right shade, they painted a small patch onto the back of their hand. The teacher then talked to them about their match, 'Was it too dark, too pink, or too pale?' They adjusted their colour mixing until a good match was gained, and then painted this colour onto a small square of paper, which was later placed on the wall. The painted papers were not arranged in order of colour from dark to light but randomly so the children could see the range. The teacher also placed large squares of white, black, yellow and pink on the display so the children could see that no one was white, no one was black and there were no pink or yellow children either. Although this activity originated in a multi-racial class it was later used by a teacher in an 'all-white' school. This was also effective as the children here had varying shades of skin colour and it also made the children aware that pink was not a good colour for self-portraits.

Teaching Example 4.2: Key Stage 1

'Senses' makes a popular topic at Key Stage 1 and it links well to children developing observation skills as they use all the senses. Although it is tempting at this stage to ask children to label drawings of the ear or eye, it is much more worthwhile to involve children in first-hand exploration using their senses.

Sight: What does the world really look like through rose-coloured glasses? Using simple cardboard frames and coloured acetate will change the way the children see the world. This is a great but simple activity to enable children to look again at their classroom, friends and school and to describe what they see.

Taste: Tasting things when blindfolded, tasting different things on different parts of the tongue, tasting lemonade, etc., with different food colouring added, are all fun things to do. Changing the colour of something can affect its taste; children can be given different coloured jelly made with vegetable gelatine, food flavours and food colouring. The children can then decide if they can identify the taste when the colour is wrong. Orange flavour jelly can be given a shot of blue food dye, whilst strawberry flavouring can be used for orange-coloured jelly. The children can then talk about what they have tasted.

Smell: Put different materials in 'smelly pots' and challenge the children to match the smell. Different smelling teas are simple, cheap and fun. Most Reception children can identify lapsang souchong, without any problems. Gunpowder tea is also easy to match to its packet. Place a small sample of tea into a black, empty film canister. Let the children smell the pot and match it to the bag or packet. Other favourites include orange pekoe, English rose and ginger teas. However, as there are more than 50 types of tea, there are many possibilities.

Hearing: Are big ears better than small ones? Help the children to make ear trumpets using sugar paper and adhesive tape. Roll the sugar paper up into a cone. Use different size pieces of paper and ask the children to see if it is better to have the big or small end near their ear. Will bigger ears funnel more sound? Then use secondary sources to see what shape animals' ears are and where they are found on the animals' head.

Touch: How well can you identify things by touch? Feely bags or boxes are always popular. Put familiar and then unfamiliar objects for description by touch, e.g. dried things, fresh leaves, etc. Encourage your children to describe the material they are feeling rather than stating what they think it is. Can other children guess the object from the description? Link to literacy: blindfold your children and provide them with letters of the alphabet cut out of felt glued onto card. Can they recognise the letter by touch alone? Similarly, in mathematics, regular shapes cut out of the bumpy part of corrugated card can be explored. Can children cut out their own shapes from card or thin fabric for others to identify? Older children can produce a 'materials trail', a path of, e.g. fabrics, card, plastics and other materials, for others, blindfolded, to explore and identify by touch (see below).

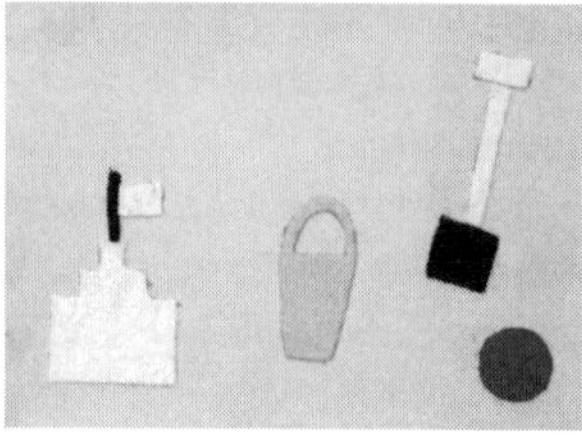

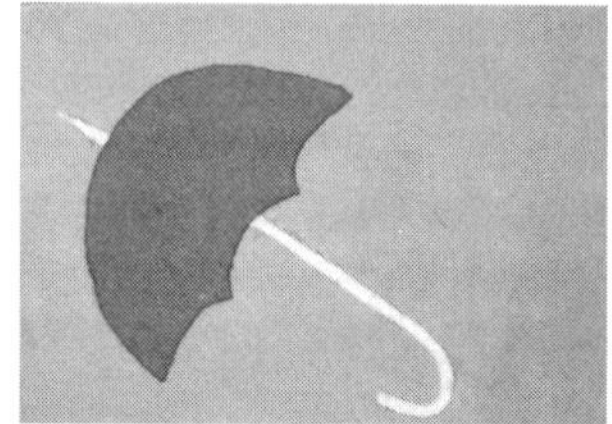

Figure 4.1 Felt shape pictures

Diet: Introduce idea of 'diet' meaning what we eat. It is useful to use a colour-coding system. Such a system has been introduced by the Food Standards agency (2006) to help adults make sensible food choices. The information below comes from their website **www.eatwell.gov.uk/foodlabels/trafficlights/**

What do the traffic light colours mean?
To eat a healthy diet, one key thing is to reduce intake of fat (especially saturated fat), salt and added sugars. With traffic-light colours, you can see at a glance if the food you're looking at has high, medium or low amounts of each of these nutrients in 100g of the food:

Red = High
Amber = Medium
Green = Low

Although a traffic-light system can be used, these refer to food groups themselves rather than just salt, sugar and fat:

- red is used for food that provides energy and movement;
- orange is used for food for growth and repair;
- green is used for food like fruits and vegetables that contain high amounts of minerals and vitamins and fibre.

In order to be healthy, a diet composed of a little red food, more orange and as much as you like of green is ideal. However, to be balanced you would have some of all. It would not be healthy to eat only vegetables or only high-fat food like cakes and biscuits.

Investigations into teeth

Teeth: care of the teeth
When children are eating their daily fruit or vegetables in the classroom there is a good opportunity to encourage them not only to chew their food properly, but to notice which teeth they use at various stages of biting and chewing food. How easy is it to bite into an apple if you have lost your 'front teeth'? Try carrots, bread, cheese and apples, cut into small pieces. Ask the children to use only one kind of tooth for each one, starting with incisor, and see what happens when they try to eat the food. Find out which teeth are more effective for each food. They can go on to think about what babies eat and why.

Other questions to ask include: 'What age does the tooth fairy come most often?' This is a survey of the children in each class in the school, who have lost a tooth that week. Collect data once a week on a Friday over a four-week period, and then collate the information into a graph. It should become obvious that front teeth (front and lateral incisors) are generally lost between 6 and 7 years of age, to be replaced by second teeth, and back teeth (molars) are lost towards the end of Key Stage 2 when the molars start to come through.

Teaching example 4.3: Key Stage 2

Teeth

Looking at own teeth

By looking in a mirror, children can count how many teeth they have and can identify the different types of teeth. They should be able to identify canines, incisors and molars and know the functions of each type.

Children should also compare human teeth with those of other animals. The diet of the animal will affect the type and numbers of each tooth. They should look at the teeth of herbivores, e.g. rabbits, which have large incisors that grow continuously through their life – they also have many molars; and carnivores such as lions and other cats which have canines to cut and tear meat.

Skeletons

Compare the human skeleton with those of other animals. This can be done by using pictures and by looking at X-ray photographs.

Diet

Case study

A trainee was asked to teach about healthy eating to her class. She was aware that her children were largely from a deprived home background and was conscious of the need to approach this topic with sensitivity. She introduced the idea of healthy eating by examining the diet of Bart Simpson, a character easily related to by all members of her class.

Food-based tasks

Plan meals for a sports person like Steven Gerrard, and the Prime Minister. What would be the same and what would be different about these meals?

Investigating in the area of humans as organisms

Too often in this aspect of science, fair test investigations are attempted. It is not a good area to try to carry out a fair test unless it is possible to have a very large sample who are happy to undertake some activities that are better carried out in laboratory. For example, there is still no proven direct link between smoking and death, as some people will smoke all their life and will not suffer bad health and others will smoke for a shorter time and will die. This is the joy of genetics. Although there is a well-known fact that smoking is bad for you, there is no direct cause-and-effect link in the way there is if you stand in front of a moving train. Therefore in this aspect of the curriculum it is better to look at surveys. A range of data is still needed and children can question the results but they are not trying to prove something by changing one factor and monitoring the effect. Using surveys and observing changes over time will develop the skills of science.

Surveying: Do the people with the largest feet have the biggest hands?

Learning intention: Looking for patterns and trends

Any survey can be undertaken, for example, 'Is the length of the leg linked to the thickness of the thigh?', 'Is the maximum span using both arms the same as the height?' Using any relationship question, it is possible to learn more about the body and growing. These activities could be undertaken using children from one class or with children from across an age range, e.g. Reception to Year 6. It is important to decide, with the children, what data should be collected and how it will be recorded, e.g. as a scatter graph for the class or for a group.

PRACTICAL TASK PRACTICAL TASK PRACTICAL TASK PRACTICAL TASK PRACTICAL TASK

Which is the best toothpaste?

Ask the children, through discussion, to decide what would make good toothpaste. Then they should bring toothpaste from home and try the froth test, by seeing how much froth can be gained when a set amount of toothpaste is shaken with water. Also fun is the idea of using different toothbrushes to see which type cleans most effectively. Coat a ceramic tile (not on the shiny side) with shoe polish and using toothpaste and brushes (that will not be used in children's mouths), find which one cleans off the most polish. To make the test reliable, talk about the amount of rubs with the brush, the amount of pressure and time to be used.

PRACTICAL TASK PRACTICAL TASK PRACTICAL TASK PRACTICAL TASK PRACTICAL TASK

Which crisps have the most salt?

As salt is an area that worries health professionals, checking the amount of salt in an everyday food can link this activity to diet. In a number of schools this activity has been undertaken as part of the creative curriculum for more than ten years. It works because there are no right or wrong answers. With the advent of the digital microscope, comparing and counting the amount of salt can be undertaken easily. Taste tests are easy but the salt could also be dissolved and then measured through evaporation. Through this latter activity children would experience dissolving, filtering and evaporating. The back of the salt packet will also tell a story and can be a useful secondary source of information. Your children may come up with far more interesting ideas; challenge them and see.

Subject knowledge that underpins the activities in this chapter

Tongue and its parts

Depending on which books are used and what research is believed, there are a range of tongue maps. The suggestion is that the tongue has different regions, with sweet and salty things being recognised by the taste buds at the tip; bitter tastes are recognised by the taste buds on the back of the tongue, and sour tastes are sensed at the sides and in the middle. What is not debated is that there are 10,000 taste buds on the tongue. Some scientists suggest that all the tongue is used for sensing different tastes. It is easy to try this with the children and to get them involved in the debate about whether there are taste zones – true or false?

The reason it is difficult to recognise taste without sight and smell is related to the link between the smell and taste. There are human olfactory receptors and chemical receptors that sense the concentrations of chemicals in food. They act together and without one the ability of the other to discriminate taste and smell is diminished. Sight too has a role in taste. Children often think that an orange-coloured liquid will taste of orange. Testing children's ability to distinguish taste can be done by providing, e.g. lemonade coloured with different food dyes, or by blindfolding children as they taste different flavoured crisps. Then ask them to hold their nose and identify some foodstuff by taste.

Task

Exploring the sense of taste provides excellent opportunities to introduce a multicultural dimension. Provide children with foods from around the world; can they describe the taste?

Teeth

Adult humans have 32 permanent teeth that replace 20 milk, or 'first' teeth. There are four different types of teeth:

- **incisors at the front of the mouth tend to have straight edges used for biting and cutting food, e.g. when biting pieces of fruit or vegetables;**
- **canines are pointed for piercing food and tearing it into smaller pieces;**
- **premolars have uneven cusps used for grinding and crushing;**
- **molars are like premolars, but are bigger and chew food.**

An adult with a full set of teeth will have 8 incisors, 4 canines, 8 premolars and 12 molars. Children usually lose their milk teeth between the ages of six and twelve. Permanent teeth replace them gradually so that usually by the time an individual is 18 they will have a complete set including the wisdom teeth (four large molars) that are the last to appear. Types of teeth and dental hygiene have been tested in the National Tests (Y6) on a regular basis. Children will give many reasons for types of teeth, including one pupil whose response on the 1998 paper, to the question 'What do canine teeth do?' was 'to stop the food falling out of your mouth'.

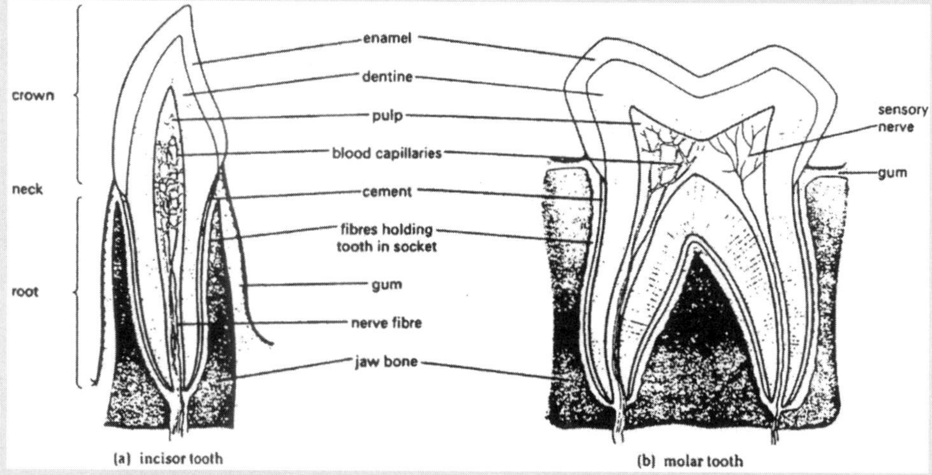

Figure 4.2 Cross sectional drawing of incisor and molar

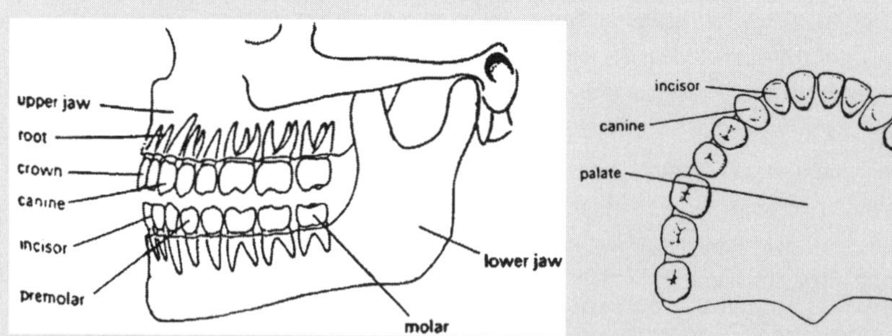

Figure 4.3 Human jaw showing the position of the teeth

Figure 4.4 The position of the teeth in a human jaw

Tooth decay is a common problem. Teeth can be kept healthy by regular, correct brushing of teeth and gums. More teeth are lost through gum decay than through tooth decay. Sweet things will change the pH of the mouth, making it easier for the plaque to multiply. Plaque is the name for harmful bacteria in the mouth. There are more bacteria in the mouth of a single human than there are people in the world. Streptococcus mutants are the bacteria that cause decay. Scientists think that it changed from being a friendly bacterium as the human diet changed to include more refined sugar.

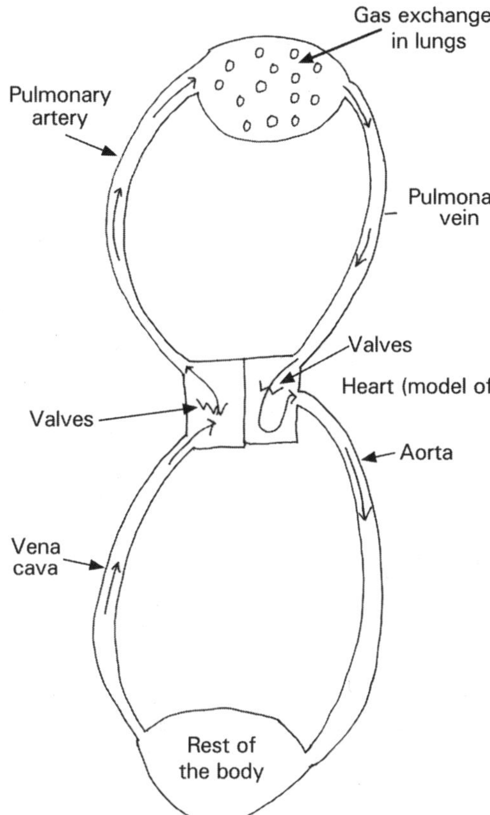

Fig. 4.5 The circulatory system

Diet

Humans need a balanced diet to keep healthy. Eating only one type of food is not good for the body because it needs a varied diet that includes the main food types: proteins, carbohydrates and fats, as well as water, vitamins, minerals and fibre.

- **Proteins are needed for growth and repair of cells**
- **Carbohydrates are needed for energy**
- **Fats are needed for energy and heat**

The circulatory system

The circulatory system is the main transportation and cooling system for the body. Using analogy again, the red blood cells could be thought of as billions of delivery vans that carry all packages of nutrients and oxygen to all the cells in the body. The white blood cells are like maintenance workers; they fight off bacteria and help to heal the body if it is damaged.

These delivery vans and maintenance workers travel down some very small one-way streets, called capillaries, as well as larger roads, like motorways. Some of the capillaries are so small only a single blood cell (delivery truck) can get through at a time. The motorways are the veins and arteries.

Veins carry blood back to the heart whilst arteries carry blood away from the heart. The heart pumps the blood away, so the arteries are always at higher pressure. This higher pressure means the arteries have to have strong walls to withstand the push of the heartbeat. The blood in the veins flows back to the heart under lower pressure so there is less pressure and the walls are thinner. The blood in the veins has delivered its oxygen and nutrients to the cells and is returning to the heart to be pumped back to lungs. It is low in oxygen and is called deoxygenated blood. The blood in the arteries is high in oxygen and nutrients and as a result is brighter red in colour. Some people think it is the amount of oxygen carried that makes it a vein or an artery, but it is the direction of travel from the heart. The vein leading to the heart from the lungs is rich in oxygenated blood but is still a vein.

The heart is a four-chambered pump, with two unconnected sides. On the right side of the heart the two chambers receive blood from the body and pump it to the lungs, whilst the left-hand side receives blood from the lungs and pumps it to the body. Children who have a condition called 'hole in the heart' have connections between the two sides that must be 'fixed' if the children are to survive. The heart is made up of involuntary muscle, which works without us having to think about it. The heart muscle is always expanding and contracting, usually at between 60 and 100 beats per minute.

In the lungs there are many small capillaries located in the air sacs, called alveoli. When the blood goes past these they pick up the oxygen parcels. The blood returns to the heart in this oxygenated form via the cardiac vein, which empties into the left-hand side of the heart. This is the high-pressure side of the heart and the blood is then pushed to the rest of the body. In the heart there are valves to stop the blood from flowing back and these are often the first part of the heart to start to wear out, thus causing heart problems.

The venous system carries the blood back to the heart. The blood flows from the capillaries, to very small veins called venules, and from these into veins. The largest veins in the body are called the superior and inferior vena cava. From the heart the whole system starts again.

PRACTICAL TASK PRACTICAL TASK **PRACTICAL TASK** PRACTICAL TASK **PRACTICAL TASK**

Look at the following animated websites:
www.healthyteeth.org/
www.kidshealth.org/kid/body/bones_noSW.html

- **How could you use these to develop children's understanding of their own bodies?**
- **Critically analyse the sites. What are their strengths and limitations?**

A SUMMARY OF **KEY POINTS**

The focus of the work in the above example was on the activities to help learners understand more about humans and other animals. In particular it has:

> **presented a number of activities on the theme of humans and other animals showing how learners' understanding of basic ideas can be developed over the primary age range.**

Moving on

One aspect of this topic briefly mentioned above was the comparison of skeletons. Using human and other vertebrate X-rays as a starting point, build up a series of lessons to investigate this important aspect of living things. For example, you might like to think about the relationship between:

- **the shape of an animal and its feeding habits**
- **the length of legs and the habitat in which the animal lives.**

Alternatively, you might be interested in linking science with design technology and in investigating:

- **the weight and strength of bones.**

This chapter has focused mainly on the vertebrate group of animals, but many other, simpler animals have features in common with humans and the other vertebrates. Taking simple ideas about living things, e.g. circulation system, what and how they eat, how they get rid of waste, as a starting point, plan a series of lessons based on children's questions about small, familiar invertebrates, e.g. snails, millipedes, worms.

How might you ask children to communicate their findings to others in this area?

FURTHER READING FURTHER READING **FURTHER READING** FURTHER READING

Peacock, G., Sharp, J., Johnsey, R. and Wright, D. (2007) Functioning of Organisms: humans and other animals, Chapter 4 in *Primary Science: Knowledge and Understanding* (3rd edition). Exeter: Learning Matters

Stringer, J. (2001) *Teaching the Tricky Bits. Science: The Human Body*. Leamington Spa: Hopscotch Educational Publishing

Wenham, M. (2005) Humans and other animals, Chapter 3 in *Understanding Primary Science*. London: Paul Chapman Publishing

Children's books

Cole, B. (1996) *Dr Dog*. London: Red Fox

Hayes, S. (1996) *Eat up, Gemma*. Falmouth: Walker

5
Green plants as living things

By the end of this chapter you should:

- **be aware of some of the significant subject knowledge that underpins the understanding of green plants as living things;**
- **recognise some of the common misconceptions associated with green plants;**
- **understand the progression of this topic using some examples of learning activities from 3 to 11 years;**
- **identify specific basic skills, illustrative and investigative opportunities within this topic;**
- **recognise the health and safety aspects of the practical activities associated with this topic;**
- **have reflected upon the potential opportunities for first-hand observation of change over time in the local environment provided by this topic.**

Professional Standards for QTS

Q1, Q2, Q4, Q7a, Q8, Q9, Q10, Q14, Q15, Q17, Q18, Q19, Q21a, Q21b, Q22, Q23, Q25a, Q25b, Q25c, Q26b, Q27, Q28, Q29, Q30, Q31

Curriculum Guidance for the Foundation Stage and National Curriculum

In the Foundation Stage pupils should:

- **show curiosity, observe and manipulate objects;**
- **describe simple features of objects and events;**
- **examine living things to find out more about them;**
- **investigate objects and materials by using all of their senses as appropriate;**
- **find out about and identify some features of living things (QCA, 2000, p86);**
- **show an interest in how things happen;**
- **sort objects by one function;**
- **notice and comment on patterns (QCA, 2000, p88).**

At Key Stage 1 pupils should be taught to:

- **recognise that plants need light and water to grow;**
- **recognise and name the leaf, flower, stem and root on flowering plants;**
- **seeds grow into flowering plants (DfEE, 1999, p79).**

At Key Stage 2 pupils should be taught:

Growth and nutrition

- **the effect of light, air, water, and temperature on plant growth;**
- **the role of the leaf in producing new material for growth;**
- **that the root anchors the plant and that water and minerals are taken in through the root and transported through the stem to other parts of the plant.**

Reproduction

- **about the parts of the flower and the role in the life cycle of flowering plants including pollination, seed formation, seed dispersal and germination. (DfEE, 1999, pp85–6)**

Introduction

Green plants are one of the two major groups of living things. As a group, green plants are very successful. They are found in most parts of the world in almost every habitat from deserts to the tundra and from the plains to the equatorial forests.

> The diversity of green plants on the surface of the Earth today is quite simply staggering. The importance of green plants, together with other photosynthetic organisms cannot be overstated. They are the starting points for most food chains and they produce the oxygen which keeps most other living things alive (Peacock et al., 2007)

Not only do green plants produce oxygen as part of the process of photosynthesis but they remove carbon dioxide from the atmosphere. The abundance and accessibility of green plants inside and outside in parks, gardens and playgrounds and in the countryside make their study potentially very exciting for primary children. A carefully planned, practical study of green plants can provide a diverse range of opportunities for children to develop their knowledge and understanding of the characteristics of green plants, their requirements for life and how they reproduce.

It would be unfortunate if the childrens' exposure to green plants in school were limited to filling in labels on worksheets with little hands-on exploration. Many children plant seeds, but this is often limited to cress seeds and sometimes repeated from the Foundation Stage through to Year 6. With this uninspiring scenario in mind, this chapter aims to explore a whole range of activities that can provide you and your children with hours of pleasure whilst developing the necessary understanding for meeting the requirements of the curriculum and a sense of awe and wonder for green plants in the natural world.

Check your understanding

Write down what you understand to be a 'green plant'. List a few examples for later reflection.

What do you understand by the following terms? Make a note of your ideas.

Plant	Fruit
Tree	Seed
Growth	Vegetable
Nutrition	Weed
Petal	Stigma
Sepal	Style
Carpel	Osmosis

Make a list of the names of some:

1. common fruits;

2. seeds;
3. vegetables.

What are the characteristics of each that identify it as a member of the group to which you have assigned it?

Check your understanding with the Glossary.

Green plants: some basic ideas

Just like animals, green plants are living things, i.e. they grow, move, feed, respire, excrete, are sensitive to the environment and reproduce, but they perform all these processes in different ways from animals. The plant kingdom is subdivided into six main groups, including mosses and liverworts, horsetails, club mosses, ferns, conifers and flowering plants.

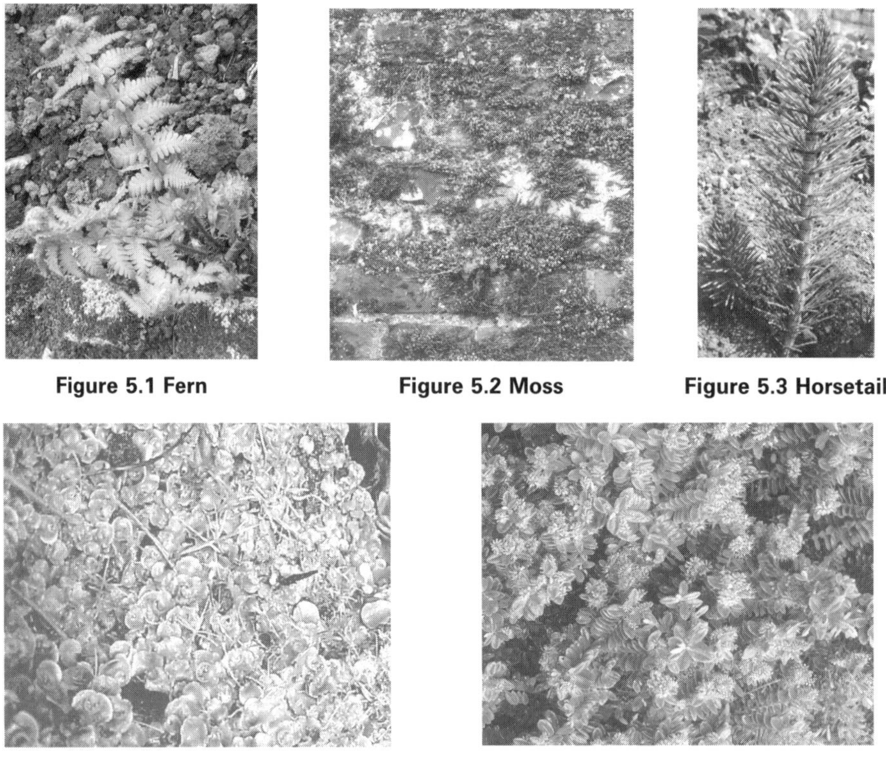

Figure 5.1 Fern

Figure 5.2 Moss

Figure 5.3 Horsetail

Figure 5.4 Liverwort

Figure 5.5 Flowering plant

In the activity above, you might have included fungi, algae and lichens as plants, but scientists do not include them in the plant kingdom. Although algae make their own food they do not reproduce in the same way as plants. They are part of a group called Protista. Fungi are placed in a group of their own called fungi; they do not make their own food and obtain their nutrition from the decaying matter upon which they live. Fungi and algae together have a symbiotic relationship. Together they produce lichens.

Green plants make their own food by the chemical change called photosynthesis, which requires energy in the form of sunlight, carbon dioxide and water. Water comes from the ground and whilst many plants will grow in soil, soil is not essential for plant growth. An essential component for photosynthesis is chlorophyll. Chlorophyll is contained in the chloroplasts in plant cells and absorbs energy from sunlight. The process of photosynthesis converts energy from the sun into sugar. Oxygen is produced as a waste product of photosynthesis. When humans and other animals eat plants, the stored energy is used to enable them, in turn, to live and grow. You can read more about this process in Chapter 7.

Sugars produced during photosynthesis are used by the plant in three ways. Some sugars are used for respiration, some are stored as starch in the plant's roots and others are used to make cellulose, which is the material that makes cell walls. Photosynthesis takes place only in the light, but respiration occurs all the time. Many plants have large leaves to increase the rate of production of sugars by photosynthesis during the day when sunlight is plentiful. The rate of photosynthesis depends on the light levels and will not occur in the dark. Some plants are adapted to use lower levels of light, such as those that live low on the ground in woodland or in tropical rainforests, where the larger plants shade out some of the sunlight. Many green plants have a cuticle, which is a shiny, water-resistant surface on their upper surface of leaves to protect the cells that contain chlorophyll. The lower surface of a leaf is often paler and less waxy and is easy to observe. The lower surface of leaves also allows the green plant to respire, or breathe. Tiny air holes in the leaf called stomata open or close to allow gases to diffuse out. Carbon dioxide is allowed into the leaf for photosynthesis; oxygen and water vapour, the gaseous products of photosynthesis, are allowed out. The stomata control the amount of water that is allowed out of the plant. This is particularly important during hot weather, when there is a danger of drying out.

Roots not only allow the uptake of minerals and water that are essential to the health and day-to-day maintenance of the plant, they also anchor the plant into the ground. You might have noticed how well plants can colonise even the most surprising places. Not only can they live in arid conditions and remain rooted in very windy weather, they even colonise dry stonewalls and other surfaces with tiny crevices where roots hold the plant tightly in position. Water and minerals are taken into the roots by a process called osmosis so they are not sucking up water. In effect, water enters the plant by itself.

Plants reproduce both sexually and asexually. Sexual reproduction involves male and female sex cells, which join together at the point of fertilisation and take on characteristics from both parents' genes. Asexual reproduction requires only one parent and the resulting new plants are identical to the parent; there is no mixing of genetic information. When plant reproduction is considered, there is a tendency for this to be limited to that of flowering plants, but flowering plants are not the only plants that pupils will encounter when exploring their environment and, confusingly, some flowering plants also reproduce both asexually and sexually.

Plants that are sometimes called spider plants (*Chlorophytum comosum*) have long grasses, green and white leaves. At the end of healthy branches small new plantlets are formed; these will root if they touch the soil, or can be taken off and planted to make new plants.

PRACTICAL TASK PRACTICAL TASK PRACTICAL TASK PRACTICAL TASK PRACTICAL TASK

Find out the names and functions of the different parts of the flower. Look at different flowers, e.g. tulip, daffodil, apple blossom, dog rose, sweet pea, and, for each, identify each part. Read more about the mechanics of fertilisation of a flowering plant. It is important that you understand this process and how seeds are formed.

PRACTICAL TASK PRACTICAL TASK **PRACTICAL TASK** PRACTICAL TASK **PRACTICAL TASK**

Identify some common plants, including trees that reproduce by:

- **insect pollination;**
- **wind pollination;**
- **self-pollination;**
- **cross-pollination.**

Locate examples of each in the local environment of a school known to you.

RESEARCH SUMMARY RESEARCH SUMMARY **RESEARCH SUMMARY** RESEARCH SUMMARY

Green plants

Research suggests that many children have a limited knowledge and understanding of plants. A commonly held view is that green plants are just 'flowers' or are 'grown in pots'. Children may not think that plants are alive. The SPACE project (Science Processes and Concepts Exploration) in the 1990s found that very young children are more likely to say that some non-living things, e.g. a teddy bear, a fire or a car, are alive than to suggest that a tree is living. They may not know what factors affect growth nor understand how they reproduce. Children may have a limited idea of the diversity within the plant kingdom. They may hold stereotypical images of plants as merely 'flowers' and not consider trees to be plants. 'Fruit' might be thought of merely as apples and oranges. They may not understand that plants are alive because they do not obviously move or make noise. Some children may also think that plants die in winter, especially when a tree loses its last leaf.

Teaching example 5.1: Foundation Stage

You may well find children's ideas about plants and living things amusing, but young children draw their conclusions about things around them based on their experience. That is why it is important to provide different experiences to challenge these ideas and to extend your children's ideas about the world. Some ideas are easy to challenge and easily changed through discussion. In this way, children will adopt the idea without the need for much persuasion. However, many children find the notion of tree-as-plant quite challenging and the idea that plants move and feed may be even more problematic. Therefore it is important that from a very young age, children are introduced to and observe the changes that occur at regular intervals through the year and that the changes are revisited through the primary years.

Exploring green plants

Learning intention: To collect and sort parts of green plants

Changing seasons offer new opportunities for exploration of the world of plants.

Very young children will not find it difficult to adopt the idea that a tree is a plant if you introduce this idea at a young age. Changes in trees are very noticeable and young children will be eager to collect fruits of trees such as the horse chestnut, sycamore and lime. Fruits can be displayed for examination and discussion, taking, of course, the necessary health and safety precautions, and can be sorted into groups based on simple criteria.

Similar explorations can be made of the falling leaves in autumn. Here, the variation in the size and shape of leaves falling from the same tree can be examined and explored.

Young children are fascinated by the changing colour of the leaves falling from the trees as the tree prepares itself for dormancy during the winter. Although it is easy for young children to think that trees die in winter, when encouraged to look they can notice the leaf scar where once a leaf was attached to the tree and the signs of new life in the form of winter buds.

Changes in leaves over time are very obvious and provide opportunities for simple recording where children are regularly asked to look for and report on the changes they notice for themselves. Fruits like sycamore seeds can be used for simple observations at the Foundation Stage. There is an excellent opportunity here for young children to develop simple scientific vocabulary, to look at the fruits of sycamore and the various parts of the seed inside the hard case of the fruit. How the seed falls through the air can be noticed and compared with other winged fruits and others without wings. Such exploration builds up a young child's ideas of plants and extends their understanding at a simple level. These will form a sound basis for later, more sophisticated exploration and investigation of trees and their parts. Lots of fun can be had when leaves are falling quickly in the autumn. On a fine day children can be asked to make general observations, for example, notice if big leaves fall faster than small leaves. A cross-curricular link can be made here with music and dance when children are encouraged to imagine themselves as leaves falling from a tree and being blown along by the wind.

Young children need to begin to understand that not all trees are the same. The activities here will raise awareness, for example, that the leaves of different trees are not all the same, or that the fruits of different trees are not all the same, thereby gradually building up ideas of variation within groups.

Bark rubbing is a popular activity for a dry day. Here again is an opportunity to discover that not all bark patterns are the same. Bark rubbings can be shared and compared. If your class has access to a number of different trees in a safe environment, children can be challenged to match a bark rubbing made by another child to the tree from which it came. There is the opportunity here for displaying the rubbings, perhaps alongside a picture of the tree and other collected parts. 'Tree hugging' (feeling and putting hands and arms around a tree) whilst wearing a blindfold is also a fun way of getting children to notice that types of trees are different.

Planting tree seeds can prove very productive as they germinate quite easily in pots with compost as the growing medium.

Seed dispersal: dandelion clocks

Children need to build up their understanding of seeds. In the early stages, they can be familiarised by handling larger seeds and sorting a range of seeds into groups.

When exploring the outside environment in summer, young children love to pick wild flowers such as the dandelion. You need to be careful about the liquid than runs from the stem because it can stain fabrics and there is an 'old wives' tale' surrounding flowering dandelions. A very pleasurable activity is to see how many puffs it takes to release the seeds from a dandelion clock (more scientifically termed seed head). Observation of this form of seed dispersal can be extended to include thistle seed heads and the rose bay willow herb, as these are frequently found on waste ground in urban areas.

Teaching Example 5.2: Key Stage 1

Learning at Key Stage 1 can easily build on that at the Foundation Stage. More detailed observations of trees and other plants can be made. Your children might be interested in finding out, for example, what happens to leaves that have fallen from trees in autumn. Simple investigations could focus on how long it takes for leaves to rot, or to investigate if they could stop the drying out of leaves over time. With your children you could design a simple experiment to find out which leaves decay most quickly. All these activities not only reinforce the properties of leaves, but could also lead to a very interesting way to reinforce the use of a fair test.

Photographs like the ones below can be used as a starting point for matching.

Figure 5.6 Photographs of tree bark

If children are given pictures of bark and asked to match it to a real tree in the school grounds or on a walk, they will notice the differences between species and simultaneously develop their observation skills.

Sorting fruits and vegetables

Learning intention: To sort and classify fruits and vegetables

You will have realised that there is potentially much confusion about what might be called a fruit and what a vegetable. It is obviously important that you are aware to which group commonly termed fruits and vegetables belong before teaching.

Starting with discussion and observation and observational drawings of a wide range of fruits will reinforce the scientific idea of fruits. Cutting the fruits to expose the different parts, i.e. the skin, flesh and seeds in the case of apples, pears, courgettes, cucumbers, bananas, etc., followed by looking at peaches and perhaps avocados and mangoes, etc., will extend learning in the right direction. Linking this to the planting of seeds can be very rewarding.

Learning intention: To be able to recognise and name the leaf, flower, stem and root
Pupils can easily learn the parts of the plant by rote, and often do, sometimes leading to boredom, but exploration can be so much more motivating and exciting if children are given the opportunity to examine at first hand, a range of plants. Observing and comparing a range of plants complete with root, stem and leaves will provide another opportunity for children to appreciate the wide range and variety of living things within a single group.

Scenario
A teacher of Year 1 children had been reading *The Enormous Turnip* to his class. Following this, the children were taken out of school to uproot some plants from the school's wild area. Armed with plastic gloves for health and safety reasons, each child in his class was allowed to uproot a weed. Working in small groups, each group was challenged to collect a range of different weeds complete with roots, stems, and leaves.

Back inside the classroom, the children not only had to show where the root, stem and leaves were on each, but further had to describe, in simple terms, the similarities and differences between the plants parts. Which weed had the longest stem? Which the shortest? Which had the fattest root? Which the slimmest? Linking with mathematics, the weeds could be ordered in different ways.

Children looked for patterns and relationships; for example, did the weed with the longest stem have the longest roots? This activity could be extended and made more challenging for older children by the use of standard measures, rather than those based on observation of length, etc., of features. As a homework activity, the class were challenged to bring into school a dandelion with the longest root with the promise of a small prize for the child who brought in the longest. These activities provided a fun way not only to reinforce the parts of the plant, but also provided opportunities for simple pattern finding investigations.

Health and safety: check the kinds of plants that are safe to collect.

Teaching example 5.3: Key Stage 2

Naming the parts of the flower
Children often are introduced to the 'typical' flower and asked to name the parts. All too often, the only opportunity to learn about this aspect of science is through labelling a stereotypical cross-section drawing of a flower. While children may well learn to name the parts of a flower as required for national tests, this often not only fails to raise children's awareness but also fails to help them recognise parts when they are met in their environment. In other words, children may well be able to recall for the test, but simultaneously fail to understand and recognise the process in real life.

Germination
Children are often very familiar with seeds around them such as chick peas: these are popular in oriental food. In fact, bean sprouts are germinated seeds and popular in Chinese cooking. Germination is very easy to observe in the classroom. Broad bean, cress and mung beans are easy seeds to germinate. Using rabbit food placed on wet paper towels or cotton wool can help children to see that not all things that look like seeds are able to germinate. Monkey nuts, providing they have not been cooked, also germinate quickly. Parsley is very slow to germinate and should be avoided with young children.

Ripening fruits: an investigation
Chidlren at Key Stage 1 will have been introduced to seeds and fruits. Ripening is the process by which fruits become ready to disperse their seeds. Ripening is a chemical process that produces seeds ready to germinate when the conditions are right. Children could undertake repeated observation of a number of fruits ripening over time, noting and recording the changes. Over-ripe fruits become inedible. Observation of this process can lead to an interesting study of change over time. To add interest your children might have noticed that fruits in a fruit bowl with bananas tend to ripen more quickly than those without. In fact, as they ripen, bananas produce ethylene gas which causes other fruits to ripen more quickly. Children could be asked to find out if this it true.

The shelf life of fruit and vegetables is an important idea for children to understand. Many root vegetables these days are pre-washed for convenience before being sold in shops. However, research reportedclaimed that the storage life of raw root vegetables, e.g. potatoes, carrots and parsnips, can be extended by keeping them unwashed, e.g. covered in soil. Linking to literacy older children can plan and carry out an observation to investigate this.

PRACTICAL TASK PRACTICAL TASK PRACTICAL TASK PRACTICAL TASK PRACTICAL TASK

Following work on seeds, a good way to assess your children's learning is to ask them to create their own, imaginary seed and to explain details about it such as 'What it would look like', 'What colour it would be', 'How long would it take to germinate?', What would the flowers look like?', 'What colour would they be?', 'How would the seeds be dispersed?'

Subject knowledge that underpins the activities in this chapter

Photosynthesis

Photosynthesis takes place mainly in leaves, but energy in the form of the sugars produced is needed in all parts of the plant to provide fuel for other essential factors for life and growth.

Light energy from the sun $6CO_2 + 6H_2O \longrightarrow C_6H_{12}O_6 + 6O_2$

Respiration is exactly the opposite process:

$$C_6H_{12}O_6 + 6O_2 \longrightarrow 6CO_2 + 6H_2O + 2900 \text{ Kilojoules (kJ)}$$

Transportation system in plants

Just like animals, plants have their own, but different, internal transportation system. Plants need food to grow and also need to get rid of waste materials. In animals, the blood system transports food and removes waste from different parts of the body. In plants the transport system is made up of many tubes, some called xylem, which carry water and minerals from the root hairs up through the plant to the leaves. Others, called phloem, carry the food around to all parts of the plant. The waste products, oxygen and water vapour, are excreted from the leaves.

The plant's transportation system carries and distributes the water and dissolved mineral salts such as very small amounts of magnesium, nitrogen, phosphorus and potassium through the plant. These minerals are taken into the root of the plant through the small hairs on the root's surface. Hairs increase the total surface area of the root. Water is transported through the roots into small tubes in the stem and up into other tubes that transport the water and nutrients into other parts of the plant where it is needed.

Soil

Some plants thrive in water with a high concentration of minerals without the need for soil. Others need neither soil nor for their roots to be immersed in water. These, called air plants or epiphytes, absorb what they need through their leaves not their roots and have adapted to living in very harsh, dry environments.

Plant reproduction

Asexual

Many green plants can reproduce asexually. This is where new plants grow out from a parent plant; for example, strawberry plants send out 'runners', or side branches that grow over the ground to form new plants. Other plants such as snowdrops, crocuses, tulips and daffodils reproduce asexually by growing from old corms, sometimes called 'bulbs'. New corms form on old ones and become new plants. Other new plants form from 'tubers'. Tubers, e.g. potatoes, are swollen underground roots. New plants grow from the 'buds' on the tuber. You will be familiar with the formation of buds from the eyes of potatoes left in the dark over time. Other new plants, e.g. iris, grow from 'rhizomes' or underground stems that are a rich store of food for new plants.

Sexual

Many plants reproduce sexually by producing flowers. This form of reproduction is very different to those described above. Flowering plants produce both male and female sex cells where pollen cells are the male sex cells and the females sex cells are ovules. When a pollen grain fertilises an ovule a seed is produced. This is called pollination.

Pollination

There are two main methods by which pollination can happen: transfer of pollen by insects or by the wind. Sometimes, pollen from one flower lands on the stigma of the same plant; this is called self-pollination. When pollen from one flower fertilises an egg from another flower on the same plant, this is called cross-pollination. Insect-pollinated flowers tend to be highly coloured and scented to attract insects. Wind-pollinated flowers, often the flowers of trees, tend to be less showy and often are hardly noticed or not recognised as flowers. A good example of this is the horse chestnut tree, which has big green candles of flowers; these are good to point out to children as they are interested in the conkers that will form later in the year.

Fruits and seeds

Scientifically speaking, the terms 'fruit' and 'seed' have very specific meanings. Following fertilisation in the flowering plant, seeds are formed. Each seed consists of an embryo, a store of food and a seed coat called a testa. The ovary forms the fruit. The role of the fruit is to spread the seeds. The spreading of seeds is called dispersal.

Fruits such as apples and pears are easily recognised as fruits, because the term 'fruit' is usually associated with sweet-tasting material surrounding the seeds in the middle and protected by a soft outer layer known as a 'skin'. It is very easy to be confused about seeds and fruits because of how the terms are used in everyday life. Some fruits, like strawberries, have very small seeds on the outside of the fruit. Others, like raspberries and blackberries, have lots of small units, each containing a seed that together make the fruit. Some fruits are not considered to be fruits at all; for example, fruits such as tomatoes, courgettes, aubergines, and peppers are known as vegetables in everyday terms, but should be thought of as fruits because they contain seeds. Pips are also seeds. Other fruits often classified as vegetables include pea and bean pods. Although inedible, sweet peas are also fruits for the same reason. In these examples, the pods are the fruits and the seeds are the pulses.

Fruits such as peaches, nectarines and plums are made up of the skin containing a soft fleshy material and the 'stone'. Together these form the fruit. Here, the seed is contained within the thin testa where it is protected until conditions are ripe for germination. Other edible materials like the avocado and mango are also fruits, with a stone surrounding the seed inside. When eating peaches, for example, you may eat all or part of the 'fruit' but discard the hard stone part that contains the seed.

Figure 5.7 Peach stone showing seed inside

Figure 5.8 Apple fruit

Figure 5.9 Banana fruit

In other examples the seed itself is eaten and the outer stone which protects the seed is discarded. This is rarely considered to be part of the fruit. Many other fruits, e.g. rose-hips or yew fruits, are not usually eaten raw by man; in fact, yew fruits are highly poisonous, but birds like fieldfares love them. You might be surprised to know that the inside of nuts, like the hazelnut, walnut, coconut or brazil, should be called seeds. When these are eaten the hard stone that forms the fruit is discarded.

Seed dispersal

Flowering plants are able to colonise new areas by seed dispersal. This not only prevents overcrowding, but also helps them to compete for light, water and space. Some seeds are attractive to animals including man, and are taken away from the parent plants to possibly germinate far away from 'home'. Seeds like acorns and hazelnuts are collected by squirrels and buried in secret places where some will be forgotten and germinate to form new plants. Some fruits are often brightly coloured like the rose-hip and are attractive as food and eaten by animals. These have a very hard fruit that stops the seed from being digested inside the animal. Later the seed is passed out, unharmed, within the faeces excreted by the animal.

Other fruits, like teasels or burdock, have small hooks all over them. These attach themselves to an animal's body and are transported away from the parent plant. Some seeds are so light, e.g. dandelions and thistles, that they are easily carried away and dispersed by the wind. Some tree seeds like sycamore or ash have wings so that the wind can carry them away to possibly become new trees in a different location. Yet more plants, such as the pea or the gorse, explode their seeds away from themselves when the fruit case splits. A poppy head dries out and the seeds are spread by a 'pepper-pot' action. The top of the head has tiny holes and when the wind blows the poppy head the seeds are scattered through these.

Germination

Germination is a very important concept in the world of plants. The seed is really a rich source of stored food ready to feed the developing embryo. When the seed starts to grow, it is said to germinate. This only happens successfully, when the conditions are exactly right, i.e. when water is available for the seed to swell and burst open, when oxygen is available for respiration and when the temperature is right for growth. Immediately following germination, a new shoot and root appear. It is important that you remember that soil is not essential for germination and neither is light for most seeds.

Web activity

Ideally you should provide your children with first-hand experience of a wide range of 'plants' but, failing this, it is easy to download pictures of each type of plant to supplement the more hands-on activities you provide for your children.

Could you turn those pictures into a game for matching or sorting?

Search the internet for websites that provide information about each group of plants.

- **Draw up a list of names of plants from each group.**

This list may well provide you with information as to the kinds of plants you might wish to collect within your school.

- **Can find out more about these separate groups?**

PRACTICAL TASK PRACTICAL TASK **PRACTICAL TASK** PRACTICAL TASK **PRACTICAL TASK**

There are many schools broadcast programmes provided by the BBC and Channel 4 on this topic. View and critique some appropriate to your preferred age range.

- **What additional aspects do these programmes offer to your pupils in terms of potential learning?**
- **When do you think it would be best to show these to your children i.e. before, or after teaching?**
- **Why would this be your choice?**

A SUMMARY OF **KEY POINTS**

The focus of the work in this chapter was on the activities to help learners understand more about green plants. In particular it has:

> **presented a number of activities showing how learners' understanding of the basic ideas about green plants can be developed over the primary age range;**
> **highlighted the fact that plants show the same characteristics of living things as animals and that similar processes are involved in both plants and animals;**
> **linked simple practical exploration and pattern-finding investigations to simple ideas about plants;**
> **raised awareness of the need to consult with health and safety guidelines when preparing for pupils to explore parts of plants.**

Effective teaching of this topic, at whatever phase, requires you to be able to recognise members of each group of plants and to locate examples from each group in your local environment. When planning to teach aspects of this topic, you should include opportunities for the exploration of as wide a range of examples of each, as possible. This is not too difficult a task today, as there is much interest in gardening television programmes and, even in towns and cities, there is a wide variety of plants available in supermarkets and local garden centres.

Moving on

Traditional science has treated plants and animals as very separate aspects of the living world. There has been a tendency to treat each discretely within schemes of work rather than teaching in a way that would help children to identify similarities between plants and animals as well as differences. You might like to consider how you might present aspects of plants and animals to make the links more obvious to your children. Earlier in this chapter, some of the activities suggested involved simple chemical changes within the plant. How do these ideas link to those presented in Chapter 10?

FURTHER READING FURTHER READING FURTHER READING FURTHER READING

Association for Science Education (2001) *Be Safe*, 3rd edition. Hatfield: ASE

Peacock, G., Sharp, J., Johnsey, R. and Wright, D., (2007) Functioning of organisms: green plants, Chapter 2 in *Primary Science: Knowledge and Understanding*, 3rd edition. Exeter: Learning Matters

6
Variation and classification

By the end of this chapter you should:

- **be aware of significant subject knowledge that underpins the understanding of variation and classification;**
- **recognise common misconceptions associated with variation and classification;**
- **understand the progression of this topic using some examples of learning activities from 3 to 11 years;**
- **identify specific basic skills, illustrative and investigative opportunities within this topic;**
- **have reflected upon the links between science, mathematics and the subliminal messages transmitted by some learning resources.**

Professional Standards for QTS

Q1, Q2, Q4, Q7a, Q8, Q9, Q10, Q14, Q15, Q17, Q18, Q19, Q21a, Q21b, Q22, Q23, Q25a, Q25b, Q25c, Q26b, Q27, Q28, Q29, Q30, Q31

Curriculum Guidance for the Foundation Stage and National Curriculum

In the Foundation Stage pupils should:

- **show curiosity, observe and manipulate objects;**
- **describe simple features of objects and events;**
- **examine living things to find out more about them;**
- **investigate objects and materials by using all of their senses as appropriate;**
- **find out about and identify some features of living things (QCA, 2000, p86);**
- **show an interest in how things happen;**
- **sort objects by one function;**
- **notice and comment on patterns (QCA, 2000, p88);**
- **show interest in the lives of people familiar to them (QCA, 2000, p94).**

At Key Stage 1 pupils should be taught to:

- **recognise similarities and differences between themselves and others, and to treat them with sensitivity;**
- **group living things according to observable similarities and differences (DfEE, 1999, p79).**

At Key Stage 2 pupils should be taught:

- **to make and use keys;**
- **how locally occurring animals and plants can be identified and assigned to groups;**
- **that the variety of plants and animals makes it important to identify them and to assign them to groups (DfEE, 1999, p86).**

Introduction

Most people, even the very youngest, are interested in themselves, other people and the animals they find around them. Indeed, the urge to make friends and communicate with other people is a natural instinct. Infants in their earliest years have a tendency to be egocentric, but can be easily encouraged to interact with others. Older children and the general population are social animals and are interested in all aspects of life around them.

People have possibly never been more exposed to, and aware of, the massive variety of life on Earth. Television presenters like David Attenborough have captured the interest by bringing wonderful programmes about life on Earth into everyone's homes. Developments in photography have brought intricate details about the lives of animals and plants to those who might otherwise not be exposed to, or begin to understand, the complexity of life and its interdependence. Never has there been such a wealth of readily available resources for use in school or to extend the casual learner.

The ideas that children and adults hold about animal and plant groups are often inaccurate. Learners appear to become more confused about the relationships between some animals as they get older. So, for example, common sense tells children that a worm is similar to and related to a snake, that a bat is a bird not a mammal, and that a whale is a fish like the shark. You will need to expose and challenge ideas like these when you come across them in your teaching. Yet, despite the difficulties, a systematic approach based on first-hand experiences and the use of secondary sources can make this topic fascinating. Starting with a topic on 'Ourselves', children's understanding can be easily extended by looking at the similarities and differences between themselves and people that they know and of the animals in their local environment.

This topic not only has outstanding interest value, but also provides the opportunity for children to begin to appreciate the variation between humans of different ethnic origins within a safe, caring, sensitive environment, particularly if the differences between familiar animals like cats and dogs can be compared at the same time. Noticing gross and fine differences and similarities between individuals can lead to simple classification and an appreciation of the wide variety of living things. This chapter will consider how this important aspect of science can be introduced at an early age and developed, systematically and progressively within the primary science curriculum.

Check your understanding

What do you understand by the following terms? Make a note of your ideas.

Variation	Classification
DNA	Genetic engineering
Species	Mutation
Asexual reproduction	Natural selection
Evolution	

Check your understanding with the Glossary.

Variation and classification: some basic ideas

The variety of life

From the beginnings of life on Earth in the 'primeval soup' there has been a continuous development of living things from unicellular and simple multi-cellular organisms to the multitude of different plants and animals that are now found on Earth. It may be difficult to understand how the species called *Homo sapiens* has come about as a result of this process. Indeed, it is amazing to think that all the different forms of life have evolved from simple ancestors.

Man has lived on the Earth only for the last 100,000 years. Before that, dinosaurs and other animals roamed. Whilst some are now extinct, other creatures like alligators and horseshoe crabs have been around for much longer than humans. Through fossil records, the development of animals and plants has been traced back through geological time. The puzzle of life on Earth has stretched the minds and imaginations of people for hundreds of years. This development in the diversity of life has involved processes of continuity and change so that today, many different identifiable species of plants and animals live, many of which depend on others and sometimes each other for existence.

Although most life has evolved naturally, some changes, particularly to domestic animals and plants, have been brought about by simple 'genetic engineering', more usually called 'selective breeding'. Here humans have intervened in the natural process. Some animals and plants have deliberately been bred together in order to develop particular characteristics. This has developed strains that are sometimes more aesthetically pleasing, for example in the case of dog or cat breeds or to produce hardier or stronger breeds. Race horses are bred to produce faster, swifter animals whilst different characteristics are selected for shire horses. In plants, the same process has led to the creation of more resistant species. Selective breeding of plants has produced more fragrant roses or ones that have a particular colour. This involves some 'tampering' with genetic information, or DNA, that is passed on from generation to generation within a species.

A species is a particular group of organisms that are able to interbreed to produce offspring that can then reproduce themselves. Within a single species there is variation. DNA is a genetic material that controls the working of cells and organisms and controls the characteristics within a species. In earlier chapters you met the idea that reproduction can occur in two basic ways, i.e. asexual reproduction and sexual reproduction. During reproduction, DNA from the parent in the case of asexual reproduction, or parents, in the case of sexual reproduction, is passed on by the sex cells to the young and future generations.

Before reproduction can occur, the genetic material in an organism is replicated. At this point natural mutations can occur which can cause variation in the offspring. So the offspring, whilst still being the same species, can have slight differences from the parents. In asexual reproduction the parent cells split to form genetically identical offspring, resulting in no variation, and the offspring look exactly like the parent. On the other hand, in sexual reproduction, the slightly different genetic material from two different parents results in differences between the offspring and their parents.

Normally, for example when a ram and a ewe mate, their genetic material will be different from each other. This results in the lambs being similar, but not identical to either one of their parents. However, in the case of the highly publicised cloning of 'Dolly' the sheep, Dolly was identical to her mother, because at conception, she received only the genetic material of her mother.

Scientists generally believe that natural variation is caused both by genetic mutation and recombination of genetic material (genes) during sexual reproduction and some variation caused by adaptation to the environment, 'natural selection' and evolutionary change. Nuffield Primary Science (1997) usefully describes this process as the 'evolution of variety'. Darwin suggested his theory of evolution when he found that the animals on the Galapagos Islands were slightly different from ones found elsewhere. However, whilst scientists mainly agree about how continuity and change has arisen over time, some religious groups, even today, reject this view and it may well be that you will have pupils in your class who are not allowed to be taught about this aspect of scientific theory.

Classification

The wide variety of living things are classified into two main groups called kingdoms: the plant kingdom and the animal kingdom. Within each of these major groups there are subgroups, for example, animals are further divided into two further groups: vertebrates, animals with backbones; and invertebrates, those without backbones. Similarly, the plant kingdom is subdivided into six main groups (see Chapter 5) on the basis of similar characteristics. Further subdivisions are based upon finer differences between animals or plants sharing similar characteristics, so for example, a frog is at the same time an animal, a vertebrate, and amphibian, and different frogs can be grouped into even more subgroups based on finer differences between species. Similarly, a chestnut tree belongs to the plant kingdom, it is a flowering plant and is further sub-grouped based on the similarities and differences between species.

It has already been established that living things of the same kind vary. Just as scientists were able to classify the elements they discovered into the periodic table, by noting their atomic number and the differences in their properties, scientists have noted, over a period of years, the similarities and differences between animals and between plants and classified them based upon observable characteristics. It is very easy to confuse newts and lizards. The potential for confusion is not helped in the Early Years by animal models that do not distinguish sufficiently between the animals. Invertebrates provide even more cause for concern and confusion. Worms are often confused with snakes and slow worms that are a type of legless lizard. X-ray photographs of some vertebrates are readily available from the internet and help pupils to understand more about those animals which cannot easily be brought into the classroom for first-hand exploration.

PRACTICAL TASK PRACTICAL TASK PRACTICAL TASK PRACTICAL TASK PRACTICAL TASK

Read the following:

Peacock et al (2007) Chapter 4 Continuity and change, pp47–59, *Primary Science Knowledge and Understanding*, 3rd edition. Exeter: Learning Matters.

This chapter provides a more in-depth treatment of how variation occurs, how DNA replicates itself, how characteristics are passed on from one generation to another and the evidence for evolution.

- **How might you explain these basic concepts to your gifted and talented pupils who might want to debate the creation *v* evolution argument with you?**

RESEARCH SUMMARY RESEARCH SUMMARY **RESEARCH SUMMARY** RESEARCH SUMMARY

Variation and classification

Little research has been carried out into pupils' ideas about continuity and change. Johnsey et al. (2007) report that this is due mainly to a lack of specific reference to variation in the National Curriculum at Key Stages 1 and 2. However, experience tells us that there is much confusion amongst children, trainees and some practising teachers about animal groupings.

Teaching example 6.1: Foundation Stage

Ourselves

Learning intention: To notice key characteristics of themselves and others

Although very young children are egocentric they are usually interested in finding out about themselves and their friends. Early explorations of the similarities and differences between themselves and others can start by having a closer look at themselves, for example, with a mirror, and talking about their own eye colour.

Drawing around their own hands or feet and taking simple measurements of the length and width using multilink cubes as non-standard measures, can lead to comparing their own hand or foot size with hands or feet of others. Body size can be compared by drawing around each other whilst lying down on a large piece of paper. This might lead to a simple survey investigation to find out whether there is a difference between the sizes of boys or girls in the class.

Other animals

Learning intention: To notice similarities and differences

Even very small children can recognise the difference between dogs and cats and can also identify the similarities between lions, tigers and domestic cats and the similarities between dogs, wolves and foxes, and may well realise that there are different breeds of horses or that a zebra is related to the horse. At this stage you might like to build on casual learning by introducing children to some of the wide variety of animals that can be found in different climates. Although their experience of real animals might be limited, they may well have learnt about different animals on children's TV.

Sorting pictures of animals into groups can provide an early introduction into animal classification.

Plants

Learning intention: To notice similarities and differences

A collection of leaves in the autumn can provide a start to a more formal study of variation. Rubbings of leaves or bark can introduce the idea that even things that look basically the same can have small differences. Using rubbings made by a friend, children can try to match the rubbing to the original. Using the rubbings within a display can make the collected information available to a wider audience and can provide the opportunity for even the youngest children to communicate their findings and develop their basic skills.

Growing bulbs and looking at twigs that are about to burst into leaf are popular activities in the spring in the Reception class. Looking at and noting the changes over time of different twigs offers opportunities to discuss not only what is happening but also to introduce the idea of differences between species.

Keys

Learning intention: To be able to use keys

Simple keys can be introduced using a few, very different animals or plants for identification. You might want to encourage older children at Key Stage 2 to make a very simple key for younger children to use. Not only would this familiarise your children with this basic skill in science, it simultaneously provides a useful context for even the least able pupils designing the key.

PRACTICAL TASK PRACTICAL TASK **PRACTICAL TASK** PRACTICAL TASK **PRACTICAL TASK**

Children of all ages love to play games. You will probably have enjoyed a simple dice game like those used in 'Beetle drives', where a die is thrown and legs are added to beetle.

- **Create a game based on the characteristics of animals that links aspects of mathematics to aspects of science within this chapter.**

Ladybirds are often used in mathematics worksheets to reinforce number. This sometimes leads to subliminal messages being received by children about real-life ladybirds.

- **Find out about the number of spots real ladybirds have.**
- **Look in mathematics schemes for this sort of use of animals.**

Record your findings.
How might you challenge this misrepresentation?
Think of how you might link mathematics and animals and plants in a display for your classroom. Make sure you make accurate representations of the animals or plants that you use.

Teaching example 6.2: Key Stage 1

Ourselves

Learning intention: To identify simple similarities and differences between people

Building on earlier explorations of simple characteristics of themselves and others, fine differences such as fingerprints or the lines on the palms of hands or the soles of feet can be investigated using simple equipment. To increase the challenge, standard units can be used for measurement and comparisons of hands, feet and bodies. Using paint on white paper or talcum powder on black sugar paper can provide a messy, but fun way to start to compare hands or feet.

Once these initial 'prints' are made, children can make measurements of the different hand and foot prints, e.g. the length, the width and area and the girth, either using lengths of tape or measuring in centimetres. Simple survey investigations can be carried out and conclusions drawn about the relationship between various features; for example, do the people with the longest foot also have the widest foot? Do people with the widest girth also have the biggest area of the sole? Do taller children have the bigger feet?

Drawing faces and looking carefully at eyes can be hugely fascinating for children. How many children in the class have blue eyes? How many brown? Asking the question, 'What other colour eyes do children in the class have?' can lead to a discovery that some children have hazel or grey eyes. Relationships between hair colour and eye colour can lead to conclusions about characteristics of human beings. Children might also be interested in who has the longest tongue.

'Guess who' is a popular game produced commercially. Pupils love providing information about features of a person for another to guess the identity. It is easy to stick in pictures of animals or plants to extend their learning. At an even simpler, but no less challenging level, this idea can be used as a lesson starter, rather like a yes/no game where one child chooses a person and others try to determine by questioning, the person selected.

Other animals

Noting similarities and differences between familiar animals, e.g. cat, dog, horse, elephant and themselves will provide an opportunity for profitable discussion of features. A visit to the zoo can provide an enjoyable day out, but school trips like this may lack focus and often lead to much note taking on paper using clipboards, but with little systematic learning. Children may well see a huge variety of animals, but it may be more productive to focus on one group, e.g. reptiles, and to notice finer similarities and differences.

Photographs of real animals saved into the memory of an interactive whiteboard can be sorted into groups by children. Here more detailed observations and comparisons can be made with motivation and interest maintained through the real-life, shared experience. On a smaller scale, mini-beasts collected in the school ground or local woods could be compared and similarities and differences being noted. Sorting photographs or pictures of animals into groups, useful though it might be, may only lead to familiarisation rather than more in-depth learning.

Children are often fascinated to find out finer details about well-known animals, e.g. that elephants have eyelashes just like themselves. Later they can compare animals that are of the same species, e.g. the similarities and differences between cat breeds or dog breeds will introduce a greater appreciation of variation. Practical exploration for the environment could then lead to discovering the vast variety of life to be found in gardens, woodlands and the school grounds. Further observation and research may lead to the discovery that some woodlice can roll into a ball while others cannot, some are brown and others almost black. Variation between species and variation within species are important concepts in science.

At Key Stage 1, the kinds of animals collected should be ones that can be observed using magnifying pots, e.g. millipedes, snails, slugs, woodlice, worms, centipedes, and leaving smaller creatures that might required to be collected with pooters to be looked at in more depth at Key Stage 2. Children can easily identify the similarities and differences between species and variations within species, e.g. a snail and a worm and the differences between a ram's horn snail and a common snail. In recent years, digital microscopes have revolutionised what is possible. It is very easy for children at Key Stage1 to view the details of a particular creature, to make a small video of its movement and for this to be shared with the rest of the class on the interactive whiteboard. There has never been greater opportunity for children to develop their understanding of this aspect of science. However, take note of the health and safety implications: children should wear plastic gloves and you should ensure that they wash their hands after this kind of activity. All animals should be returned to where they were found.

PRACTICAL TASK

Animals

A simple game of Snap played with pictures of animals can help reinforce the names of animals. Increase the difficulty by using invertebrates as well as vertebrates. A further development of this could be to make a game of 'Happy Families', using 'families' of animals from the same group, e.g. a family of horses, with a family of sheep, with a family of dogs, etc.

- **How could you make this game more difficult to meet the needs of your higher-ability children?**
- **Create a game using downloaded pictures of animals from the internet.**

Plants

Working outside in the wider environment, and linked to earlier activities, older children can try to identify trees using photographs of bark patterns, or they can collect and put winter buds into groups based on their own chosen criteria. Alternatively, you can group leaves or winter twigs and ask pupils to tell you what criteria you have used to group them. Sorting and grouping plants and animals using Venn or Carroll diagrams links with mathematics and provides opportunities for close observation of similarities and differences.

Smelling things is a popular activity linked to our senses, for Key Stage 1. Here herbs and spices can be put into small film canisters, covered with a small piece of cotton cloth and held in place with an elastic band. Herbs such as mint, coriander and basil are readily available from supermarkets. Learning can be extended beyond the basic favourite smells, by asking children to match the smell to the plant. This provides an alternative activity that involves familiarisation with a variety of plants.

PRACTICAL TASK

Survey your local environment for animals and plants your children might collect during a later lesson. Using the internet, CD-ROMs, other secondary sources and keys, at your level, note down important information about each organism. You may find commercially produced keys useful. Make sure that you note the important features that help to identify each organism and then:

- **make a key for use in your classroom by your pupils.**

You may expect more able or gifted and talented pupils to be able to use the commercial keys without support, but for others, a simple key, containing only organisms that are found locally, will be easier for most children to use.

REFLECTIVE TASK

Use of ICT

Visit the following website, which is designed to help with the construction of keys:
www.smithlifescience.com/McDlitUnitBChap2ClassLivingThings.htm#TR

Would this site, aimed at helping teachers, be useful in your teaching?

- **Reflect on your use of ICT in this aspect of science.**

Teaching example 6.3: Key Stage 2

Ourselves

Older primary children may well be self-conscious about their features and more aware of having, for example, a large nose or chin or a broad forehead. Girls might be interested in the shape of faces as some are heart-shaped, while others are oval. Both boys and girls will be interested to find out if their ear lobes have a particular shape. Ear lobes generally fall into two categories: those that are prominent, i.e. separated from their face, or fixed. Another characteristic that varies is the ability to roll the tongue. Some children can fold their tongues in half, others cannot. How many of each group are there in your class?

Making keys

By the time they reach Key Stage 2, children should be familiar with the major groups of animals and be able to group them using more scientific criteria. They should also be able to use simple keys, for the identification of both plants and animals. Once you have revised this skill with them, you can extend their learning by asking them to apply this knowledge by making their own key. Start by giving them a small number of very different animals or plants and asking them to work in pairs, noting the differences and similarities between the animals or plants. Using this information, they can be challenged to make a key and to test it out on their friends. Learning can then be extended by increasing the number and type of individual animals or plants to be included in the key.

Task

Once your children are familiar with the process, ask them to make a simple key for use lower down the school.

- Arrange for your children to work alongside younger children when keys are being used.
- Reflect on the benefits of peer grouping in this way.

PRACTICAL TASK PRACTICAL TASK PRACTICAL TASK PRACTICAL TASK PRACTICAL TASK

Look at the following pictures. Can you spot any inaccuracies, or the potential for subliminal messages and the reinforcement of misconceptions? What messages do they give to you and other potential readers?

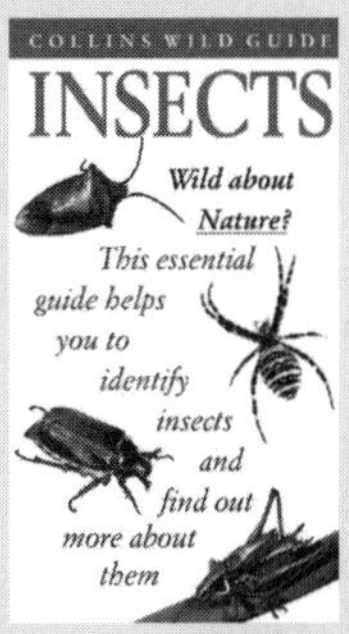

- **Collect together all the resources you can find within this topic, e.g. books, stories, CD-ROMs, etc.**
- **Critically evaluate them for their accuracy.**

If you are a student interested in promoting a modern foreign language in your classroom, look at the resources available in the language of interest. Analyse these for any undesired subliminal messages.

- **Ask older children to critique books and other resources about animals and plants for slight inaccuracies and to talk about these to children lower down the school.**

Subject knowledge that underpins the activities in this chapter

The animal kingdom

Living things are grouped together on the basis of common characteristics. This is called classification. 'Taxonomy' is the term used for the hierarchical system of classification based on a wide range of characteristics. Here, each organism has its own unique classification. Classifying organisms in this way helps us to understand how a particular group has evolved, including fossil evidence and DNA analysis.

Ponsonby and Dussart (2005) state that it was Plato (429–347 BC) who provided the first written definitions of abstract classification terms, but that his pupil, Aristotle, produced the first classification system based on appearance (anatomy) and function (physiology). Crude and incomplete by our current standards, it survived for more than 2000 years. Under the modern system of classification, based on the work of Karl Linnaeus in the eighteenth century, each living organism has two names, a generic name and a specific name. For example, *Homo sapiens*, which is the name for man.

A species is a group of organisms which share a great many characteristics or features and which can normally interbreed successfully, but Ponsonby and Dussart (2002) say that biologists still argue over the definition of a species.

The animal kingdom is divided into two groups: invertebrates and vertebrates.

Invertebrates are creatures without backbones. They belong to a number of different phyla:

- ***Animal-like protists* – microscopic, live in water and have only a single cell e.g. amoeba, hydra;**
- ***Porifera* – sponges that live in water;**
- ***Coelenterata* – these animals with a simple nervous system, have tentacles with stinging cells and have a single opening for food intake and waste output, e.g. sea anemone and jellyfish;**
- ***Platyhelmintha* – these flatworms have a head end and tail end to the body, some live in fresh water, some are parasites, e.g. tapeworm;**
- ***Mollusca* – the body is usually soft, not segmented and often protected by a shell. Most have a muscular foot and an identifiable head, e.g. snail, slug, octopus, oyster, winkle, whelk and limpet;**
- ***Annelida* – these trueworms have bodies divided into portions called segments and have a simple gut, blood and nervous system, e.g. common earthworm, lugworm and leech;**
- ***Arthropoda* – these are animals with jointed legs. This phylum is divided into four classes:**
    1. **Miriapoda** – usually found on land and usually amongst rotting plants. They have many legs and a long body e.g. centipedes and millipedes;
    2. **Crustacia** – have many legs and are usually found in the sea e.g. crabs, lobsters. The woodlouse is a crustacean that lives on land;
    3. **Arachnida** – all have eight legs e.g. spiders and scorpions;
    4. **Insecta** – all have six legs and three parts to their bodies e.g. crane fly, dragonfly, butterfly, moth;
- ***Echinoderma* – have no head or tail end and live in the sea e.g. star fish and sea urchin.**

Vertebrates are animals with backbones, two pairs of limbs and a head with a brain. They all belong to the phylum:

- ***Vertebrata* which is divided into five different classes:**
  1. **fish** – are cold-blooded, i.e. have a variable body temperature and have scales over their bodies;
  2. **amphibians** – are also cold-blooded, have soft damp bodies and can breath on land and in water, e.g. frogs, toads, newts, salamanders;
  3. **reptiles** – also cold-blooded, live on land, have a dry skin with scales, e.g. snakes, lizards, slow worms, crocodiles, turtles, tortoises;
  4. **birds** – are warm-blooded, i.e. have a constant body temperature, are covered with feathers and have a toothless horny beak e.g. blackbird, flamingo, heron, penguin;
  5. **mammals** – also warm-blooded, have some body hair and feed their young on milk produced by special glands e.g. elephants, kangaroo, sheep, man, bats, whale.

Man (common name)

Kingdom: animal
Phylum: Chordata
Class: Mammalia (mammals)
Order: primates
Family: Hominidae
Genus: *Homo*
Species: *Homo sapiens*

So, although it may seem very confusing, each different living organism is classified in a systematic way which can help to identify the bigger groups to which animals and plants belong for example.

This system can also distinguish between animals or plants that are very similar; for example, variations within a species. Kangaroos and wallabies are very similar animals but belong to different genus.

Look at the table below. The grey kangaroo, the red kangaroo and the short-eared wallaby are distinguished from each other based on the fine differences between them so that both the grey and red kangaroo belong to the same genus, but the short-eared wallaby to a different genus.

Taxon	**Grey kangaroo**	**Red kangaroo**	**Short-eared wallaby**
Kingdom	Animalia	Animalia	Animalia
Phylum	Chordata	Chordata	Chordata
Class	Mammalia	Mammalia	Mammalia
Order	Diprotodontia	Diprotodontia	Diprotodontia
Family	Macropodidae	Macropodidae	Macropodidae
Genus	*Macropus*	*Macropus*	*Petrogale*
Species	*fuliginosus*	*fufus*	*brachyotis*

Classification of kangaroos (based on Ponsonby and Dussart, 2005)

Some groups of animals have even more levels of classification within their taxon whilst others have less. This relates to the level of complexity of the animal. Look at the table below.

Taxon	Atlantic cod (*Gadus morhua*)	Sea lettuce (*Ulva lactuca*)
Kingdom	Animalia	Protista
Phylum	Chordata	Chlorophyta
Super class	Gnathostomata	
Class	Osteichthyes	Chlorophyceae
Sub class	Actinopterygii	
Superorder	Teleosteii	
Order	Gadiformes	Ulvales
Suborder	Gadoidei	
Family	Gadidae	Ulvaceae
Genus	*Gadus*	*Ulva*
Species	*morhua*	*lactuca*

Linnaean classification of the Atlantic cod, *Gadus morhua,* and the sea lettuce, *Ulva lactuca*: (Ponsonby and Dussart, 2005)

PRACTICAL TASK PRACTICAL TASK PRACTICAL TASK PRACTICAL TASK PRACTICAL TASK

Classification of animals

Look at the table above showing the classification of the red kangaroo, the grey kangaroo and the short-eared wallaby. Visit the following websites:

Grey kangaroos

http://www.yptenc.org.uk/docs/factsheets/animal_facts/grey_kangaroo.html
http://www.dierinbeeld.nl/animal_files/mammals/kangaroo/index.html
http://www.giftlog.com/pictures/kangaroo_facts.htm
http://images.google.co.uk/images?svnum=10&hl=en&lr=&q=%22grey+kangaroo%22&btnG=Search

Wallabies:

http://www.calm.wa.gov.au/plants_animals/mammals_rock_wallabies.html
http://animaldiversity.ummz.umich.edu/site/accounts/information/Petrogale_brachyotis.html
http://images.google.co.uk/images?hl=en&lr=&q=%22short-eared%22%20wallaby&btnG=Search%C2%A0within%C2%A0results&ie=UTF-8&oe=UTF-8&sa=N&tab=wi

- **Locate photographs and information about these animals. Can you identify the differences between these animals that place them in different groups?**

Classification of plants

Look at some simple information books aimed at Foundation Stage, Key Stage 1 or Key Stage 2. Choose some pairs or trios of common plants, e.g. horse-chestnut tree and sweet chestnut tree; blue ash, European ash and the white ash; Holm oak, English oak, White oak. Use identification books to compile a simple taxon for your chosen plants as below.

Taxon	Horse chestnut	Sweet chestnut	
Kingdom			
Phylum			
Class			
Order			
Family			
Genus			
Species			

A SUMMARY OF **KEY POINTS**

The focus of the chapter was on the activities to help learners understand more about variation and classification. In particular, it has indicated where there are close links between science and mathematics, and between science and literacy. Although the links can be useful, there is also the possibility of the assimilation of inaccurate information by use of some popular resources in mathematics and the use of both fact and fiction books in literacy which appear authoritative.

There are many opportunities to reinforce increasingly complex ideas inherent in this chapter through simple games which can help develop pupils of science alongside literacy and mathematics. It has also highlighted the need to analyse critically resource material across the curriculum for the subliminal messages they may transmit. This is not to say that the resources should not be used, but confusing or wrong information should be used productively to aid learning.

Moving on

Although the knowledge of science is not static, many basic ideas remain the same over time. The appropriate use of secondary resource materials can provide interest and for optimum learning.

With this in mind you should be collecting ideas from many sources during your training to use in your later career.

FURTHER READING FURTHER READING FURTHER READING FURTHER READING

Nuffield Primary Science (1997) The variety of life, in *Science Process and Concept Exploration: Understanding Scientific Ideas*, pp30–1. London: Collins

REFERENCES REFERENCES REFERENCES REFERENCES REFERENCES REFERENCES

Beverley, C.V. and Ponsonby, D.J. (2003) *The Anatomy of Insects and Spiders*. San Francisco, CA: Chronicle Books, Australia: Penguin Books, Sweden: AlphaBeta Publishers, Spain: Lisma, France: Marabout

Ponsonby, D.J, and Dussart, G.B. (2005) *The Anatomy of the Sea*. San Francisco, CA: Chronicle Books, France: Marabout, Sweden: AlphaBeta Publishers

Children's books

Burnie, D. (2005) *Nature Activities: Bug Hunter*. London: Dorling Kindersley

7
Living things and their environment

By the end of this chapter you should:

- **be aware of significant subject knowledge that underpins the understanding of living thing in their environment;**
- **recognise common misconceptions associated with living things and their environment;**
- **understand the progression of this topic using some examples of learning activities from 3 to 11 years;**
- **identify specific basic skills, illustrative and investigative opportunities within this topic;**
- **have risk-assessed a visit to a local environment;**
- **have reflected upon the opportunities for links with environmental education and the global dimension associated with this aspect of science.**

Professional Standards for QTS

Q1, Q2, Q4, Q7a, Q8, Q9, Q10, Q14, Q15, Q17, Q18, Q19, Q21a, Q21b, Q22, Q23, Q25a, Q25b, Q25c, Q25d, Q26b, Q27, Q28, Q29, Q30, Q31

Curriculum Guidance for the Foundation Stage and National Curriculum

In the Foundation Stage pupils should:

- **describe simple features of objects and events;**
- **find out about, and identify, some features of living things (QCA, 2000, p86);**
- **show an interest in why things happen;**
- **talk about what is seen and what is happening (QCA, 2000, p88);**
- **sort objects by one function;**
- **notice and comment on patterns (QCA, 2000, p88).**

At Key Stage 1 pupils should be taught to:

- **find out about the different kinds of plants and animals in the local environment;**
- **identify similarities and differences between local environments and ways in which these affect animals and plants that are found there;**
- **care for the environment (DfEE, 1999, p86);**
- **ICT opportunity: multimedia sources to make comparisons;**
- **Use data collected to compile a class database.**

At Key Stage 2 pupils should be taught:

- **about ways in which living things and the environment need protection;**

Adaptation

- **about the different plants and animals found in different habitats;**
- **how animals and plants in two different habitats are suited to their environments;**

Feeding relationships

- **to use food chains to show feeding relationships in a habitat;**

- **about how nearly all food chains start with a green plant;**

Micro-organisms

- **that micro-organisms are living organisms that are often too small to be seen, and that they may be beneficial (for example, in the breakdown of waste, in making bread) or harmful (for example in causing disease, In causing food to go mouldy) (DfEE, 1999, p88);**
- **ICT opportunities pupils could use video or CD-ROM to compare non-local habitats;**
- **ICT opportunity: pupils could use simulation software to show change in the populations of micro-organisms in different conditions.**

Introduction

Earlier chapters looked at differences between animals and plants and explained grouping based on common characteristics. The similarities and differences within and between animal groups and those within and between plants groups were also considered. This chapter focuses on where particular animals and plants live, how they are suited or adapted to their preferred environment and the interdependence of life within habitats.

Whilst the availability of TV programmes, books, CD-ROMs and other information sources related to this topic have never been better or more numerous, children lack first-hand experience of simple habitats. Consequently, many children have limited understanding of the relationship between plants and animals in simple and more complex habitats. This may always have been true for some, i.e. those living in densely populated urban areas, but never before have so many children living in more rural and other potentially rich environments been discouraged from the kinds of exploration once thought normal in previous generations. The increase in the urban sprawl, the move towards 'designer gardens' and the fear of pupils being outside alone, mean that the responsibility of the school curriculum to introduce pupils to life in natural settings has never been greater.

Many children appear to have little understanding of where their own food comes from beyond the local supermarket. Outdoor exploration is limited in the curriculum because of the perceived lack of time available. One of your most important roles in teaching science in the primary sector, therefore, is to open your children's eyes to the life around them and the interdependency of life in both their local habitats and those farther away.

Check your understanding

What do you understand by the following terms? Make a note of your ideas.

Habitat	Camouflage
Environment	Adaptation
Competition	Feeding relationships
Ecosystem	Food chain
Food web	Interdependence of living things
Primary producers	Primary consumer
Herbivore	Carnivore
Predator	Prey
Omnivore	Secondary consumer

Check your understanding with the Glossary.

How much time have you spent outdoors with your children during the formal school day?

Living things in their environment: some basic ideas

The basic needs of all living things are met within their local environment. If needs are not met, individuals either move to other areas or perish. There are huge variations in the environmental conditions found in different places on Earth, but even the harshest environments provide a home for some organisms. All plants and animals live together in a community within a habitat: a place where animals and plants live together with some degree of interdependence. An ecosystem is a system of relationships where animals and plants coexist and where there are simple and sometimes more complex feeding relationships between them.

The number of different habitats is vast. Habitats can be quite small in size, for example. a garden pond or a piece of old bread; or large, like a desert or jungle. The specific conditions that exist in the habitat make up the environment. Nuffield Primary Science (1997, p24) explains that living things exploit their environment. Although the environment can be a place of danger for the inhabiting organisms, the environment also provides:

- **a source of energy;**
- **a source of new materials;**
- **a place to be;**
- **a place that provides shelter;**
- **somewhere to dump waste.**

All environments are affected by:

- **how much light is available;**
- **changes in temperature and weather conditions over time;**
- **how much shelter is available;**
- **the chemical substances present;**
- **the range of other plants and other living things present in the environment which interact both with their own and other species.**

In some habitats the physical conditions are generally stable, but in others there are daily, seasonal or yearly changes. For example, tides can cause significant changes to a coastline over time. Whilst plants are the primary producers of food, not all animals eat plants. In a habitat all organisms are linked and damage to one species can have a devastating effect on the whole system.

Although humans have no large predators in developed countries, mosquitoes, midges and bacteria live in and on Man. Some parasites live on our bodies; for example, head lice or fleas picked up from pets. Others live inside the body; for example, small parasitic thread worms that sometimes cause problems in primary age children. In poorer countries tape worms and other water-borne parasites often lead to serious illness, particularly when there is a lack of a clean water supply.

Plants vary according to where they live; for example, those that live where there is plenty of moisture and little light tend to have many large leaves to increase the amount of sunlight they can absorb to generate their food. In the desert where the sunshine is bright and moisture scarce, leaves are often reduced to small spines like those on a cactus.

Each different living thing has specific characteristics to allow it to survive the local conditions. If the balance within a habitat changes, even slightly, there may well be long-term and significant consequences for the variety and size of populations the habitat supports. Life on Earth depends on the constant supply of energy from the Sun. Energy passes in one direction and raw materials that living things get from their environment have to be recycled around each ecosystem. When living things die, they decay, releasing the basic materials of life back into the environment to be used by others. Some materials decay quickly but others break down into their constituent materials over a long period of time

Children's ideas

The SPACE project (Science Processes and Concepts Exploration), reported in Nuffield Primary Science (1997), found limited ideas amongst children but that most could give examples of where plants and animals live and identify good places for particular animals to live. Their explanations, however, often reinforced the children's initial observations, e.g. 'Worms live under the soil because it's dark and because worms like it dark' and 'A stick insect could go on a tree 'cos it could hide from things and animals couldn't reach it.'

Children often think that plants need only water, soil and sunlight to live. Some children think that plants get their food from the soil through their roots. Some children do not seem to know that plants make their own food. Sometimes they suggest that the plant will need leaves to get air, that roots collect food and that the stem is there to carry the food to the flower. Children's ideas about what animals need to live often reflect those for plants, with food being the most important.

You might find that your pupils are aware of major environmental seasonal changes in habitats, but may have stereotypical, generalised ideas about the seasons, e.g. the sun shines in summer and it is cloudy or rainy in winter. Obvious changes in leaf colour and leaf fall may be noticed, but they may not notice the appearance of flowers, fruits and seeds. Many children of all ages think that all plants die during the winter.

REFLECTIVE TASK

Read the following:
Roden, J. (2005) Children's ideas, Chapter 5 in *Primary Science Reflective Reader*. Exeter: Learning Matters

The SPACE research within this topic relied heavily on children's drawings to elicit their ideas. Many children were found to have many limited ideas about plants and animals in their preferred habitats.

Thinking about plants and animals in their local environment, reflect on the following:

1. Why might children's ideas be limited in the way revealed by the SPACE project?
2. When planning aspects of this topic, would you build in time to elicit your children's ideas? Why?

Teaching example 7.1: Foundation Stage

Exploring habitats

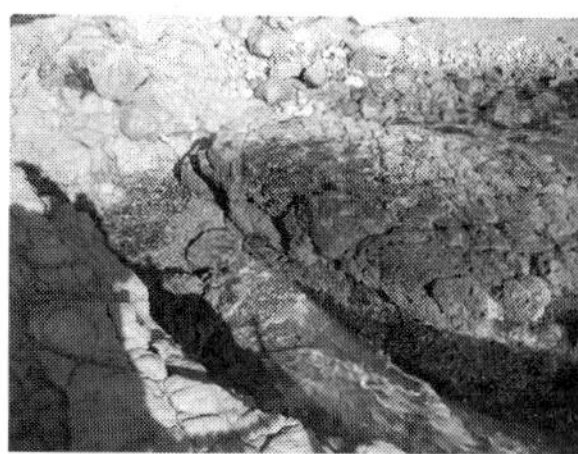

Figure 7.1 Rocky shore

Figure 7.2 Pond

Figure 7.3 Waterfall

Learning intention: To become aware of the variety of plants and animals in their local environment

Success criteria

- To identify a range of familiar animals.
- To recognise simple plants.

Very young children will be familiar with mammals, e.g. dogs, cats, and possibly hamsters, guinea pigs, rabbits, and may have seen birds and squirrels in gardens, the street or park at first hand. Some may have seen ferrets, pigeons or be familiar with exotic animals such as tarantulas or small lizards kept as pets. Some may have visited a zoo or wildlife park or have seen fish and other animals in an aquarium. However, many may be unaware of the multitude of animal life in many different natural habitats. Your children's experience of plants may be even more limited. At this stage, they need to look at and talk about plants and animals and what they require to live and so begin to realise that not all animals rely on Man for their daily survival.

Bringing small mammals into the classroom can widen children's understanding, through discussion of the similarities and differences in what they eat and what their needs are. You can then extend this idea to animal homes in the wild, e.g. where does a squirrel, a frog, a duck live? How many different kinds of ducks have they seen on the pond? What sorts of animals and plants live in a pond, a wood, a wall, or in the soil? What is it about these animals and plants that helps them live where they do? Distinct differences between plants can be noticed such as: are the plants found by the side of the pond in the park the same as those in the rest of the park? Asking children to talk about the ways in which they are the same and the differences helps with grouping. Also you will be potentially extending the number of plants and animals noticed and recognised by children. This will also raise awareness, in a simple way, that different habitats have different ways of meeting the needs of the plants and animals that live there.

Simple activities can include matching animals to a habitat, e.g. duck to a pond, rabbit to a rabbit warren, birds to a nest in a tree, etc. Questioning whether or not, e.g. all birds live in trees, can extend children's understanding. They can be encouraged, using BluTack to stick pictures of different animals on a display featuring different habitats. Which animals and plants would like to live, e.g. on wood, in the pond, etc.?

The study of animals should not be limited to vertebrates, in particular, mammals, and a range of invertebrates should be introduced at this stage. 'Change' walks, popular in many schools, can provide an excellent opportunity to notice a range of plants and animals in context, looking carefully at where different invertebrates are found and recording this information later by painting a picture of an animal and the plant on which it was found. Looking at others' paintings can provide an opportunity for comparing the kinds of animals found in different habitats at an appropriate level. More able children can consider whether specific animals and plants could live successfully in other habitats and asked to give their reasons.

Simple adaptations can be discussed, e.g. ducks' feet enable them to travel quickly in the water; slugs have slimy bodies that can help them travel over dry surfaces. Identifying how animals move, and where, is also useful.

Teaching example 7.2: Key Stage 1

Learning intention: To name some plants and animals that live in local habitats

Success criteria

- List and identify different animals and plants that live in a variety of habitats.

Building on experiences in the Foundation Stage, children at Key Stage 1 should carry out more detailed and systematic studies of the animals and plants found in a range of different, but local habitats. Importantly, plants and animals should be studied *in situ* rather than collecting and taking examples back to the classroom. Different groups of children in your class could focus on different habitats to communicate findings and make comparisons. Ideally, habitats should be visited at different times of the day and in different seasons.

Ask your children to list the found animals and plants in their habitat to talk about later. Recording by sketching or photography is preferable to removing living things from their habitat and reinforces basic ideas of conservation. Recording by digital photography makes comparisons of changes of habitats over time very easy. These can be stored electronically or put in a scrap book. Later discussion might provide answers about how the animals and plants are adapted to their habitat. You should encourage your children to ask and answer their own questions. Research using secondary sources may be required to find the answers to some of their questions but these would be based on their real observation of cohabiting living things within an ecosystem.

If children undertake surveys of the number of animals and plants in a particular habitat at different times of the year, patterns in behaviour can be identified. This will help develop an understanding of the requirements for life and the interdependence of living things at first hand. Every year the Royal Society for the Protection of Birds (RSPB) involves the public in counting the numbers and types of birds in the garden. Children can also survey the range of places that woodlice or snails are found in different seasons, or the number of caterpillars on particular plants. They can answer the question, 'What happens to animals and plants in winter?' and decide if some plants and animals live in the same place all year. This provides excellent opportunities for discussion and the opportunity to challenge the idea that plants die in winter.

Teaching example 7.3: Key Stage 2

Exploring habitats

Progression in this aspect of science can come not from providing totally different activities, but by increasing the demands on the children and extending the range of habitats selected. In terms of cross-curricular links to geography, older children could place the different habitats on a map constructed by them of the local or global area. So for example, study of local areas may include ponds and woodlands. This can provide the context for identifying the animals and plants in the habitat and discovering their feeding preferences. Similar teaching points and questions can be asked as in Key Stage 1, but in addition, Key Stage 2 pupils need to construct food chains, ideally using the plants and animals already explored in their habitat. These ideas can be extended to habitats and ecosystems in the wider world linked to the geography programme of study.

Learning intention: to construct a food chain for two contrasting habitats

The science National Curriculum at Key Stage 2 requires pupils to be familiar with at least two contrasting habitats. This provides the opportunity for your pupils to apply ideas learned previously in their local environment. If the pupils cannot visit the habitat at first hand, split the class into two groups, each group taking a different habitat to research from secondary sources. Pupils always work best when there is a challenge and an identified audience for their research. Focus the learners on the way the energy moves through the system. It starts with the Sun: green plants use its light to make food. Which plants are eaten by which animals? What happens to those animals next? Having made the food chain and food web, they could be asked to incorporate their found information into a simple play, where all pupils in the group are required to take roles. Props can be made in Design and Technology and there are links here to drama and role play. The teacher should pose such questions as, for example: Could any of the organisms live in more than one habitat? Is there anything about the organism that helps them to live in a particular place? Alternatively, pupils could prepare a wall display to reveal their findings.

Investigating

Learning intention: To find out what food or what conditions small animals prefer

Success criteria

- To find ways of answering questions.
- To take readings and observations to answer questions.
- To draw conclusions from their work.

Simple investigations can be made by constructing choice chambers for particular small creatures. Once set up, a number of individual creatures in question are introduced randomly to the various chambers. At predetermined, standard points in time, pupils can count the number of individuals in each chamber, thereby building up, over time, an idea of the animals' preferences. Although woodlice are usually used, water shrimps or the Mexican bean beetle, *Epilachna varivestis*, which unlike other members of its family attacks plants. All these are equally good and extend opportunities for investigations.

One point of consideration is how open to allow this work, to ensure that there is little or no danger of harm coming to the creatures. Although pupils might like to find out if caterpillars like cup cakes and salami, ethically, this is not a good idea. Sensitivity for the needs of living things is one attitude that is crucial in a study of living things in their environment. Setting up a local habitat in a large aquarium can provide almost endless interest for pupils. Experience demonstrates that pupils will continue to bring small pieces of dead and living things into school for the habitat weeks after the formal study of it has ended.

Micro-organisms can be investigated using a pack lunch box that has been left over time. Make sure the sandwiches and fruit are all in sealed small bags. Include things like crisps, chocolate, etc. Compare the lunch box with one that has not been left. Let the children see the type of micro-organisms by colour and size. Health and safety: never allow children to open the bags after sealing, and dispose of the rotten food carefully.

PRACTICAL TASK PRACTICAL TASK PRACTICAL TASK PRACTICAL TASK PRACTICAL TASK

It is crucial that you risk-assess prior to any visit to habitats both inside and outside your school grounds.

Visit www.rospa.com, the website of the Royal Society for the Prevention of Accidents, which provides advice to teachers about visits out of school.

- **Undertake a risk assessment of a visit that you are likely to undertake in the future.**

PRACTICAL TASK PRACTICAL TASK PRACTICAL TASK PRACTICAL TASK PRACTICAL TASK

ICT Task

Micro-organisms

Your children need to realise that some micro-organisms can be harmful, but that others can be helpful to man. In Sc1 there is a requirement that pupils at Key Stage 2 be taught that science is about thinking creatively to try to explain how living and non-living things work, and to establish links between causes and effects (DfES, 1999, p83). Louis Pasteur (1822–1895) investigated this aspect of science and demonstrated that micro-organisms cause the souring of some substances including milk, and that germs from the environment sometimes cause illness. He used his theory to explain the causes of many illnesses, such as anthrax and smallpox. How he came to prove, despite opposition to his ideas is fascinating and can help your children to understand the process of progress in science.

- **Undertake research yourself into Pasteur's work.**
- **How could you use this information to enhance your children's understanding of the development of scientific ideas, science as a creative activity and the notion of ideas and evidence in science?**
- **What strategies, e.g. hot-seating, could you use to promote these ideas? Hot-seating puts the child in the role of the scientist, and other children have to ask them questions about their work, ideas or discoveries.**

Camouflage

One way that some animals are adapted to their environment is by colour. Children of all ages are fascinated by the idea of camouflage, for example moths on tree bark in unpolluted areas, or zebras on the African plain. Ask children to create a background of a range of colours of green and brown in blobs and stripes and then place objects of different colours on to this background. When they walk away, which colours can be seen most clearly? The arctic hare changes the colour of its coat from brown with flecks of black during the growing season to a pure white coat in winter.

Other adaptations

A look at birds' feet can provide further insight into how familiar animals are adapted to their environment related to where they live, how they move, what they eat. Do all sea birds have the same kind of feet?

PRACTICAL TASK PRACTICAL TASK PRACTICAL TASK PRACTICAL TASK PRACTICAL TASK

In order to see if your children have grasped basic concepts in this topic, give your children the following ecosystems:

- **arid desert;**
- **polar region;**
- **tropical rainforest;**
- **grassland.**

Then ask them to create an animal that would live in one of these. They would have to say what it would look like, what it would eat, who would eat it, and they would have to draw it and give it a name.

PRACTICAL TASK PRACTICAL TASK PRACTICAL TASK PRACTICAL TASK PRACTICAL TASK

Thinking about a habitat within a scheme of work that you have taught or will be teaching, plan how your pupils could investigate the idea of camouflage in the classroom.

Subject knowledge that underpins the activities in this chapter

Food chains and energy transfer

Food chains describe the energy changes within an ecosystem and usually start with the Sun as the source of energy.

The Sun provides the energy for plants to make their own food and to provide food for other living things. Green plants are called **producers** because they make their own food from sunlight and other basic materials. All animals are consumers because they cannot make their own food.

Producers are important, because although not all other living things eat plants, they ultimately provide food for the other members of the community. Animals that eat plants for their basic energy needs are called **primary consumers** or **herbivores.** Animals that do not eat plants themselves rely on eating those that do for their survival. These are called **secondary consumers** or **carnivores**. Animals which then eat the secondary consumers are called **tertiary consumers**. Only plants can be primary producers because animals cannot make their own food directly. Decomposers are microbes that feed on dead and decaying material. Most of these are bacteria (single-celled organisms) and more complex fungi (moulds and mushrooms). These live by decomposing dead material. As they consume, decomposers produce waste materials (chemicals) that are needed by plants in order to grow. Decomposers recycle the materials essential for life. Decomposers sometimes cause problems like mould on bread, but they need the right conditions to grow like other living things.

Food chains indicate feeding relationships in a habitat. They show the direction of the energy transfer from one organism to another.

The most common example given in most textbooks is

Grass → rabbit → fox

An important concept in science is related to the impact on other species if there is a population explosion, or a significant reduction in one part of a food chain. For example, what might happen to the fox population if the rabbits decreased in number because of sickness?

Leaves → moth caterpillar → sparrow → owl
Dandelion leaves → snail → thrush

Food webs

Most animals will eat a variety of other animals. This more complex relationship is shown diagrammatically in a food web.

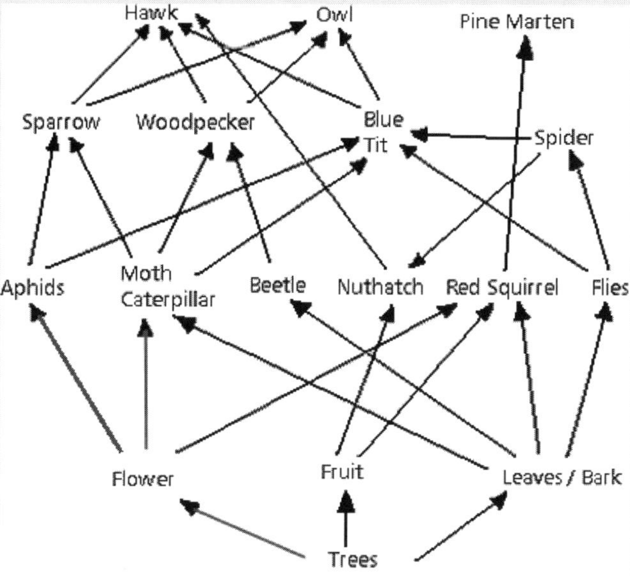

Task

Traditional textbooks tend to give the same examples. More child-friendly ones can be found on **http://ecokids.ca/pub/eco**. Visit the site and evaluate its potential for use in your classroom.

An interesting slant on this idea is provided if you start with children's lunch boxes and ask them to work back from each piece of food, thinking about the food chains involved.

Predators and prey

Predators are animals that hunt and kill other animals for food for themselves or their families. Animals that are hunted are called **prey.** In a food chain the predator always is shown **before** the prey. The arrow in a food chain **always** indicates the direction of the energy transfer. So, in the example above, the stored energy in the fruit is transferred to the nuthatch when the nuthatch eats the fruit. Feeding relationships within ecosystems are important and sometimes very finely balanced. If one animal is more successful and there is an increase in its population, this may well have an adverse effect on the animals and plant species further down the food chain. For example, if lions breed well in one year, there may be a corresponding decrease in the wildebeest population, which might then impact in turn on the lions and other animals, e.g. vultures and other animals that rely on scavenging for the remains left by lions after the kill. Starvation might be the result. Changes in one feeding system can also affect other feeding systems and populations can impact on other levels, even in the case of animals that get their energy from plants, i.e. primary consumers. If we think about this in terms of Man's reliance on plants for food, particularly in some parts of the world, the food chain is short; when the rains fail to arrive, the crop fails, and starvation results. Omnivores obtain their energy from eating both animals and plants.

It is easy to see, however, how important the Sun is in this process. Some scientists believe that although there were dinosaurs that ate only plants and others that ate only other dinosaurs and other small animals, the reason why dinosaurs as a group died out was because of the climatic changes that occurred over many years. This affected the amount of plant material available to be eaten by the dinosaur herbivores. Hence, over a long period of time, because the food chain was affected, all dinosaur species died out because their food source decreased in abundance.

The final links in the food chain are the decomposers. Decomposers are living things that can be thought of 'dirty rotters' because of the way in which they get their energy from dead and decaying material. Some decomposers are plants, some are animals and some bacteria. Decomposers you and your children are likely to encounter in local and near habitats include fungi, insect larvae like maggots, woodlice, millipedes, earthworms. Decomposers get their energy by chemically breaking down dead plant and animal material and other detritus such as excrement (chemical reactions). Sometimes, as in the case of earthworms digesting dead plant material, essential minerals and nutrients are returned to the soil, thereby 'recycling' material ready to be used again within other life processes.

The idea of a food chain is easy, but often, experience suggests that children are not taught that the arrows within a food chain represent the energy transfer and **not** which animal eats which plant or animal. You need to bear this in mind in your teaching.

Adaptation

Over millions of years, animals and plants have evolved slowly to meet the sometimes changing demands of their particular environment. This has happened because a new characteristic has enabled some species to survive better. Such changes are termed adaptation to their environment. Animals and plants that are better adapted to their environment are more likely to survive, reproduce and pass on their genetic material to the next generation. Particularly when times are hard there is competition both within and between species and the strongest, best-adapted of the species will survive. This is sometimes termed the 'survival of the fittest'.

The seashore

The seashore is potentially a very harsh habitat, particularly for those animals and plants that live amongst rocks between high and low water. Here there is a great risk of dehydration and heat stroke at low tide and an increased risk of being eaten by visiting predators such as seagulls. Unsurprisingly perhaps, the range of plants found in this habitat is limited. Seaweeds have adapted so that they tend to have very thick outer coverings that allow them to withstand periods exposed to wind and sun without drying out, and air sacs that allow the seaweed to float higher in the water and nearer to the sun to help with photosynthesis.

Similarly, some simple animals, such as limpets and mussels, have adapted by having hard shells, which while they may not protect them from the most determined of sea birds, safety in numbers reduces the risk of an individual being eaten. Soft-bodied creatures like crabs have their own shells for protection, or if they have none of their own, inhabit those discarded by other creatures, e.g. hermit crab. Other shellfish which inhabit sandy beaches are often not visible until you dig down into the sand. Some, like cockles, have adapted to enable them to bury themselves in the sand by a process that is fascinating to watch, ideally at first hand or on video. Here animals' lives are affected more by the changing of the tides than the changing of the seasons, for the temperature of the sea changes more slowly than the air above it. They have to survive in an environment of high salt content. Sea anemones, which have poisonous tentacles, put them out to catch smaller prey at high tide and draw them inside themselves if there is a risk that their bodies will be exposed to the air at low tide.

A study of a transect from the sea to the far reaches of sand dunes on a sandy beach would reveal a wide variety of plants and animals potentially found from, in the sea, free-swimming animals and plant plankton to fishes and other animals such as jellyfish; on the rocks and in pools, crustaceans such as shrimps, lobsters crabs, shellfish such as mussels and limpets, seaweeds, sponges; on to the sand, further shellfish, worms like the lugworm; and into the sand dunes, mites and other insects and other plants that colonise the seashore such as the grasses with tough, strong roots to hold them securely and help them to get water to survive.

Coniferous forests

Coniferous forests provide an equally harsh, but very different habitat. Many in the UK were originally planted to provide a quick, replenishable supply of wood and consist of mainly one species of plant, which grow close together thereby excluding light from the forest floor. In other parts of Europe, coniferous forests are widespread mainly because they are tolerant plants and able to live in poor soil. They are often found extensively on the sides of mountains and hills. Coniferous forests tend not to support a high variety of animals. This is mainly because their leaves, or rather, adapted leaves – needles allow little water loss in areas where the rainfall is poor and allows little to grow, excepting brackens on the forest floor. This means there is little food available for herbivores. Nevertheless the increasingly successful grey squirrel, originally introduced to the UK from North America, is in competition with red squirrels and is, in some places, exterminated to protect the red. Deer thrive in the cool of the coniferous forest and evidence of foxes, badgers and hedgehogs can be found. In the autumn fungi abound. The number and type are amazing and well worth a survey, always remembering though, that some harmless-looking varieties can be deadly. Mosses and liverworts, too, abound on the floor of the forests playing their part in the ecosystem.

PRACTICAL TASK PRACTICAL TASK PRACTICAL TASK PRACTICAL TASK PRACTICAL TASK

The whole of life revolves around the transfer of energy. Make two lists of primary producers, primary consumers and secondary consumers you have encountered in two of the different habitats within this chapter. Download some pictures of the animals and plants on your list and cut out some arrows to show the relationships between your chosen living things.

Having made your list, draw some food chains to show the feeding relationships within the ecosystem.

Ask your class to download or otherwise collect pictures of animals to show in food chains. Use role play, perhaps using masks made by your pupils, to reinforce the direction of the energy transfer. Some children could act out the food chain with arrows as props to show the direction of the energy transfer.

Could you make a game using this simple idea to reinforce this idea to aid your pupils' learning?

PRACTICAL TASK PRACTICAL TASK PRACTICAL TASK PRACTICAL TASK PRACTICAL TASK

Look at the following website, which provides some delightful information on camouflage and a whole range of information about different environments and teaching about environments including some imaginary animals. **www.torontozoo.com/pdfs/TorontoZoo-Grade2-Workshop.pdf**

- **How could you use this in your teaching?**

The BBC and IBA provide an enormous array of wildlife programmes throughout the year, not exclusively schools broadcasts. Whilst it is not suggested that you show long programmes, it is good to select short snippets of video to introduce into your teaching to reinforce points of learning.

- **Scan the schools broadcast schedules for programmes associated with habitats and ecosystems.**
- **View those you are particularly interested in and include them in your scheme of work at an appropriate point.**

A SUMMARY OF **KEY POINTS**

The focus of the work in this chapter was on the activities to help learners understand more about living things in their environment. In particular it has:

> **presented a number of activities on the theme of living things in their environment showing how learners' understanding of the basic ideas related to living things and their environment can be developed over the primary age range;**

> **emphasised the need for pupils to have much first-hand experience of exploring a number of different habitats and to think about the feeding relationships between different kinds of animals, plants and micro-organisms;**

> **demonstrated how different living things rely on each other for survival and how some are adapted to their environments;**

> **shown cross-curricular links to geography and how a study of local and distant environments can nurture a sense of responsibility for the local environment and an awareness of the global impact of environmental issues.**

Moving on

This chapter has considered a range of habitats and two in particular. It has looked at the feeding relationships between different members of two habitats. With the increasing emphasis on global awareness, you need to ensure that you are familiar with a whole range of habitats and ecosystems and to incorporate a study of these into your teaching, particularly at Key Stage 2. Today, the media provide children with a whole range of information about the plight of endangered species such as the orang-utan or, nearer to home, the greater crested newt and the slow-worm.

Think about how, in your planning, you could link this topic directly to the issues that we know are currently of interest to your pupils, e.g. recycling, global warming.

Today it is often said that global warming is the most difficult problem facing man now and in the future. The government-commissioned STERN Review examines and presents the available scientific evidence in relation to the economic problems that lie ahead. Its stance is that global warming is caused by Man's interaction with the environment. However, the extent to which man can be blamed for global warming is debatable. Fossil and other evidence suggests that natural variations in sea level and mean temperature of the world have varied since before life on Earth began. As a reflective practitioner, you need to be aware of and have examined the arguments and be able to debate the issues either with your pupils or colleagues and other professionals.

REFERENCES REFERENCES **REFERENCES** REFERENCES **REFERENCES** REFERENCES

Nuffield Primary Science (1997) *Science Process and Concept Exploration: Understanding Scientific Ideas*. London: Collins.

FURTHER READING FURTHER READING **FURTHER READING** FURTHER READING

DfES (2005) *Developing the Global Dimension in the School Curriculum*. London: DfES

Howe, A., Davies, D., McMahon, K., Towler, L. and Scott, T. (2005) Living things in their environment, Chapter 10 in *Science 5–11 A Guide for Teachers*. London: David Fulton

Peacock, G., Sharp, J., Johnsey, R. and Wright, D., (2007) Ecosystems, Chapter 5 in *Primary Science: Knowledge and Understanding*, 3rd edition. Exeter: Learning Matters

The STERN Review (2006) on **www.ttrb.ac.uk**

Children's books

Donaldson, J. and Marks, L. (2005) *Sharing a Shell*. Eastbourne: Gardners Books

Websites

www.kentwildlifetrust.org.uk Kent Wildlife Trust
www.eco-schools.org.uk Eco Schools (Ecology, recycling)
www.naturegrid.org.uk Nature Grid (environment, living things)
www.rspca.org.uk Education

Part 3
Materials and Their Properties

8
Properties of materials

By the end of this chapter you should:

- **be aware of some of the significant subject knowledge that underpins the understanding of the properties of materials;**
- **recognise some of the common misconceptions associated with the properties of materials;**
- **understand the progression of this topic using some examples of learning activities from 3 to 11 years;**
- **identify specific basic skills, illustrative and investigative opportunities within this topic;**
- **recognise how pupils can record, in different ways, some of their activities within this topic;**
- **have reflected upon how you can involve parents and carers in this aspect of children's learning.**

Professional Standards for QTS

Q1, Q2, Q4, Q5, Q6, Q7a, Q8, Q9, Q10, Q12, Q14, Q15, Q17, Q18, Q19, Q21a, Q22, Q23, Q24, Q25a, Q25b, Q25c, Q25d, Q26a, Q27, Q28, Q29, Q30, Q31, Q32

Curriculum Guidance for the Foundation Stage and National Curriculum

In the Foundation Stage pupils should:

- **examine objects to find out more about them (QCA, 2000, p86);**
- **notice and comment on patterns (QCA, 2000, p88).**

At Key Stage 1 pupils should be taught to:

- **use their senses to explore and recognise the similarities between materials;**
- **sort objects into groups on the basis of simple material properties;**
- **recognise and name common types of material and recognise that some of them are found naturally;**
- **find out about the use of a variety of materials and how these are chosen for specific uses on the basis of their simple properties (DfEE, 1999, p 80).**

At Key Stage 2 pupils should be taught:

- **to compare everyday materials and objects on the basis of their material properties, including hardness, strength, flexibility and magnetic behaviour, and to relate these properties to everyday uses of the materials;**
- **that some materials are better thermal insulators than others;**
- **that some materials are better electrical conductors than others;**
- **to describe and group rocks and soils on the basis of their characteristics, including appearance, texture and permeability;**
- **to recognise differences between solids, liquids and gases, in terms of ease of flow and maintenance of shape and volume (DfEE, 1999, p87).**

Introduction

Generally thought of as part of chemistry, 'Materials and their properties' is a topic that is very extensive in scope. There are many different kinds of materials existing in the world. A study of materials can be very wide ranging from what substances are made from, i.e. the nature of matter including atoms, molecules, mass and weight, to physical changes and chemical reactions. Importantly, all materials are made up of building blocks known as elements and, together or singly, elements make up all the different materials known to Man. A study of relevant materials is fundamental to all sciences from astrophysics to biochemistry.

You might have found your own study of materials difficult, tedious or boring. On the other hand, your teachers might have approached the topic with enthusiasm using models and practical activities to introduce and reinforce the important basic abstract ideas. This area of science can be confusing, but this does not need to be the case if it is taught in well-planned, short, but linked, chunks. A study of materials in the primary school offers many different opportunities for practical 'hands-on' exploration where pupils can progressively find out about the world around them. This process builds naturally on the way that children learn, from their early exploration of materials by putting everything in their mouths, to finding out what happens to some materials when they are placed near to a magnet.

Check your understanding

What do you understand by the following terms? Make a note of your ideas.

Material	Atom	Absorption
Naturally occurring material	Molecule	Compound
Synthetic material	Element	Strength
Durability	Viscosity	Mixture
Hardness		Ductile

Check your understanding with the Glossary.

Properties of materials: some basic ideas

The classification of materials is fundamental to science and important at all levels. Materials are classified in many ways. However, a key feature is whether they occur naturally or not or on the basis of their chemical make-up. If the classification is based on chemical make-up, materials can be composed of single substances, a mixture of two or more single materials existing together or composed of a number of materials combined together chemically. Wood, stone, pebbles, coal, flint, bone, wool fur and other animal hair, cotton, flax, linen and silk, asbestos, metals like gold or silver all occur naturally. Plastics, concrete, bricks, glass, some wood products such as chipboard or hardboard and synthetic fibres like nylon or rayon are not naturally occurring. Peacock et al. (2007) state:

> All materials are made up of a combination of one or more of just over 100 elements. The resultant variety is staggering. Materials can be transparent, brittle, toxic, soft, good conductors of electricity, etc., etc. The same material can behave differently when it exists as a solid, liquid, or gas (try crunching liquid water!). Some materials can react with others to produce new materials and by-products. Without materials, life would not be. (p.72)

Constructed over many years, the periodic table of the chemical elements is a highly complex system. The periodic table organises elements into patterns of elements based on their atomic structure. Chemists discovered that substances with similar atomic structure had similar, but not identical, properties. They discovered trends in their properties. On the periodic table today, elements are grouped together into periods (rows) that run across the periodic table and groups (columns) to reflect their relationship with others.

In the everyday world, materials can be grouped in many different ways based on different criteria. Although the term 'solid' can be problematic, basic sorting and recognition of the different properties of solids, liquids and gases are important in science and relevant to a study of materials in the primary school. Similarly, the notion of particle size is important. Many basic related ideas are explored in Chapter 6 of Peacock et al. (2007) You might find reference to this text useful, to check and extend your understanding, as you work through this chapter and the following chapters in this section.

Children's ideas from research

Materials

Children will usually associate the term 'material' with fabrics. Younger children will initially choose to sort materials by their directly observable features, e.g. colour, shape, size, whether they can be bent or produce sound. You may find that older children will sort by function, e.g. whether it is a foodstuff or construction material, and they tend also to generalise about materials, e.g. metals are strong, shiny and sharp.

Interestingly, children often think that particles in solids, liquids and gases are different according to their shape, i.e. gas molecules are round, molecules of liquid have an irregular form and molecules of solids are cuboids (Hader and Abraham, 1991, cited in Peacock et al. 2007, p83). Molecules are thought to be largest in solids and smallest in gases (Pereira and Pastana, 1991, cited in Peacock et al., 2007, p83).

Children identify solids as hard, that they can be held or touched and are heavier than liquids, e.g. children will usually say that a large block of ice is heavier than the same quantity of water. Liquids can flow and be poured; they run and are heavier than gases. Children find liquids easier to classify than solids and relate these to water. Thicker liquids, e.g. treacle and honey, cause problems. Children often think that all gases are poisonous, coloured and that all gases will kill you. Air is often just one substance and is different to other gases. Sprays, mists, smoke and flames are regarded as gases. Gas is a dangerous fuel. Gas, air and oxygen are often thought of as all the same thing.

'Difficult' substances

Children find pastes, foams, powders and soft substances difficult to classify. They may be classified as something between a liquid and a solid. The bigger the particle, the more likely the material is to be classified as a solid. Use of the term 'particle' here means a grain of sand, sugar, coffee, etc. When children are taught that liquids flow, they then include sand, flour, talc, etc., as liquids. Children's ability to classify sometimes seems to deteriorate with age, e.g. when sorting shopping, young children never classify rice or flour as a liquid, possibly because they associate liquids with wetness, but older children often do. Children often think that weight increases when a liquid changes to a solid and decreases when it changes back to a liquid. They often think a gas has no weight.

Teaching example 8.1: Foundation Stage

Play

Learning intention: To explore materials through play

The Foundation Stage classroom provides many opportunities for children to explore the properties of materials through everyday play activities, e.g. the water tray, sand tray, manipulating clay and play dough or the 'home corner'. You might find it highly surprising then if you hear some Early Years teachers stating quite forcibly that 'we don't do science' in the Foundation Stage, Nursery or Reception class. Indeed babies, even before birth because they are immersed in fluid, 'explore' the properties of materials inside their mother's womb. Early Years science aims to build on this learning, which is further extended immediately after birth as new-born babies meet both naturally occurring and not naturally occurring materials for the first time in their new environment.

Hands-on displays of specific materials, e.g. metals or plastics, where children can explore when they wish, can help them to progress their understanding of the properties of particular materials. They can also extend their vocabulary, e.g. linking the feel of soft, hard, bendy, stretchy, materials to the word, and challenge their ideas about the properties of materials. Whilst a teacher or helper may not 'teach' a formal lesson about the properties of materials to the Foundation class, informal opportunities present themselves every day through involvement in child-initiated 'play' activities. In this situation it is important for you and the other adults to observe and listen to your children as they play. With experience, you will come to recognise the opportunities presented to you for extending their scientific vocabulary, knowledge and understanding of materials at a simple level. Each of the above examples focuses on properties of materials in a natural, play-based way and without realising it the children will be extending their learning through discussion.

Basic skills: Sorting and classifying materials

Exploring materials and sorting materials into different groups starts with observation, when it is safe and appropriate, using all the senses. This leads to simple classification, and to an understanding of the differences and similarities between materials. The youngest children can begin to identify different materials by sorting a small number of objects with very obvious differences between their properties, e.g. shape, colour and texture. They will engage in the activity through discussion in small groups and recording will be visual by placing objects with similar properties into two hoops.

Scenario

A Foundation class was looking at liquids. The trainee had collected together a number of bottles of 'bubble bath' and other washing liquids in small bottles produced by manufacturers to appeal to young children. Paying close attention to the possibility that children might try to drink the liquids in the bottles, an adult helped the children. They first explored and described the colour and smell of each liquid and then noticed the 'runniness' (the viscosity) of each and put them into order based on this property.

Investigations

Exploration of materials through play can lead to simple investigations that are based on observation of things set in a context and will appeal to the youngest children. For example, 'How can we keep Teddy dry? Teddy needs to go out in the rain but lost his umbrella. What materials could he use to keep him dry?' Using simple familiar resources such as 'compare bears', a plastic container (to place the bear in), a variety of materials such as fabrics, or paper, etc., elastic bands and droppers for dropping water on Teddy, children can try and find out. You can ask the children, working with an adult, to investigate simple variables such as different types of materials, number of layers of materials or the amount of water. Recording can be made in a simple chart with small samples of the material stuck onto a piece of paper and the children simply tick or cross (✓ or ✗) whether Teddy gets wet or stays dry. The table can then be developed into ranking using an arbitrary scale. This is a suitable investigation for Foundation Stage children because there are few variables. If it can be started with a story, even better.

Easily available today are teddies that can be heated in a microwave, e.g. to keep hands warm. Simply heating Teddy, adhering strictly to manufacturers' directions, can lead to finding out how long Teddy will keep warm. Teddy can be heated for different lengths of time (up to the maximum time allowed) and children can, if a number of teddies are available, compare how quickly the bears cool down. Simple comparisons of the insulating properties of materials can be made if each teddy is placed in a 'bed' wrapped in different materials. 'Which material keeps teddy warm the longest?' In this case, not only are the children learning about heating, cooling temperature and insulation, but also about the properties of the 'stuffing' inside Teddy.

Beware! Do not encourage your class to put their own teddies in the microwave! You may need to keep parents and carers aware of your 'explorations' in science.

Artificial and natural sponges can be used to introduce the idea of absorption. The question, 'Which sponge holds the most water?' provides a starting point for direct observation and measuring amounts of liquid. The independent variable is the type of sponge or size of sponge, and the dependent variable is the amount of water the sponge holds. This can be measured by ranking using a series of clear plastic bottles. It is helpful to place a drop of food dye in the bottom of the bottle to help the children to see the volume of water and to make ranking easier. The activity could arise directly out of child-initiated play if sponges are placed in the water tray.

Consider carefully the number and type of articles provided in the water tray. Although it is tempting to put many different toys or materials into the water tray at once, reducing the type and number of articles will provide greater focus for the play and the specific properties of selected materials. Whilst the materials are in the water tray your pupils could also start to explore the different properties of solids, liquids and gases. Provide balloons filled with air, water and ice for your young scientists to play with in the water. Using these balloons they will see that they all float, but at different levels. They can also 'feel' forces when they push them down into the water. They can talk about what they feel. It is useful to provide some digital pictures of the balloons in the water. Use these to help children create a floor book to help develop their vocabulary.

Teaching example 8.2: Key Stage 1

Basic skills: sorting and classifying materials

Learning intention: To be able to sort materials into observable features

You might think that sorting objects is merely an activity for the youngest children, but in fact it is a skill that needs practice throughout the primary years. Recognition of some properties of materials in the Foundation Stage can lead to sorting by different criteria at a later stage. Older children can sort materials into those that are naturally occurring and non-naturally occurring categories, but this can lead to confusion when they are faced with materials that fall into two categories, e.g. a wooden clothes peg. Children are even more confused if the term 'man-made' is used instead of 'not naturally occurring'. Because wooden clothes pegs are not found shaped like that in nature, so a man must have made them. However, pegs are made from wood, which occurs naturally.

Older children should be encouraged to choose their own categories for sorting materials. Occasionally they should be challenged to sort in a particular way, or asked to make a key relating to a group to materials, for instance through close observation of very similar, but different materials, e.g. rocks, white powders of different substances, or metals.

The variety of materials and their uses

When children are able to recognise and name common materials, they can undertake a material trail and apply their understanding of materials in a new setting. Pairs of children can explore the classroom and, with supervision, other areas of the school to identify where particular materials are used and for what purpose.

Investigation: absorbency

Learning intention: To compare materials and communicate their findings

An investigation focused on the absorbency of kitchen towels provides an opportunity for children to build on earlier experience and further explore the properties of materials. The global question, 'Which is the most absorbent kitchen towel?', provides the opportunity for children to plan with their teacher. The independent variables include the type of towel, size of towel, number of layers of towel, amount of liquid and type of liquid. The dependent variables, depending on how the investigation is set up, could be the observation, or simple measurement, of the size of the puddle left after the spilt liquid is mopped up. The success of this activity depends on accurate measurement and observation. If pupils are going to compare by observation, the addition of a little food dye to the water can provide greater visibility. If the type of liquid is changed rather than the type of towels, this becomes a really useful activity to develop children's understanding of liquids other than water. So, simultaneously, ideas about absorbency and viscosity of liquids can be developed. Changing the demands of the investigation introducing measurement in standard units makes this activity suitable also for older children. Beware, however: some children confuse strength of the towel with its ability to absorb liquids, but discussion can easily remedy this problem.

Durability of materials
Starting with a story such as *New Clothes for Alex* (Mary Dickinson and Charlotte Firmin, Hippo, 1986), children could investigate the durability of fabrics using the global question: 'What materials would we use to make Alex's new clothes?' This fair test investigation provides an opportunity for older Key Stage 1 children to begin to identify the independent and dependent variables. The independent variables might include the type of fabric, the number of layers, the size of sample, the place tested, the size of stone used for rubbing the fabrics and the type of surface for rubbing. Possible dependent variables include the number of rubs or observation of the fabric after a set number of rubs of the stone. Here is an opportunity for simple graph work. If children are allowed to design their own investigation, there is the opportunity for different responses and the communication of findings, which is an important aspect within the National Curriculum.

Teaching example 8.3: Key Stage 2

Strength of materials
Learning intention: To make simple generalisations about materials and record results in a table

Success criteria
- to find ways of testing for hardness;
- to record the measure for each material in a table;
- to compare and discuss findings, drawing conclusions based on evidence.

Before you start on an activity like this, you need to consider health and safety. As the children will drop weights on materials and be looking at the impact and then grading this, they should wear safety glasses. Also, the materials should be placed in the middle of a mat. This will ensure that if the material breaks, the pieces are localised.

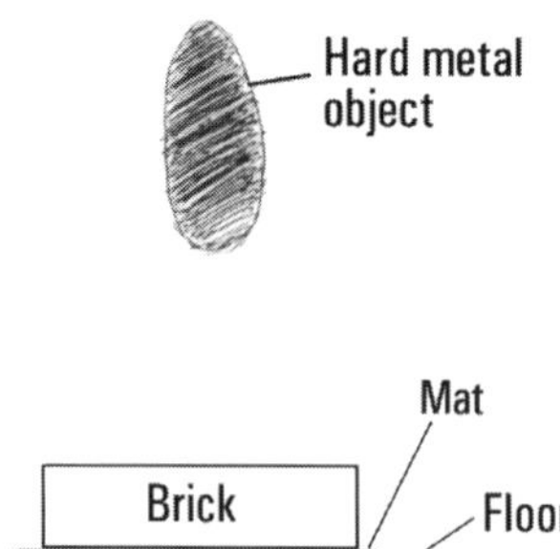

Testing strengths of materials
Point to note: A material's hardness will depend on its type. Minerals are measured by their ability to resist scratching, whilst metals are judged on the depth of impression when a load is applied. Although children will want to test many different materials and rank them in order of hardness, materials that shatter, like glass, should not be included in the sample, unless supervision rates are high. This activity should not be undertaken as a fair test but instead as a range of surveys.

Independent variables: The types of materials, the type of weight that will be dropped on the materials, the height from which the weight is dropped, the type of materials used to scratch the surface, the number of scratches and the pressure applied.
Dependent variables: There are no scientific measures for hardness (see further information at end of chapter) and in all cases observations and arbitrary scales should be used. It is possible to look at the amount of weight an object can withstand before breaking.

The children can test materials by:

- dropping weights from a set height and discussing the impact on the materials' surface, then ranking the impact;
- scratching the material with a nail and comparing the amount and depth of the scratches;
- adding additional weights and seeing the weight needed to break an object (old metal weights are ideal for this);
- dropping the weight from increasing heights and ranking and comparing impact damage.

The results of these tests should be recorded in tables and secondary research used to find out about the way in which materials are formed. Looking at the material using the digital microscope, to see if there are any relationships between the hardness rating and its observed physical properties, will help children to draw conclusions.

Teaching example 8.4: Key Stage 2

Learning intention: To be able to test and measure, using standard units, the strength of materials

Context: Shopping bags

Success criteria

- To use standard units of measurement.
- To record results in more than one way.
- To draw conclusions based on evidence.

This activity is simple to undertake and can be linked to the wider curriculum if the cost of the bags and their effect on the environment are also taken into account. The independent variables might include the type of bag, the type of load used to test strength, age of bag, size of bag, the material the bag is made from; and the dependent variables are the amount of tins added, or the number of books that can be carried, before the bag or handles break, or the time used before the bag wears out.

Suspend the bag from a thick broom handle balanced between two tables or chairs. Ensure that children's feet and hands are not underneath the test area. Using weights or a number of tins (e.g. beans) as non-standard weights, continue to place items in the bag until the bag handles, or the bottom of bag, can no longer withstand the weight. Record and evaluate the material used and the amount of weight withstood.

PRACTICAL TASK PRACTICAL TASK PRACTICAL TASK PRACTICAL TASK PRACTICAL TASK

Involving parents and carers in their children's learning
Children should be encouraged to talk to their parents or carers about the science they have been doing in school. Equally, you too, should encourage parents and carers to build on and to extend their children's scientific learning out of school.

Thinking about the shopping bag activities above:

- **How could you encourage pupils to test out durability of bags in everyday life?**
- **Do 'bags for life' really mean life?**
- **How many bags are used within their households each week?**
- **What types of bag are used at home?**
- **What vocabulary could be reinforced?**
- **What other simple activities could you set for your children to extend their learning of this aspect of science outside school?**

PRACTICAL TASK PRACTICAL TASK PRACTICAL TASK PRACTICAL TASK PRACTICAL TASK

Look at website **www.chem4kids.com/**
This is an American site, where materials are called matter. However, if you follow the links you can test your subject knowledge of atoms and particles.

- **Decide if you think this site would be one you would use in school.**
- **Would you suggest parents and children use it together?**

Now visit **www.webelements.com** Amongst a fascinating variety of information about elements in the periodic table, pertinently it gives the valency of each element, what the element looks like and offers sound as well as visual models.

Subject knowledge that underpins the activities in this chapter

The activities in this chapter are essentially concerned with the different properties of materials. The reason for their properties is the building blocks from which they are made. All materials are made from atoms. The term 'atom' comes from the Greek word meaning smallest thing. We now know that atoms are not the smallest things but in ancient times the Greeks also thought that some materials such as water and salt were atoms. Before our current understanding of science many scientists thought that everything was made up from the elements of earth, fire, water and air. It is known now that air and water are composed of atoms of different types and are in fact compounds.

> The chemical elements are composed of ... indivisible particles of matter, called atoms ... atoms of the same element are identical in all respects, particularly weight. (Dalton,1809 cited in Royal Society of Chemistry (2007))

The building blocks of all materials are called elements. Earlier the analogy was used of Lego pieces; another analogy could be that of the alphabet. There are only 26 letters in the alphabet, but they can be put together to make all the words we use. There is a chemical alphabet of more than 100 elements and they are used to make all materials known and yet to be created. The atoms of each element are all the same. Zinc, copper, gold, and helium are examples of elements. An element cannot be broken down into simpler substances by ordinary chemical means, so acids, heat, light or electricity will not break them down. Elements are listed on the periodic table.

The periodic table demonstrates how all the elements relate to each other based on their atomic structure. The first element is hydrogen, which has an atomic number of 1. This indicates that all atoms of hydrogen have one electron and one proton. All atoms in an element have the same number of protons and electrons and are electrically balanced, i.e. they have no charge in their uncombined normal state. The number of protons an element has determines its atomic number. Helium, atomic number 2, has two protons and two electrons. Oxygen, atomic number 8, has eight protons and eight electrons. When all the elements were placed in order it was found that they could be grouped according to their properties and the system helped scientists understand relationships and trends in properties of similar elements and also to predict some of the properties of elements that had not yet been discovered.

When Mendeleev developed the periodic table in the 1870s his system was based on atomic weights. This meant that some elements did not fit the expected patterns. When the English scientist Moseley confirmed that it was the atomic number, not the mass, that was important, the system used today was created. Although atoms contain neutrons, protons and electrons, it is the electrons that determine their behaviour.

Initially it was thought that electrons merely spun around the nucleus containing the protons and neutrons in a swirl. However, it is now known that electrons have set positions called shells. They are drawn in two dimensions as rings around the nucleus. Their position and the number of electrons in the outer shell determine the property of the material. The first shell of an atom can only contain a maximum of two electrons. The number of electrons that can be found within a shell is determined by the $2n^2$ rule, with n being he number of the shell. The first shell ($n=1$) will contain two electrons. The second shell ($n=2$) can contain up to 8 electrons. A substance like lithium has an atomic number of 3, so will have one full first shell and one electron in the outside shell. The number of electrons in the outer shell determines the behaviour of the material.

Elements with full electronic shells are stable and do not react; ones with spaces for electrons to be gained or lost are reactive. The most reactive substances either have to gain only one electron, for example the halogens such as chlorine, which have 7 electrons in their outer shell; or lose one electron like the group 1 metals such as lithium or sodium. When two or more elements combine they make new materials. Compounds are made of more than one element. A compound can have very different properties from the elements it is formed from. For example, the highly reactive metal sodium reacts with poisonous green gas called chlorine to produce sodium chloride, common salt (see Figure 8.1).

Elements can join together in a number of ways. Hydrogen atoms only have one electron. This should make hydrogen very reactive as it has a lone electron in its outer shell, but hydrogen atoms combine in pairs and share their lone electron, making each pair of hydrogen atoms stable. Hydrogen shares electrons in a covalent bond. Covalent bonds are formed when one or more pairs of electrons are shared between two atoms. Ionic bonds are formed when one or more electrons are removed from the atom and attach to the non-metal atom resulting in a positive and negative ion, which attract each other. Sodium chloride is an example of ionic bonding, with the lone electron on the outer shell of sodium filling the space in outer shell of the chlorine atom.

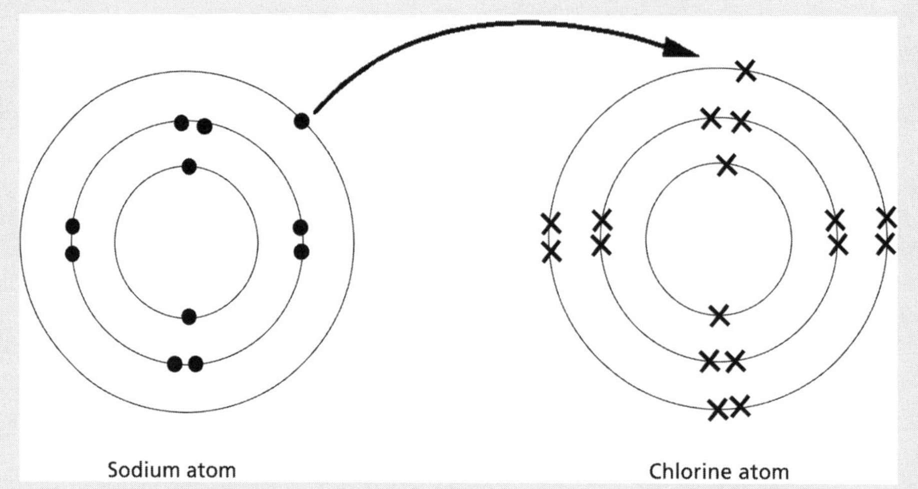

Figure 8.1 Reaction between sodium and chlorine to form a compound.

If elements were not able to join to other elements then there would be a limited number of materials. The elements, however, can exist on their own and in a seemingly never-ending range of possibilities. How they are linked together creates their properties. The resulting substances are termed compounds and mixtures.

Water, salt and sand are all compounds; they are made up of more than one element chemically combined. Water, which consists of two atoms of hydrogen and one of oxygen, is a very special substance with very particular properties because of the hydrogen bonds that cause strong forces of attraction between each molecule. These bonds allow some other materials to dissolve easily within it, cause the surface tension that allow insects like pond skaters to move quickly across its surface, and also account for the peculiar behaviour of water as it freezes and expands (Figure 8.2).

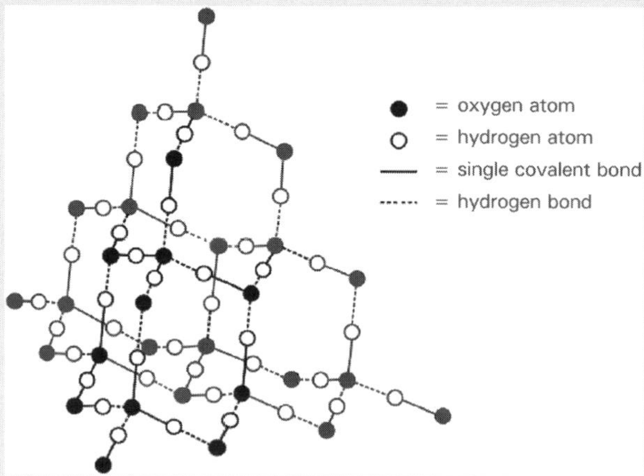

Figure 8.2. Bonds between hydrogen and oxygen in water.

If electricity is passed through water at a high enough voltage, separate atoms of oxygen and hydrogen are formed, so the water molecules can be split into their component parts by simple chemical means. If water is heated the compound stays as a compound and only water vapour is produced (see Chapter 9). Compounds are always found in the same proportions, e.g. there are always two hydrogen atoms to every one oxygen atom in water and always two oxygen atoms for every carbon atom in carbon dioxide, and they are linked by either covalent or ionic bonds.

The properties of particular materials depend on the bonds made between the atoms within them and the way in which individual atoms are arranged within elements. The properties of the materials are determined by the way in which atoms are joined together and the number of electrons involved. Some substances which are not combined chemically are called mixtures. Mixtures do not have set compositions and can be separated easily.

Carbon (C) is an interesting element as it can take a number of forms and can demonstrate key principles. Each form of carbon has very different properties. These differences depend on the arrangement and structure of the individual atoms that make up the structure. Carbon is a non-metallic element, its atomic number is 6 and it has six protons and six electrons (2, 4). There are four electrons in the outer shell that are able to form bonds with other atoms.

In graphite, commonly called 'lead' in pencils, only three of these electrons form bonds, giving strength in horizontal organisation but no strength in the vertical plane. The properties of all materials are influenced by the organisation of the atoms and their bonding. In graphite the bonding of its atoms makes a good material for pencils because as you write, layers of atoms are left on the page. Graphite is soft and dark in colour; its colour is also determined by the structure of the atoms stopping light from passing through it.

Diamond is also made totally of carbon atoms but has very different properties. Here, all four atoms in the outer shell share their electrons with other carbon atoms. This makes very strong bonds in all planes and a tetrahedral shape. The bonds are also covalent, which makes diamonds very strong. The structure of diamonds is one of repeating sets of eight atoms in a diamond-shaped formation. This structure enables diamonds to have strong crystal form. It is the atomic bonding that gives diamonds their physical and chemical properties; diamond is very strong and transparent.

The final form of carbon has a strange name and a stranger formation. It is called Buckminsterfullerene and is a 60-atom molecule with a shape like a soccer ball. This latest form of carbon was discovered in 1985. Carbon, like all material has its own particular properties because of the way its atoms behave. A few materials can exist in more than one form: this is called allotropy.

The way that atoms of carbon join together in different formations, demonstrates how the physical features and properties of substances will depend upon the way the atoms link together. The number and position of electrons are the most important part of this bonding process.

Sodium (Na), atomic number 11, has 11 electrons and 11 protons. This means it has an electron shell configuration of 2, 8, 1 (see Figure 8.1 on page 100). There is one electron in its outer shell, so sodium is a Group 1 metal and like other elements in the group, is very reactive. Chlorine (Cl), atomic number 17, has 17 protons and 17 electrons. The electron shell configuration is 2, 8, 7. Chlorine needs one electron to fill the outer shell, so it too is highly reactive. Elements with seven electrons in their outer shell are called halogens and belong to Group 7a. If sodium and chlorine are joined together then a new substance, the compound called sodium chloride, is formed. The sodium chloride compound demonstrates how the structure of atoms in materials reflects their properties. Chlorine is a poisonous green gas, the outer shell is not full and it is a highly dangerous material. Sodium is also highly reactive, with only one electron in its outer shell. When these two elements are combined the resulting compound is salt.

Salt contains ionic bonds: each sodium atom has donated the electron in its outer shell to chlorine, which now has a full outer shell, so salt is a stable and inert solid. Here, the sodium becomes a positively charged ion because of the loss of one electron. Similarly, the chlorine becomes a negatively charged ion as it has gained one electron. However, although these are electrical charges, when salt is dissolved in water to produce salt water this is still not dangerous or reactive. If salt water is heated, the salt remains behind after the water has evaporated because dissolving is a physical not a chemical change. (See Chapter 9 for more details.)

Thermal insulation and conductivity

The structure of the atoms within a material determines the properties of that material, including important properties like thermal insulation and conductivity. Unfortunately, it is impossible to discuss all the properties of materials and how these are determined in each case. However, thermal insulation and conductivity can be problematic ideas for children. Generally, plastics, which have many different forms and therefore very varied properties, are complex materials that are usually poor conductors of heat. Poor conductors are called insulators. The atoms of solid plastic are not ordered and regular but are long, tangled chains of molecules. They do not have free electrons; the electrons are tightly held.

Other materials, particularly metals that are the most conductive materials, conduct heat well because heat energy is transferred either by the passing of it from one free electron to another or by the energy making individual atoms vibrate. If the organisation of the material is regular, then the transfer of heat by vibration works more effectively. The units of vibrational energy are called phonons. Plastic materials have no free electrons and no atomic order to support phonons, so heat transfer is poor and these materials are insulators. Air is a poor conductor of heat and many other materials, e.g. wool and other fabrics, are poor conductors of heat and good insulators because they contain air in pockets between the particles.

Hardness

Hardness of materials is measured by the material's ability to withstand local penetration, scratching, machining or wear. There is no clear definition of hardness and no scale to measure it. Hardness may not be a fundamental property of a material but is a composite one that includes strength, which can be measured using the Rockwell hardness scales. This has no units and is measured on depth of impression when a load is added. The greater the load, the higher the grading of hardness.

REFLECTIVE TASK

The science National Curriculum at Key Stage 1 requires children to think about the use of a variety of common types of materials and how these are chosen for their specific use.

- **How might you present this aspect of the programme of study to your children? What activities might make this fun?**

Similarly, at Key Stage 2 there is a requirement to describe and group rocks and soils.

- **Starting with observation, how might you develop this aspect of science in your Key Stage 2 classroom?**

A SUMMARY OF KEY POINTS

The focus of the work in this chapter has been on activities to help learners understand more about some properties of materials. In particular, it has:

> **presented a number of activities that show how learners' understanding of the basic ideas presented can be developed over the primary age range;**

> **demonstrated that exploration of materials through sorting and classifying materials is important at each phase of the primary years and not just at the Foundation Stage;**

> **explained that the term 'materials' describes a multitude of different substances whose properies depend on the ways that the atoms and molecules within the material are structured: crucial to this process is the way that substances react or not when they are put together;**

> **shown that whether or not a substance reacts with another to form a new substance depends on the subatomic particles and their arrangement within individual atoms;**
> **shown the importance of thinking about how to encourage learners to engage in scientific activities at home with a view to involving their parents or carers and raising their awareness of the importance of science.**

Moving on

Review the strategies you could use to develop your relationship with your children's parents or carers. How could you modify your approach to encourage your children to engage with science at home? Could you arrange some opportunities for peer tutoring within your classroom?

FURTHER READING FURTHER READING FURTHER READING FURTHER READING

Smyth, A.L. (1997) *John Dalton 1766–1844: A Bibliography of Works By and About Him*, revised edition. Aldershot: Ashgate.

Howe, A., Davies, D., McMahon, K., Towler, L. and Scott, T. (2005) Materials and their properties, Chapter 5 in *Science 5-11 A Guide for Teachers*. London: David Fulton

Peacock, G., Sharp, J., Johnsey, R. and Wright, D. (2007) Materials, Chapter 6 in *Primary Science: Knowledge and Understanding*. 3rd edition. Exeter: Learning Matters

9
Physical changes in materials

By the end of this chapter you should:

- **be aware of some of the significant subject knowledge that underpins the understanding of physical changes in materials;**
- **recognise the common misconceptions associated with physical changes in materials;**
- **understand the progression of this topic using some examples of learning activities from 3 to 11;**
- **identify specific basic skills, illustrative and investigative opportunities within this topic;**
- **have reflected upon classroom organisation when teaching this topic.**

Professional Standards for QTS

Q1, Q2, Q4, Q7a, Q8, Q9, Q10, Q13, Q14, Q15, Q17, Q18, Q19, Q21a, Q21b, Q22, Q23, Q25a, Q25b, Q25c, Q25d, Q26b, Q27, Q28, Q29, Q30, Q31

Curriculum Guidance for the Foundation Stage and National Curriculum

In the Foundation Stage pupils should:

- **show curiosity, observe and manipulate objects;**
- **describe simple features of objects and events;**
- **examine objects to find out more about them;**
- **investigate objects and materials by using all of their senses as appropriate;**
- **find out about and identify objects and events they observe (CGFS, p86);**
- **look closely at similarities, differences, patterns and change;**
- **ask questions about why things happen (CGFS, p88).**

At Key Stage 1 pupils should be taught:

- **to find out how the shapes of objects made from some materials can be changed by some processes, including squashing, bending, twisting and stretching;**
- **explore and describe the way some everyday materials change when they are heated or cooled (DfEE, 1999, p80).**

At Key Stage 2 pupils should be taught:

- **to describe changes that occur when materials are mixed;**
- **to describe changes that occur when materials are heated or cooled;**
- **that temperature is a measure of how hot or cold things are;**
- **about reversible changes including dissolving, melting, boiling, condensing, freezing and evaporating;**
- **the part played by evaporation and condensation in the water cycle;**
- **how to separate solid particles of different sizes by sieving;**
- **that some solids dissolve in water to give solutions but some do not;**
- **how to separate insoluble solids from liquids by filtering;**
- **how to recover dissolved substances by evaporating the liquid from the solution;**

- **to use knowledge of solids, liquids and gases to decide how mixtures might be separated (DfEE, 1999, p87).**

Introduction

'Materials' is a very broad topic involving some very complex scientific ideas. Materials can change in a number of different ways. Changes in materials usually fall into two categories: physical changes and chemical changes. It is easy to become confused about these two different types of change. Building on the last chapter, in this chapter you will explore the ideas of changes in materials that can be reversed by physical means.

Many people find the idea of physical change confusing, particularly when thinking about what happens when things are mixed together, or what counts as a mixture, a suspension or a solution. This chapter aims to explain, in simple terms, the difference between the various physical changes and to provide some simple activities that can be provided to help your children develop their understanding of this aspect of science.

The most important point for you to remember is the precise definitions of the significant terms and to check your understanding before teaching. Even more than in other topics, it is very easy to teach the 'wrong' idea about materials whilst being convinced that your ideas are correct. Crucially, you need to understand the difference between physical and chemical changes and to raise the awareness of children to everyday examples of each type of change.

Check your understanding

What do you understand by the following terms?

Physical change	Dissolving	Solution
Reversible change	Suspension	
Solvent	Evaporation	Change of state
Solute	Condensation	Mixture
Melting	Latent heat	Emulsion

Check your understanding with the Glossary.

Physical changes in materials: some basic ideas

Some materials can be changed physically by squashing, twisting, bending or stretching. Some soft substances, e.g. clay, play dough or plasticine, change physically by being warmed and moulded to form an object of a particular shape. Other materials such as aluminum foil can be changed by being scrunched up. Depending on their size, rubber objects can change by being pushed or pulled. Some materials are magnetic – they are attracted by a magnet – and others are not. Simple changes like these can easily be explored in the classroom.

Many solid materials can be added together to form mixtures, e.g. salt and sand, sand and rocks. Some rocks, called conglomerates, are mixtures of different materials. The individual materials that make up the mixture can be separated by physical means and mixing can be reversed. Some mixtures can be separated very easily; for example, a mixture of iron filings and sand can be separated physically by the use of a magnet.

Dissolving is a process that happens when some solids are mixed with liquids. Some solids like salt or sugar change physically when they are mixed with some liquids. This is called dissolving, and a solution is formed. Solids that dissolve in a liquid usually produce a transparent, but sometimes coloured, solution. When salt, the solute, is dissolved in water, the solvent forms a transparent and colourless solution. Copper sulphate solution is transparent and blue. Substances like sand, wheat flour, cornflour, pepper, wood, metals, glass, plastics or wax do not dissolve in water and are said to be insoluble in water.

Other substances when mixed together, e.g. powder paint with water, produce a dense, opaque suspension. This is when the solid paint particles 'suspend' or hang in the liquid with which they are mixed. Over time the solid particles in the suspension fall to the bottom of the container leaving a thick-looking layer at the bottom and a coloured, almost transparent layer above. The liquid layer can be decanted and the paint can be recovered by leaving the remaining water to evaporate over time. The paint particles in powder paint mixed with water can often be noticed if you look carefully at the mixture.

Many people confuse melting and dissolving, partly because the terms are used interchangeably in everyday life, but also because in science they have very precise meanings. Melting and dissolving are both examples of physical change and are reversible. Chocolate, wax and ice change physically when they are heated and melt. They turn from a solid to a liquid. Some materials do not melt when heated, they burn: a chemical change. Melting is one of a number of reversible physical changes that involve a change of state. Other familiar changes of state include evaporation, condensation and solidification (freezing).

Sometimes it is very difficult to imagine just how a mixture of materials can be separated. Some materials cause even more confusion, as they react chemically when mixed with water.

Children's ideas from research

When children see substances dissolve, they often say that the solid material has 'disappeared', or confuse the process with melting as it appears that the solid has turned into a liquid. Both these ideas are incorrect as the substance is still there; it cannot be seen with the naked eye but can be tasted.

Learners often think that melting is the term used only for the change from ice to water and not for other substances, for example wax or metal. They also think that when paraffin wax or butter melts, water or a similar substance is formed or they say that it has turned into water. Children use the terms 'dissolving', 'melting', and 'turning into water', to mean the same thing.

Evaporation is similarly problematic. Younger children may say that water disappears through the table or goes into the ground or floor. Older children may explain evaporation as something transferred into the air or the sky. Very few describe water as changing to a vapour into the surrounding air. Your children might say that water has been absorbed by the container or disappeared into the cooker. Even adults often say that water disappears during drying.

The gaseous state of water is often described as invisible water particles or a mixture of air and water or water changed into air. Few children accept that there is always water vapour in the air and that water vapour could change into liquid water. Steam is often thought of as the mixture of condensing water particles mixed with air produced when a kettle boils, rather than the invisible area between the kettle spout and the 'cloud'. Condensation of water on cold surfaces is very difficult for children to understand. Many children think that the reason why water droplets can be seen on the outside of a cold container is because water that was inside the vessel has moved to the outside.

Trainees like yourself often have significant problems understanding that some mixtures, e.g. a fruit smoothie, are examples of a physical change because they fail to understand that the individual fruits remain unchanged chemically.

Teaching example 9.1: Foundation Stage

Changing materials by stretching

Figure 9.1 Changing materials by stretching

Learning intention: To explore how things change by stretching

What happens to the shape drawn on a balloon when it is inflated?

This investigation requires adult assistance but involves children in direct observation. Children can draw their own shape on a deflated balloon, make simple recordings of the shape and then observe and record the changes to the balloon with each pump of the air using a balloon pump. Sequential drawings of the shapes can be made as the balloon is inflated. Ask the children to observe the changes in size of their shape with each pump from a balloon pump. This activity requires only simple resources, i.e. balloons, balloon pump, ball-point or felt-tipped pen, and only requires a short period of time to complete. Children will be fascinated by the activity which becomes more systematic with adult help and questioning to aid the observation of changes taking place.

The manipulation of play dough and clay are both very popular play activities in the Foundation Stage. Both provide opportunities for introducing and reinforcing vocabulary and for observations leading children to notice the result of the material being stretched or squashed.

Making butter

Learning intention: To communicate observations

It is relatively easy and quite fascinating to make butter using a simple recipe and for children to watch the changes that take place as the milk changes to butter. With the help of an adult, children can notice the characteristics of the milk or cream at the start and how it slowly changes as the container is shaken. This can be achieved by using the top of ordinary milk shaken with a pinch of salt in a very clean plastic pot with a screw-top lid.

CASE STUDY CASE STUDY CASE STUDY CASE STUDY CASE STUDY CASE STUDY

Interestingly nowadays, butter is not always the result when milk is shaken in the way suggested above. As part of a practical session, trainees were asked to explore butter using different types of milk and cream and were then asked the question: 'Which one would make the best butter?' One group decided to compare sour cream, double cream and top of the milk. Results showed conclusively that the top of the milk had the potential to make butter quickest, as after half an hour of agitation, the fat globules had consolidated, forming a solid and leaving a liquid (butter and buttermilk). Whilst in the process of making butter they found the following website of suggested lesson activities particularly aimed at young children: **http://teachers.net/lessons**

- **Try to find out why 'modern' milk products do not change in the way expected.**

Other trainees consulted the following websites to find out about butter and making butter in the traditional way and the equipment that was used.

www.waltonfeed.com/old/butter.html
www.newton.dep.anl.gov/askasci/chem99/chem99069.htm -
www.pcl-eu.de/virt_ex/detail.php?entry=03butter

- **What could these websites offer to your children's learning across the curriculum?**
- **Explore the difficulties you might encounter in undertaking this activity with your class.**

When asked, teachers often disagree about whether the change from milk to butter is a physical change or a chemical change.

- **Ask your colleagues what they think and why.**
- **Identify the changes from milk to butter. Why is this a physical and not a chemical change?**

Teaching example 9.2: Key Stage 1

Manipulating materials

Learning intention: To look for patterns when materials are stretched, rolled, or flattened

Which material will make the longest snake? This is an excellent activity for providing opportunities for children to make simple comparisons and measurements. The independent variables here include the type of material, size of material, how it is stretched (pulled, rolled or flattened), where it is rolled. The dependent variable is the length of the snake, involving observation and ranking or the use of standard measures with centimeters (cm). The activity is very useful to introduce simple graphs as the results can be scaffolded by adults into a graph. Here, the idea of reliability of data can be introduced as the results between girls and boys often vary greatly because of the different way in which boys and girls roll the material.

Melting can easily be explored at Key Stage 1 by putting small amounts of different substances, e.g. chocolate, butter, etc., in individual and sealed plastic bags and placing them together in a bowl of hot water. In this way children can investigate the rate of melting, noticing which materials melt most quickly and which need more energy before they change state.

Teaching example 9.3: Key Stage 2

Which are the most stretchy tights?
This is a fair test investigation where the independent variables are the type of tights, size of tights, type of mass used, amount of mass; and the dependent variable is the length of tights, which involve comparison, observation and ranking. This activity needs a great deal of space or specifically bought tights that will not stretch too much with the addition of each mass unit, but is a fun activity that needs tall children to hold the tights as tights can stretch a very long way. Small plastic bags of sand are useful as mass units.

Making ice cream
Use the following website to see how ice and salt can be used to make ice cream. Again there is a link to history as people made their own ice cream before most houses had freezers.

http://marshallbrain.com/science/ice-cream.htm

Dissolving
Dissolving can be easily investigated in the classroom using simple, safe substances like salt, sugar, Epsom salts, sodium bicarbonate and other simple kitchen powders mixed with water. Not all of these substances will dissolve; some will not dissolve at all, some may form a suspension and some will form a solution, some will undergo chemical change and form new substances. You can help your children to clarify their ideas about these mixtures by providing the opportunity to explore these ideas first hand.

Children at Key Stage 2 can be asked to apply their understanding of materials and how they can be separated by a variety of physical means. For example, if you provide a mixture of sand, salt, very small paper clips and gravel, you can challenge your children to plan, carry out a series of activities to separate the mixture and to justify the methods they will use. This can provide an excellent way to assess their understanding.

Evaporation
Evaporation is a change of state that is easy to investigate both inside and outside the classroom. In fact, to demonstrate their understanding of this concept, children need to be able to recognise evaporation in different contexts such as puddles in the playground, washing drying on a line, fruit losing weight in the fruit bowl over time, sand castles drying out over time in a sand tray, or the amount of water in a fish bowl changing over time.

PRACTICAL TASK PRACTICAL TASK PRACTICAL TASK PRACTICAL TASK PRACTICAL TASK

Planning safe activities

- **What equipment would you need to provide for your children to make these activities safe?**
- **How would you group your children for this activity? How many children would you have working together on this task?**
- **How would you organise your classroom?**

Think about the planning necessary if you were to ask your children to investigate the following:

- **Does the size of the particle affect the time it takes for a solute to dissolve (the rate of dissolving)?**
- **Does the temperature of the water affect the rate of dissolving?**
- **Does a solute dissolve quicker or slower in different liquids?**
- **How much dissolved material do different water samples contain?**
- **How could this activity be linked to the natural crystals that can be observed in rocks and minerals?**

Subject knowledge that underpins the activities in this chapter

Manipulation and stretching

When materials like play dough and plasticine are manipulated and when other materials are stretched, they are changed physically by the forces that are exerted on them. See Chapter 10 for more information.

Dissolving

When a solid, called a solute, and a liquid, the solvent, are mixed together, they form a solution. Although the solute appears to disappear, in fact it is still present chemically the same within the solution.

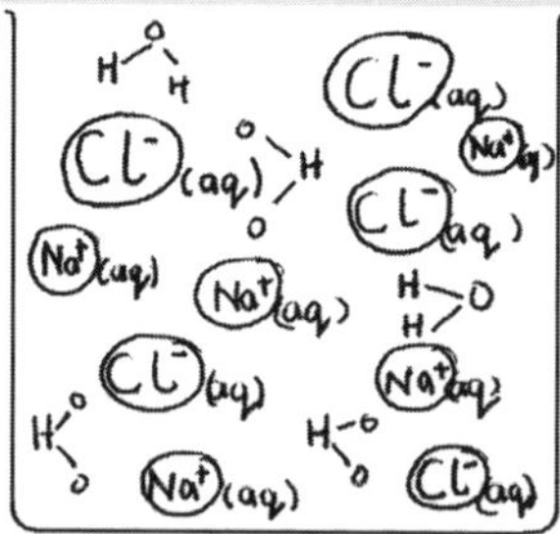

Figure 9.2 Salt dissolved in water

This physical change is easily reversible by evaporating the liquid over time, or by heating the solution gently. The resulting solid can be compared with the starting substance, if a digital microscope is used to take initial pictures of the solute (at 60 magnification) and then later when the solute is recovered by evaporation of the solvent.

The rate of dissolving can be increased by increasing the temperature of the solvent or by increasing the surface area of the solute.

Mixtures

Mixtures can be separated depending on their particle size and on the properties of the material. For example, in a mixture of sand, gravel, small paper clips (or iron filings) and salt, the iron filings or very small paper clips are magnetic and can be separated with a magnet. Gravel can be separated by picking out by hand, or by using a fine sieve that will allow the salt and sand to pass through. Knowing that salt dissolves in water and that sand is insoluble provides clues as to how these can be separated. Here again the particle size can help. When mixed with water, salt dissolves, but sand does not. When they are dissolved in water the water and salt particles in solution are very small, small enough to pass through a fine folded paper kitchen towel or filter paper. The bigger particles of sand in this mixture cannot pass through. Sand remains in the filter. Leaving the sand on the opened paper over time will allow the water to evaporate, leaving the dry sand separated. Finally, if the other separating processes have been done carefully, a transparent salt solution will remain. The salt can be separated from the water by gently heating it over a candle flame.

Figure 9.3 Evaporating a solution of salt and water

Milk is a mixture: an emulsion. The opaque mixture consisting of fat particles suspended in a watery liquid. 'Ordinary' milk will separate out over time – the fat particles floating on the top as cream, leaving the heavier liquid particles below. Simple examples like these can be translated into very productive activities which help to develop children's understanding of physical changes in materials in the primary classroom.

Change of state

Change of state is a physical change that can be reversed. It involves energy, in the form of heat given out or taken in and can be explained using a model: the kinetic theory of matter or particle theory. All matter consists of very small particles in constant motion. Particles with more energy move faster and those with less energy more slowly. In the model, solid particles have less energy than liquid particles, which have less energy than gas particles. In solids, the particles are close together in fixed positions with strong forces of attraction between them. In liquids, particles move around in a random way. In many models of a liquid there are gaps between particles. In reality there are no gaps; instead, particles slip and slide over each other at different speeds. There is some attraction between particles in a liquid and there is a fixed volume. However, because the particles can move around each other, liquids will take the shape of the container. Gas particles are very energetic so they move very fast. There is little attraction between them and they move outwards to fill the space in which they are contained. Gas particles collide with each other and in doing so exert a force on things with which they collide. Gases have no fixed shape or volume and can be squashed.

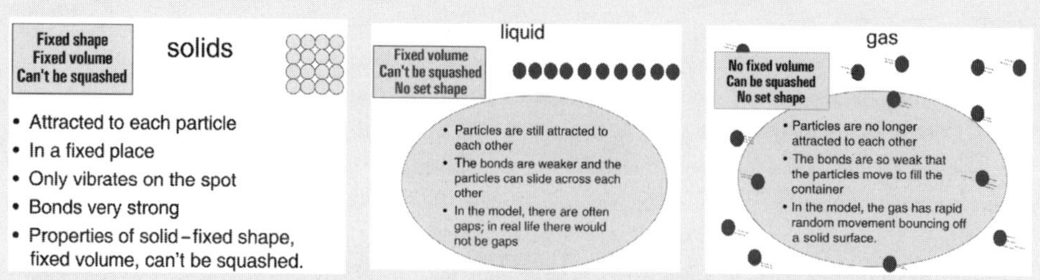

Figure 9.4 Particle arrangement in solids, liquids and gases

Change of state of happens in everyday life. The most familiar changes of state relate to water, because it changes over such a small temperature range, going from a solid to a gas between 0°C and 100°C. However, to change ice to water at 0°C requires a lot of energy. One kilogram of ice at 0°C needs 340,000 joules of energy to change it to one kilogram of water at 0°C. The energy needed to change ice to water in this way is called latent, or hidden heat. Conversely, to change water at 0°C to ice at 0°C the same amount of energy must be removed from the water. This is what happens in a freezer. The energy given to the ice here is used to break the strong links between the solid water particles to allow them to have enough energy to move around more feely within a liquid.

Heat is also needed to raise the temperature of water from 0°C to 100°C. This is called specific heat capacity. The specific heat capacity of water is 4200 joules per kilogram. This means that 1kg of water must be given 4200J of heat each time the temperature is raised by 1°. You could calculate the amount of heat needed to raise 1 kg of water from 1° to 100°. When the water temperature reaches 100° the water is said to boil. This is the boiling point of water. Under normal conditions the temperature does not rise any further. Instead, the water begins to evaporate at a very fast rate, but all the liquid water does not change to a gas instantaneously. Instead, as heat continues to be given to the water the energy is used to change water to gas at 100°. Here again we have latent or hidden heat, this time called the specific latent heat of vaporisation. The energy required to change 1 kilogram of water at 100°C to gaseous water (steam) at 100°C is 2,300 000J.

Under some conditions the boiling point of water can be raised by the addition of some substances, e.g. salt in cooking so that food cooks quicker. Under low pressure, water will boil at temperatures slightly below 100°C. This is why it is said that a good cup of tea cannot be made at the top of Snowdon. Similarly, the melting point of ice can be depressed by the addition of salt. This is why salt is put on roads in winter. The melting point of ice can also be depressed by the addition of weight, which explains why a weight-loaded wire can pass through a piece of ice apparently by magic.

Water in its three states of matter (water changing to a gas in a boiling kettle, water vapour condensing on cold windows, rain falling from clouds, ice cubes melting in a fizzy drink, ponds freezing in winter) can be seen simultaneously. Some materials easily change state with minor changes of temperature; for example, ice cream or butter melting when taken out of the fridge, or chocolate melting in the hand, or wax melting when a candle is lit and solidifying when the wax drips down the side of the candle. Different substances have different melting points and different boiling points. Gold will change state but the range of temperature from gas to solid is nearly 2000°C, making it unsuitable for use in the classroom. Most metals are solids at room temperature, but mercury is a liquid at room temperature.

It is important to stress that many common substances change state but no new substances are formed. When a substance is in different states, solid, liquid, or gas, it is still the same substance. The change from one form to another is reversible, with an associated energy change. You should encourage your class to look for and recognise different states of matter.

Evaporation

Evaporation is **not** the same as boiling. For any substance, the boiling point is a point where the liquid changes to a gas without a change of temperature. Evaporation, however, can happen at any temperature within a liquid. The higher the temperature, the faster the rate of evaporation. Temperature is a measure of the average amount of energy of the particles. Not all particles have the same amount of energy: some are moving faster, some more slowly. Those with more movement may move fast enough to escape from the attractive forces within the liquid and evaporate. As the temperature increases, more particles will have more energy so the rate of evaporation increases. When a liquid boils, it reaches the temperature where all particles have enough energy to evaporate. Evaporation causes cooling. This is because as particles escape, they take energy with them and the temperature of the remaining liquid falls. In order for more evaporation to occur, energy has to be taken from its surroundings. Eventually, all the liquid particles will evaporate in this way. Humans lose heat in this way through perspiration.

Solidification

Solidification or 'freezing' is the point at which materials change from a liquid to a solid. And this is different for different substances. Unfortunately, the term 'freezing' is often associated with the change from water to ice and therefore with cold when really, these terms relate to the physical change of any substance when it changes state from liquid to solid. Worse still, in everyday life we often say we are 'freezing' in cold weather which is, of course, an unfortunate use of the term. Surprisingly, in science, 'cold' does not exist: it is only the absence of 'hot' (or the absence of energy). Temperature is a measure of a material's internal energy.

Task

- **What activities could you provide for your class to reinforce this important concept?**

Mixtures are all around us in everyday life; they form part of the environment, for example, some toothpastes, smoke in the air.

- **Find out more about mixtures. How could children investigate mixtures in the classroom?**

Condensation

This is the reverse of evaporation and is equally important to children's understanding of change of state.

- **What experiences/activities could you provide for your children to reinforce this idea?**

REFLECTIVE TASK

Choose one of the above misconceptions.
Devise an activity or series of activities to challenge learners' misunderstanding of this aspect of changes in materials.

- **Consider the range and appropriateness of equipment to be used with learners in your activities. How could the activities be adapted, perhaps by use of different resources, to meet the needs of those with special needs, e.g. visual impairment? This is termed differentiation by resource.**
- **How could the activities be adapted to include children with particular difficulties in manipulating equipment?**
- **What questions would you ask the children in order to help them to undertake the tasks?**
- **What strategies could you help the children to use in order to develop a clear idea of your chosen misconception?**

A SUMMARY OF **KEY POINTS**

The focus of the practical examples in this chapter was to help learners understand more about physical changes in materials. Essentially the activities in this chapter were concerned with how materials can be changed by physical means. Physical change can be achieved in a number of different ways, e.g. by:

> **manipulating materials in some ways, such as bending or stretching;**
> **mixing two or more materials together where the 'ingredients' co-exist side by side, for example when flour is mixed with sand, or paint pigments are mixed with water – no chemical reaction takes place even if it difficult to see the original particles – they remain unchanged by the mixing of the particles, and still exist as the same substance and could (even if this is difficult in practice) be separated;**
> **mixing two substances together where one substance dissolves in another to form a solution;**
> **heating or cooling some substances that change from a solid to a liquid to a gas and back again, but remain unchanged chemically during the process.**

Even though it may appear to be difficult or even impossible, these changes are reversible and the initial materials sometimes can be separated in the classroom by physical means such as evaporation, filtering, chromatography or decanting.

Moving on

The National Assessment Agency (2006), reporting on pupils' performance in the science National Tests in 2006, said that in materials and their properties, pupils needed to become familiar with a range of changes, recognising which ones are reversible and which are non-reversible and particularly whether changes are non-reversible based on observations of the materials being investigated. To help improve pupils' performance, they state that 'pupils need opportunities to investigate the process of dissolving ... evaporation and condensation in different contexts and explain what is happening when these processes occur'.

Look at the QCA website at **www.qca.org.uk/itl** which provides more information on how to improve pupils' performance in the science National Tests. Then review:

- **your school's scheme of work in this area, suggesting improvements when necessary;**
- **your own teaching in this area.**

REFERENCES REFERENCES REFERENCES REFERENCES REFERENCES REFERENCES

National Assessment Agency (2006) *Science: Implications for Teaching and Learning from the 2006 National Curriculum Tests Key Stage 2*. London: QCA

FURTHER READING FURTHER READING FURTHER READING FURTHER READING

Wenham, M. (2004) States of matter and physical change, Chapter 6 in *Understanding Primary Science* 2nd edition. London: Paul Chapman Publishing

Sharp, J., Peacock, G., Johnsey, R., Simon, S. and Smith, R. (2007) Classroom organisation and management, Chapter 7 in *Primary Science: Teaching Theory and Practice* 3rd edition. Exeter: Learning Matters

Ward, H. (2005) Classroom organisation, Chapter 10 in Ward, H., Roden, J., Hewlett, C. and Foreman, J. (eds) *Teaching Science in the Primary School: A Practical Guide*. London: Sage

10
Changing and making materials

By the end of this chapter you should:

- **be aware of some of the significant subject knowledge that underpins the understanding of changing and making materials;**
- **be aware of some of the common misconceptions associated with changing and making materials;**
- **understand the progression of this topic using some examples of learning activities from 3 to 11 years;**
- **identify specific basic skills, illustrative and investigative opportunities within this topic;**
- **recognise the health and safety aspects associated with the teaching of this topic;**
- **have reflected upon the health and safety aspects of teaching this topic.**

Professional Standards for QTS

Q1, Q2, Q3b, Q4, Q7a, Q8, Q9, Q10, Q14, Q15, Q17, Q18, Q19, Q20, Q21a, Q21b, Q22, Q25a, Q25b, Q25c, Q25d, Q26b, Q27, Q28, Q29, Q30, Q31

Curriculum Guidance for the Foundation Stage and National Curriculum

In the Foundation Stage pupils should show an awareness of change (QCA, 2000, p88).

At Key Stage 1 pupils should be taught to:

- **explore and describe the way some everyday materials change when they are heated or cooled (DfEE, 1999, p80).**

At Key Stage 2 pupils should be taught:

- **to describe changes that occur when materials are heated or cooled;**
- **that non-reversible changes result in the formation of new materials that may be useful;**
- **that burning materials results in the formation of new materials and that this change is usually not reversible (DfEE, 1999, p87).**

Introduction

You will be aware that materials can change in a number of different ways. Cooking is a wonderful way of introducing younger children to chemical change, but you need to remember to include opportunities for children to engage with the processes involved in a conscious manner, for example by observing and recording changes at each stage in the process rather than merely taking part in an activity. Cooking is an enjoyable vehicle for introducing pupils to chemical changes at a very young age.

Changes in materials generally are classified at the primary stage as either physical changes or chemical changes. The last chapter looked at physical changes and included some practical activities for pupils in the classroom. In this chapter, you will focus on chemical change, which will involve an exploration of making and changing materials. Approached creatively, this topic can provide a wealth of interesting and exciting experiences for your children and for yourself.

Check your understanding

What do you understand by the following terms? Make a note of your ideas.

Chemical change	Chemical reaction
Irreversible change	Exothermic reaction
Endothermic reaction	Burning
Oxidation	Combustion
Kinetic theory	Respiration
Denature	Rate of reaction

Check your understanding with the Glossary.

Write down some examples of chemical reactions known to you.

Making and changing materials: some basic ideas

Some materials when mixed together change chemically with a change in energy, often in the form of heat, combining together to make a new substance. When plaster of Paris is mixed with water, heat is given off – an exothermic reaction. Exothermic reactions are reactions that give off heat during the change. Alternatively, when water is added to a mixture of citric acid and sodium bicarbonate a reaction occurs which results in the formation of a salt, a gas is produced and the resulting new substances get very cold. For this reaction to take place, the system needs to take in heat from the surroundings to provide the energy to make new bonds. As a result, the material feels cold to the touch and this is termed an endothermic reaction.

A very common widely-held misconception is that all chemical reactions happen very fast, even spontaneously. Fast chemical reactions can be very exciting, as when something burns; when a firework goes off it produces light, sound and heat. Whilst burning (also called combustion) is a fast process producing heat and light, many chemical reactions take place slowly and the changes taking place can be hardly noticed at all. In your past studies, you will probably have read about, or even investigated rusting as an example of a slow chemical reaction. Rusting, like burning, requires oxygen but is called oxidation rather than combustion because the reaction is slow to provide heat. You may remember that when testing for carbon dioxide in the secondary school laboratory, lime water turned milky. Respiration, although a type of combustion, is a slow reaction rather than a fast one. These are simple examples of slow chemical reactions, but there are many more that often go unrecognised as chemical reaction by the vast majority of adults and children.

Your pupils will probably be familiar with changes in fruit in the fruit bowl over time and other food rotting, plant growth involving photosynthesis, leaf fall and decay in the autumn, the growth of nails and hair on themselves and other animals. All these involve fascinating, if slow, chemical reactions which can be investigated in the primary classroom. Basically, chemical change occurs when existing chemical bonds between elements are broken and new bonds between the elements are made. See Peacock et al., (2007, pp75–81) for further information.

Change is one of the so-called 'big' ideas in science. It is important that children observe change in as many contexts as possible and that they come to realise that the many changes that take place are examples of chemical change. Whilst primary children do not need to be able to explain the specific changes in terms of the chemical elements that are involved in such chemical reactions, it is helpful if they understand at an early age that chemical change is taking place and that the 'products' of the reaction are not the same as the ingredients. Many observations of things changing over time involve chemical changes and can not only be used to reinforce this idea, but also can help children to appreciate the wonderful aspects of both the physical and the natural world.

Children's ideas from research: Changing and Making Materials

Learners often think that if wood is burning and water appears on the wood then it is because the wood has been damp; similarly gases that have formed during combustion were believed to be already in the material that is burning. So smoke formed during combustion was thought to be in the wood before combustion.

They also describe chemical reactions in terms of physical changes e.g. rusting is ageing iron rather than a chemical change. There is also a tendency to focus on the beginnings and end of a reaction and therefore learners don't notice the dynamic changes during the process. This also applies to combustion. They might only look at the physical visible properties and focus on those before and after the reaction.

Chemical reactions are often confused with mixing. So children could claim that there are some changes, e.g. colour but that the substances are still the same as before the chemical reaction. Things that give off bubbles are thought of as just an effect, not part of making new materials, so children think that the process of mixing things makes them fizz. If materials are mixed together and a chemical change occurs learners think that one material is active and the others are just affected by this active material.

Children are often aware that Oxygen in the air helps the burning process but they do not believe it is changed as a result, this is common to other materials and there is a belief that when things react they are still the same as before – so they retain their original form.

Teaching example 10.1: Foundation Stage

Bread

Learning intention: To make simple observations of the changes when bread is made

Success criteria

- To talk about the changes we see.

- To sequence pictures of bread-making.

It is relatively easy in the Foundation Stage classroom to make bread using a simple recipe and for pupils to watch the changes that take place at each stage of the process. Initially pupils can notice, working in small groups with an adult helper:

- how the texture of the flour changes when water and yeast are added;
- how the mixture becomes more firm as the dough is kneaded;
- how, when set in a warm place, the dough rises before cooking;
- how the texture and colour of the bread at stages in cooking change.

To add even more interest, changes to eggs from raw to hard-boiled can be observed.

The examples here both involve chemical changes. Changes could be recorded at each stage with a digital camera, and what could be nicer than to finish the science 'lesson' with a picnic of homemade egg sandwiches?

Make models with Soft Mo, which keeps its colour but changes consistency when heated in a domestic oven. This is a good activity that enables children to see how it becomes rigid.

CASE STUDY CASE STUDY **CASE STUDY** CASE STUDY **CASE STUDY** CASE STUDY

Making toast is a good starting point for change. It is also fun to use toast to make model houses. Some Reception classes had fun making Hansel and Gretel's house using toast and ready-rolled icing sugar and sweets. The length of time the bread was toasted for impacted upon the stability of the finished house. This formed the start of some excellent cross-curricular work.

A teacher with a Foundation Stage class started the day looking at *The Book of Wizard Craft* by Janice Eaton Kilby, Deborah Morgenthal, Terry Taylor, and Lindy Burnett.

Following this, pupils were sent off to choose from the activities provided for them to follow-up the story. The science activity follow up consisted of a corner of the classroom that provided the opportunity for them to explore 'Grandma's potions'. Here various simple 'chemicals', for example, flour, vinegar, water, oil, washing-up liquid, bubble bath and corn flour, were available for children to mix in a large shallow tray. Strict rules ensured that only a small number of children were allowed to explore the mixing of the potions at any one time.

In each of the above examples, chemical changes are taking place, but the science for children consists not of teaching about chemical reactions, but to practise the important process skills of observation, measurement and recording as well as providing the opportunity for teachers and other adults to ask the important attention focusing questions such as 'How is it the same now? ', 'How has it changed? and 'What do your think would happen if. . .'.

Teaching example 10.2: Key Stage 1

Cakes

Figure 10.1 Cakes at different stages of cooking

Learning intention: To be able to observe and record the way things change when heated

Context: Cakes baking

Success criteria
- To be able to record at least one change using their senses.
- To be able to sequence cakes (or pictures of cakes).

When baking, children do not see the changes that occur once the mixing has taken place because for health and safety reasons it usually takes place in an oven away from the classroom. Instead of baking all the cakes and making a link to instructional writing in literacy, you could try making a number of cakes, cooking each for varying amounts of time. This provides children with a real opportunity to look at the changes that are involved.

Make a batch of cake mix as usual. One cake is not put in the oven, but the rest are cooked for times ranging from 3 minutes to 40 minutes. It is usually effective to take the cakes out every 3 minutes initially and then every 5 minutes towards the end. The photographs above show the changes you might expect as a result. Using real cakes, children can sequence different cakes looking at how they have changed. More able children can sequence five or more cakes including ones that have less noticeable differences, whilst less able children may be supported and look at the changes involved and sequence three cakes (for example not cooked, 15 minutes and 30 minutes).

Health and safety: It is possible to freeze the cakes for use at another time. However, children should not eat these cakes and care should be given to children with egg allergies.

Teaching example 10.3: Key Stage 2

Marble chips
How to speed up the reaction of marble chips and acid.

Learning intention: To be able to describe the patterns and trends in their work

Success criteria
- To be able to record results in tables.
- To be able to communicate what is found, using scientific words.

Context: marble chips and liquids
The idea is that the children will focus on the size of the chip or the dilution of the liquid. It is likely that they will have already seen the effect of different liquids on marble chips prior to this activity.

Key questions could be:
What factors affect the speed that the marble chips react?
Which liquids will result in more bubbles?

Before you start on an activity like this, you need to consider what you know about your children and their existing skills. This activity could be set up together for sharing as a class or as a small group activity where each group could decide what variable to change and what to measure. Later you could ask the class to explain their investigation and discuss all their findings together.

Independent variables: Type of liquid, amount of liquid, size of chip, position of activity, type of container, concentration of liquid.

Dependent variables: Time taken for marble to change size (size over time), observation and ranking, or, more challenging perhaps, the amount of bubbles produced.

You need to ensure that a range of liquids is used in this investigation as this will provide opportunities for children to discuss their findings in a more challenging context. All the chosen liquids should react with marble (carbonate), for example, vinegar, lemon juice as well as a dilute solution of citric acid. If concentration is changed, make sure that children use one of the liquids and water in different proportions. The mixing of, for example, vinegar and water could, depending on the age of your children, be measured by spoon or using a syringe or a pipette. For example, you could use neat vinegar alone, five spoons of vinegar with five spoons of water, or nine parts vinegar and one part water.

There is no direct link between this and teeth rotting: liquids that would encourage growth of plaque will not have any effect on marble (see Chapter 5).

Teaching example 10.4: Key Stage 2

Burning

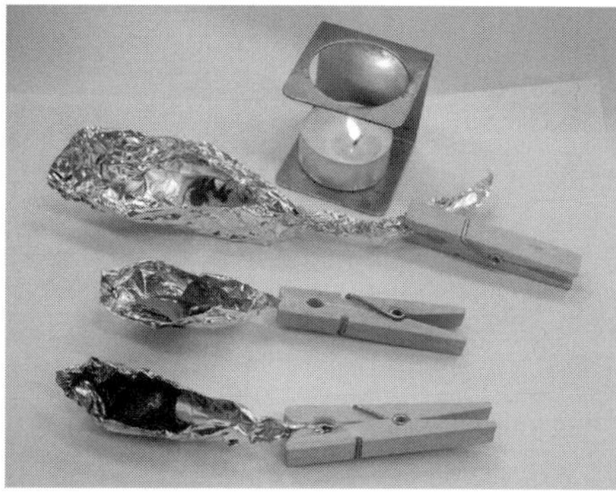

Figure 10.2 Burning using foil spoons

Learning intention: To be able to state whether burning is a reversible change using observations

Success criteria

- To be able to record a series of observations.
- To understand and explain a key feature of burning.

Burning as a chemical change is often avoided in the classroom as it is thought of as a difficult and dangerous activity. However, burning is part of the National Curriculum and there are some easy ways to ensure burning is safe.

- Use aluminium foil spoons and hold these at the end with clothes pegs.
- Use small quantities of materials to burn and do not use plastics.
- Ensure the room is well ventilated but does not have too much air flow.
- Use night lights as a source of flame and place the night light in a holder.
- Place the holder in a sand tray.

- Keep the group size small and provide roles for children.
- Have a bowl of water on the table to place the end result into.
- Ensure hair is tied up and children have discussed the rules.

Allow the children to burn a small variety of selected materials and note the changes. This could be before and afterwards with some children, and a series of observations with others. Decide on the most effective materials and include some that will not change.

Making bouncing putty

This activity requires a little time and patience but is suited to upper Key Stage 2 children. It is worthwhile making it to the recipe as an illustrative activity and then enabling the children to investigate with the proportions of borax, corn flour and PVA adhesive as an investigation.

For the Illustrative task you will need:
UPVC glue;
Borax (disodium tetraborate);
Corn flour.

First dissolve half a teaspoon of borax with two tablespoons of water. Make sure the borax has dissolved. In another cup add one tablespoon of glue and one tablespoon of corn flour. To this mixture add half a tablespoon of your borax solution. Do not stir but leave the mixture to react for about 15 seconds. Then stir until fully mixed. When it is not possible to stir any longer, take out the mixture and knead it in your hands. Although to start with the ball will be a sticky mess, it will solidify when kneaded. When it is no longer sticky, bounce the ball and discuss the changes. Make sure that you and your pupils wash your hands after use, and don't eat the materials used to make the ball or the ball itself. It is possible to change the amount of borax, cornflour and PVA glue and see the effects.

Death masks

It is possible to make a death mask with your pupils. However it is best undertaken as a demonstration with a very brave child as the sitter. You need to ensure that parental permission has been gained, or ask for a volunteer from, e.g a teaching assistant, parent or the headteacher.

Procedure

Initially, place some Vaseline over the child's face, inserting small pieces of straw in their nose to allow for breathing. Make up a thick mixture of plaster of Paris and begin to cover their face. It is vital that the child/adult has contact with the outside world by having their hand held and that you provide a 'running commentary'. It will take about 5 minutes to cover the face and another 15 minutes to dry. Remove the mask carefully. The sitter can later tell the audience about the changes they felt, as the mask will get hot before it sets. The mask then provides an image of their face, which then needs to be filled with more plaster of Paris. The result is an exact replica of their face. Links to famous death masks like Wellington or Tutankhamen could be made.

REFLECTIVE TASK

Health and safety

You should **always** consult ASE (2001) *Be safe*, 3rd edition, ASE, for all issues about health and safety in the primary classroom.

It is important that you ensure that pupils know that liquids should not be drunk. Make sure that you do not provide liquids that could cause irritation to skin.

- **What other health and safety issues do you need to consider when preparing other aspects of this topic for use in your classroom?**
- **How would you ensure that your pupils do not eat the results of their activity?**
- **How could you ensure that less water is spilt in your classroom?**
- **What temperature of water would you use to ensure that this is not a potential hazard in your classroom?**

Are there any other points that need to be thought about before your pupils work on aspects of this topic?

Refer to the information at the end of the book for acceptable responses to these questions.

PRACTICAL TASK PRACTICAL TASK PRACTICAL TASK PRACTICAL TASK PRACTICAL TASK

Web activity

Chemical changes occur as a result of heat or require children to experiment with things that burn or change. As a result there is a possibility that children would be exposed to greater risk than with an activity which did not involve heat or water. Look at the website below and think about which activities could have problems. Do not then avoid these but think about how they could be changed to limit the dangers. Use the ASE *Be Safe* book to help you with your judgements.

Look at website:

www.deakin.edu.au/education/resources/sci-enviro-ed/early_years/pdfs/chem_change.pdf#search=%22%20chemical%20change%20in%20primary%20school%22

Choose one of the activities suggested.

Does the activity involve chemical or physical changes?

How could you organise this in an upper Key Stage 2 classroom that is known to you?

What resources would you need?

What precautions would you take to ensure that this task was safe for all learners?

Subject knowledge that underpins the activities in this chapter

The activities in this chapter are essentially concerned with how materials can be changed chemically by sometimes just mixing, or by heating a mixture of materials. Whatever the method, the final product is very different chemically from the ingredients. Chemical changes often involve energy, sometimes lots of energy and changes in mass, although in a chemical reaction the overall mass remains constant. New substances are formed and the properties of the new materials are often very different from those of the original substances. Furthermore, chemical changes are usually not easily reversed. Some chemical changes lend themselves to observations over time. For example, a candle burning is an example of a chemical change taking place that can lead to many specific related observations being made.

Eggs when they are cooked change as the heat changes the protein, resulting in changes in both texture and form. In the body there are many chemical changes occurring all the time. Some of the most important involve the breakdown of food with oxygen in a process called respiration, which is the opposite reaction of photosynthesis (this is discussed further in Chapter 5).

In the bread-making activity, it is the chemical reaction involving in the sugar, yeast and water mixture that produces the carbon dioxide gas that causes the bread to rise. Yeast is a micro-organism that uses the sugar as a food source. Carbon dioxide is produced as a by-product of respiration (an example of slow combustion). When the risen bread is placed in a hot oven, the heat halts the chemical reaction. The yeast dies because the heat denatures the protein. Science in real life is the interplay between all aspects whilst school science sees biology, chemistry and physics as separate subjects.

The bouncing ball activity is a fun way of looking at polymers. These are chemicals with long repeating chains. The glue is made up of the polymer polyvinyl acetate (PVA) which forms cross-links when it is mixed with borax. The amount of each substance affects the properties of the completed material. If you use more corn flour, you can produce a stretchy substance similar to Play-Doh. If you use less borax, the ball will turn into a runny mixture like Glup (cornflour and water). To create slime, add more glue. Different amounts of substances create different forms of balls. This is a good activity for planning an investigation because of the different types of variables.

The marble chip activity looked at the rates of reaction. Although it would not be good practice to teach primary children about rates of reaction, it is likely that they will notice that as the temperature increases, the reactions occur more quickly or that as the surface area increases, there is also an increase in reaction rate. This effect may also have been noticed in activities on dissolving sugars. When two substances react their particles must collide with each other with enough energy to make the reaction happen. This is part of the kinetic theory. If the surface area is increased by grinding down the marble chip into a powder, there is greater opportunity for collisions to happen. If the concentration of the vinegar is increased there are more atoms and so a greater chance of collision. All these factors increase the rate of the reaction.

PRACTICAL TASK PRACTICAL TASK PRACTICAL TASK PRACTICAL TASK PRACTICAL TASK

Choose one of the misconceptions listed earlier in the chapter or one you have encountered in your teaching.

Devise an activity or series of activities to challenge learners' misunderstanding of this aspect of changes in materials.

Consider the following:.

- **The range and appropriateness of equipment to be used with learners in your activities. How could the activity be adapted, perhaps by use of different resources, to meet the needs of those with special needs, e.g. visual impairment? (Differentiation by resource.)**
- **How could this activity be adapted to include children with particular difficulties in manipulating equipment?**
- **What questions would you ask the children in order to help them to undertake the tasks?**
- **What strategies could you help the children to use in order to develop a clear idea of chemical change?**

A SUMMARY OF KEY POINTS

The focus of the work in this chapter was on the activities to help learners understand more about making and changing materials. In particular it has:

- **presented a number of activities on the theme of changing and making materials, showing how learners' understanding of the basic ideas of materials can be developed over the primary age range;**
- **introduced the real-life link between different aspects of school science (respiration is covered in biology but is an example of chemical change);**
- **shown that some changes in cooking occur due to changes in protein;**
- **shown that the rate of the reaction will be dependent on temperature, concentration or surface area and is linked to kinetic theory of matter;**
- **emphasised the importance of thinking about health and safety but that good fun science should and can occur.**

Moving on

You may want to check your own developing knowledge about some of the background science introduced in this chapter. It may be that you have in the past seen science in terms of biology, chemistry and physics rather than integrated as they are in the wider world. How might this impact on how you teach science in the future?

FURTHER READING FURTHER READING FURTHER READING FURTHER READING

Howe, A., Davies, D., McMahon, K., Towler, L. and Scott, T. (2005) Materials and their properties, Chapter 5 in *Science 5–11 A Guide for Teachers*. London: David Fulton

Peacock, G., Sharp, J., Johnsey, R. and Wright, D., (2007) Materials Chapter 6 in *Primary Science: Knowledge and Understanding*, 3rd edition. Exeter: Learning Matters

PART 4
PHYSICAL PROCESSES

11
Electricity

By the end of this chapter you should:

- **be aware of some of the significant subject knowledge that underpins the understanding of aspects of electricity;**
- **recognise that electricity is a form of energy;**
- **recognise some of the common problems associated with teaching about electricity;**
- **understand the progression of this topic using some examples of learning activities from 3 to 11 years;**
- **identify specific basic skills, illustrative and investigative opportunities within this topic;**
- **have reflected upon the importance of the nature of scientific ideas.**

Professional Standards for QTS

Q1, Q2, Q4, Q7a, Q8, Q9, Q10, Q14, Q15, Q17, Q18, Q19, Q21a, Q21b, Q22, Q23, Q25a, Q25b, Q25c, Q25d, Q26b, Q27, Q28, Q29, Q30, Q31

Curriculum Guidance for the Foundation Stage and National Curriculum

In the Foundation Stage pupils should:

- **show an interest in why things happen and why things work;**
- **talk about what is seen and what is happening;**
- **ask questions about why things happen and how things work (QCA, 2000, p88).**

At Key Stage 1 pupils should be taught:

- **about everyday appliances that use electricity;**
- **about simple series circuits involving batteries, wires, bulbs and other components (for example, buzzers, motors);**
- **how a switch can be used to break a circuit (DFEE 1999, p81).**

At Key Stage 2 pupils should be taught:

- **to construct circuits, incorporating a battery or power supply and a range of switches, to make electrical devices work, for example buzzers and motors;**
- **how changing the number or types of components (for example batteries, bulb wires in a series circuit), can make bulbs brighter or dimmer;**

- **how to represent series circuits by drawings and conventional symbols, and how to construct series circuits on the basis of drawings and diagrams using conventional symbols (DFEE, 1999, p88).**

Introduction

Electricity is a form of energy; it runs machinery and can be transformed into other types of energy such as light, sound and heat. Electricity is a fascinating phenomenon and has been intriguing mankind since the Greeks found that when amber was rubbed it could be made to attract feathers and other items. The Greeks had discovered static electricity. Electron is the Greek word for amber. Indeed, all familiar words that start with 'electr' like electricity, electron and electronic come from the Greek word *elektor*, which means 'beaming sun'. In most textbooks static is called such because the charge does not move, but this is untrue as static electricity is just the presence of an unbalanced charge.

Electricity can be defined as: *phenomena arising from the existence of charge;* or *Any effect resulting from the existence of stationary or moving electric charge* (Oxford Concise Science Dictionary, 1984). However, although it is a commonly used term in the curriculum, scientists claim that 'electricity' does not exist as a single entity and should only be used in its adjectival form with a noun; for example, electrical current, electrical energy and electrical circuit, almost in the same way as the word 'gravity' should really be called 'gravitational attraction'.

When scientists discovered that electricity could be generated and transported relatively easily into homes and factories, everyday life was revolutionised. Today all children and most adults in developed countries take electricity for granted. They enjoy the convenience, the comforts and the entertainment that electricity provides without thinking for a moment about how it is produced, how electricity makes things work and what life would be like without it.

Teaching about electricity to primary children can be challenging, not necessarily because of understanding of the concepts involved, but more often because of the inappropriate equipment available in schools to teach it. With this in mind, this chapter will focus mainly on electrical charge and electrical energy and will highlight the situations to avoid when teaching about electricity in your classroom.

Check your understanding

What do you understand by the following terms? Make a note of your ideas.

Electrical charge	Electrical energy
Electromagnetism	Electrons
Electric current	Voltage
Electrical power	Sparks
Ohms	Volts
Kinetic energy	Potential energy
Battery	Circuit
Cell	

Check your understanding with the Glossary.

PRACTICAL TASK PRACTICAL TASK PRACTICAL TASK PRACTICAL TASK PRACTICAL TASK

Without the aid of a bulb-holder, use a battery (one with both terminals at the top – a flat 4.5-volt battery is most suited to this activity) and one 3.5 volt bulb and make the bulb light without any additional wires.

Now answer the following questions:

- **Which arrangement of parts of the bulb and battery together make the bulb light?**
- **What parts of the bulb need to be touching the terminals?**
- **What will happen if the glass is touched against the terminal?**
- **Which parts of the bulb are made of materials that are conductors and which parts are made of materials that do not conduct electricity?**

Introduce wires and a bulb holder.

- **What are the advantages of using wires and bulb holders?**
- **What problems might be caused for children's understanding of this aspect if additional materials are placed into the circuit?**

Make a note of the arrangement you found to work and note your answers to the questions. Then:

- **Draw what you think is inside a battery (cell). It does not matter what size battery but draw one used in a household appliance rather than in the car.**
- **How can electricity be produced from a potato or a lemon in a 'potato clock'?**
- **When electricity flows through wires, draw what you think is inside the wires.**

Compare your response to that in Appendix 3.

N.B. There are many aspects of science where undertaking a 'hands-on' practical task will help children develop their understanding, but health and safety requirements dictate that we can not carry them out. Remember to check with the *Be safe* publication from the ASE before trying unusual activities. One such activity concerns what you think might be inside a battery. Children could understand the thinking task, but it would be dangerous to cut open a battery. You may be able to show them using a website.

Electricity: some basic ideas

The traditional model of the atom composed of protons, neutrons and electrons will be used in this book to explain electricity. Scientifically this model of the atom is no longer the only accepted one. Present understanding of atoms is far more detailed including six interestingly named quarks, called up, down, charm, strange, top and bottom. Even these names have changed over the recent past, with the bottom quark also known as 'beauty' whilst the top quark is sometimes called 'truth'. It was in the 1970s that scientists found that protons, electrons and neutrons are not the smallest particles but that they are composed of quarks.

It is helpful here to define the term 'model', as in fact most scientific explanations are models that attempt to simplify real life. All models, including the one used here, are only approximations of the real world, this world being far more complex than perhaps the human brain can comprehend. Any model potentially can make a scientific idea simpler to understand, but will only reflect current thinking and therefore will only be valuable until new information is found which challenges the way the model works. In the case of the above, the model has not been challenged in its entirety; it has just been made more complex. In order to understand most aspects of electricity the simple model still holds true. However, *Six easy pieces*

(Feynman, 1998) is recommended if being told 'you do not need to know' makes you want to know 'what' and 'why'?

The model often called the 'solar system' or Bohr model used here, was refined in the early 1900s and explains atoms as being made up of three types of particles; protons, neutrons and electrons. Neutrons and protons are located in the nucleus of the atom each having a relative mass of 1 amu. The abbreviation amu stands for atomic mass unit, which is a relative mass unit, related to the carbon^{-12} atom. The unit is written as u; it is one-twelfth of the mass of this atom. Neutrons and protons each have a mass of 1 u. Electrons spin in shells around the nucleus and have negligible relative mass. Electrons were always said to be weightless, but physicists did not agree, arguing that it must have mass, even if a negligible one, because electrons exist and all things that exist have mass. They calculated that 1836 electrons were equal in mass to 1 proton.

Electrons and protons are both charged particles whilst neutrons carry no charge. The charge on one proton is positive and the charge on one electron is negative. Two particles that have similar charges, either both negative or both positive, interact by repelling each other: two particles with dissimilar charges (one positive and one negative) interact by attracting each other. If there is an excess of electrons, the body will be negatively charged; if there is an excess of protons the body will be positively charged. The flow of charged particles, especially electrons, constitutes an electrical current. Charge is measured in coulombs. How tightly these electrons are held in the electronic arrangement within materials affects whether the material conducts electricity or not.

Electricity and static

Static electricity is the electricity discovered by the Greeks when they rubbed amber and the ancient Egyptians when they rubbed cotton, and accounts for effects seen during thunderstorms. When some materials are touched, the rubbing causes an imbalance of charge with either a build-up of an overall positive charge (more protons), or a build up of overall negative charge (more electrons). The problem with rubbing is that it could be thought that friction causes the unbalance charge, whilst in fact it is the property of the material itself. Many materials merely need to be touched by another to alter the balance of protons and electrons in them. Some materials will always give off electrons, to become positive, such as dry skin and others attract electrons, becoming negatively charged, such as Teflon. The Triboelectric series lists common materials in order of how well they become charged. Gold and platinum are nearly as good as polyester for becoming positively charged, whilst steel and cotton are neutral – they do not gain or lose electrons. For an electric current to flow there must be a potential difference, i.e. areas of positive and areas of negative charge, and a way for the electrons to move. Static electricity is more likely to happen on dry days. When there is a lot of moisture in the atmosphere, water vapour (a polarised molecule) will form on the surface of materials and prevent a build-up of charge. Lightning is also the same phenomenon, but this is more complex as there is an induced opposite charge created at ground level which produces an electric force field, which in turn creates the tension in the otherwise neutral molecules in the air. When the field is great enough the air molecules break down into ions which then allow the conduction of electricity.

Conductors

Materials that conduct electricity are called conductors. Not all substances conduct electricity. Electrons in an atom must be able to move from their place around its nucleus for the material to be a conductor. In order for this to happen there must first be an uneven balance of charge produced by chemical cells or electro-potential or by mechanical generators. Some materials, particularly metals such as copper and a few non-metals, e.g. graphite, have low resistance which means they have electrons that can move easily. Other materials like rubber and wood have high resistance, meaning that their electrons cannot move easily and are held tightly in position by the protons. Chapter 8 explained that all materials have electrons. It is the electrons' ability to move freely within a material that determines whether it conducts electricity or not. Electrical current is created when electrons begin to flow. Metals are very good conductors because they have many electronic shells containing electrons. The electrons in metals are able to move from one atom to another almost like a sea of electrons.

In order to create electrical current there must be a potential difference: an area with excess negative charge and areas of excess positive charge. The flow can only start when the circuit is complete. The electrons are already in the wire but there is no electrical current. The battery provides an area of electrons (negative terminal) and an area of positive ions to attract these electrons. Provided there is somewhere for the electrons to go (a complete circuit) a force is set up, the electrical charge flows and an electrical current can be measured.

A complete circuit

A circuit connects electrical components in a closed path or loop. It includes a source of energy or electromotive force (emf), one or more switches, interconnecting wires and an electrical appliance such as a bell or a light bulb. A complete circuit is needed for the electrical charge to flow.

Batteries and cells

Batteries are the sources of electricity most often used in a study of electricity in the primary school. These are relatively safe to use because the current involved is quite small. Scientifically one 'battery' should be called a cell, because in science a battery is a number of cells grouped together. Batteries supply direct current, where the electrons flow in only one direction. Mains electricity provides alternating current, where electrons change direction frequently every second. The alternating current is caused by spinning a large magnet in a coil of wire, which excites the electrons in the wire and starts the current flowing.

Children's understanding of electricity

Much research has been undertaken into children's ideas about electricity. This has found that children's ideas are remarkably similar and consistent across countries in the developed world. Children's ideas about electricity are often incomplete, they hold misconceptions or 'alternative frameworks'; their ideas are radically different from those of scientists, but remarkably similar to each other. Challenging children's ideas can help to change unscientific alternative frameworks into ones that are more in line with scientifically accepted views.

Children often think that the bulb or other components in a circuit consume electric current and that the current flows in two directions simultaneously. Sharp (2007) advises that finding out children's ideas prior to teaching in this topic can be very productive and that even when pupils can construct circuits well, they may not understand the basic principles involved. Children often talk about the battery 'running down' and may have different ideas about what is happening inside a wire. Many adults have also been found to hold misconceptions in this topic. If you are worried about teaching this aspect you should, as with all topics, research basic ideas at the planning stage and continue to check your understanding as you work with your pupils.

Teaching example 11.1: Foundation Stage

There are no specific requirements for children in the Foundation Stage to learn about this topic. However, as the use of electricity features in their early lives it is one aspect of their environment that they should be encouraged to explore in terms of being safe when using electricity and also to think about how, for example, a torch works and what happens if the battery is taken out. Children could also undertake a simple classification of toys that work with batteries and by other means.

Play

Children should know that electricity can be dangerous and there are things connected with its use that should not be touched. They should also look at toys that use electricity in the form of batteries as well as ones that do not. Electricity by its very abstract nature is not suited to Reception and Foundation Stage children. Teachers sometimes think that because they understand electrical work, their children will, but this indicates a failure to understand that the children are not working at that level. This misunderstanding is sometimes compounded by teachers using an analogy of electricity acting like cars on a racetrack. This is inappropriate for any work on electricity because of the misconceptions introduced by its use. Electrons do not come out of the battery and go round the circuit to the other terminal, using the wires as a track; there are already electrons in the wire which are caused to move when a circuit is completed.

Teaching example 11.2: Key Stage 1

Look around the school and list all the things that would not work if there was a power cut. When children are asked to do this they will include on their list some things that do not use electricity.

What do you need to make the bulb light brightly?

Ask the children to draw a picture of how they think they could make a light bulb work using a bulb, battery and wires. When all the children have drawn a picture of what they would do, they can try out their ideas. This activity usually illustrates the misconceptions that children hold in this topic, such as: the one-wire theories (you only need a battery a wire and a bulb as the electricity gets to the bulb to light it) or the drawings that have gaps in the circuit (as the children are not aware of why the circuit needs to be complete). Undertaking this activity in the classroom often produces at least six different pictures that the rest of the class can try. The drawings can be placed in order on the interactive-whiteboard and the children told that these are the 'ideas' that they must try, as scientists did in the past. By trying these ideas they will find the evidence of which ones will work. They have to follow the instructions by only using the things drawn and by putting them in the same places as they are in the plan. After the children have tried out each plan, they should come back to the carpet to discuss the evidence they have for whether that idea worked or not. This is a more effective way for children to explore with the electrical equipment than a trial-and-error approach, where some children never really systematically work through the options and others get the bulb to light by mistake but do not remember what they did.

Build a torch or a lighthouse

When children have made circuits and additionally placed components like buzzers and motors in their circuit to see the effect, they should be given the opportunity to practise this knowledge and use it to problem-solve. This will provide further opportunity for experimentation and exploration. Can they make a lighthouse or a torch? Below are examples of torches made by children. It takes more time than just making simple circuits but the resulting science knowledge and understanding are more secure.

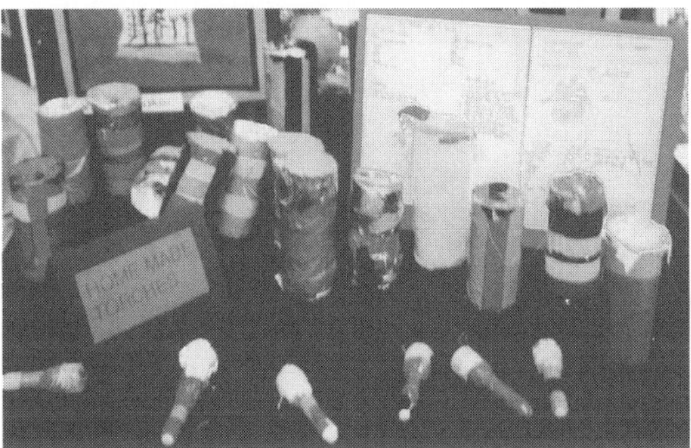

Figure 11.1 Torches made by children

Teaching Example 11.3: Key Stage 2

What factors affect the brightness of the bulb?

This activity is fun and enables children to think about how to change the components or the organisation to affect the brightness of the bulbs. Using light sensors will provide a quantitative reading to measure the brightness of the bulb. For all work simple electrical equipment is suggested, not commercially produced electrical kits.

Independent variables

Thickness of wire, length of wire, type of bulb (2.5, 3.5 or 6 volt bulb), type of battery (1.5V, 3V, 4.5V or 6V), type of wire.

Dependent variable

The brightness of the bulb.

The children can select the variables to change and will measure the brightness of the bulb by using either an arbitrary star rating scale or a light sensor attached to a data-logger. They should change only one factor and measure the effect. If copper wire is used it will take about 60 metres to see any real change in the brightness of the bulbs. As much of the wire used in primary schools is only thin strands wound together, the wire might look thicker but is in fact many wires together. A better effect is gained if a single piece of wire is used. Copper wire is an excellent conductor and if the length of the wire is the factor selected to be changed, it is useful to use a high-resistance wire, like nickel chrome wire, that will show the brightness of the bulb changing noticeably over a one metre length.

Teaching example 11.4: Key Stage 2

The chirpy chick in a circuit

Toys that work by connecting terminals can be used to show that a break in a circuit will stop electricity from flowing. Ghost balls, light-up ducks and chirping chicks all work on the same principle: they have a battery and the circuit is completed when the terminals are joined. It is fun to use a large circle of people holding hands. Place the toy into the circuit between two children; each child holds one terminal and the chick but they do not touch each other. Then all the children link hands and when a complete circuit is made either the chick will chirp, or the toys will light. If the circuit is broken then the chick does not chirp and if a conductor is introduced to the circuit by asking other children to hold each side of it in the circuit, the electrical current will still flow. If an insulator is placed in the circuit the electricity will not flow and there is no chirping or light. It is fun to ask children to hold either end of everyday objects in the circle and see the effect. This is a really easy and fun way for children to see that a complete circuit is needed and to test insulators and conductors.

Figure 11.2 Using a toy to show the need for a complete circuit for electricity to flow. Students trying out the activity.

Problem-solving investigations

Due to the nature of electricity and its complexity, after simple circuit work it is expected that children will be able to use their knowledge to build models that require electricity to make them work, e.g. fairground rides, games, burglar alarms or lights for a dolls' house, etc. The additional element that children need to be taught is about communicating their understanding by using scientific conventions of circuit notation.

Progression in learning

Since the National Curriculum was introduced in 1989 the structure and content of the science components have been revised a number of times. The last major one affecting primary science was in 2000. Although the Key Stage 4 curriculum has been radically overhauled since that date, there have been no changes to the primary curriculum. Initially the 17 science attainment targets set out in detail the knowledge and understanding that children were expected to acquire during the primary years. Teachers tended to use the attainment targets for planning purposes. In the latest revision the statutory order for the science programme of study is organised into four aspects that are less detailed and prescriptive. In the early years of the science National Curriculum teachers found great difficulty in covering all the knowledge in terms of both level and amount. At each revision, teachers were asked for their opinions in consultation documents.

Electricity is one of the many ideas and concepts in science that is too abstract for many children. The effects of electricity can be observed, but electricity itself cannot be seen directly. This is one reason why in the 1994 consultation process it was suggested it should be taken out of the programme of study at Key Stage 1 and only taught at Key Stage 2. However, teachers responded negatively to this suggestion and, as a result, electricity remained at Key Stage 1.

Currently, the statutory orders require children to be taught about the observable features of electricity. There is no requirement at Key Stages 1 or 2 to understand where electricity comes from or how it is made. Pupils should be taught how to make a complete circuit, to know that switches break circuits and what happens when more bulbs are placed within a series circuit (like a daisy chain). However, children ask questions and it is important that teachers are aware of the simple scientific answers. As with all abstract ideas, scientists have developed models that explain what we cannot see. All models are approximations that enable scientists and others to turn very complex phenomena into understandable processes. As all models are approximations they may change or become refined as knowledge improves. There are a number of simple models to explain electricity. This chapter has been using these models throughout. However, another way of explaining circuits is by using an analogy of water and water pumps.

PRACTICAL TASK PRACTICAL TASK PRACTICAL TASK PRACTICAL TASK PRACTICAL TASK

Imagine a series of pipes that are filled with water and are all linked together in a square.

The black square is the water pump. The pump is off and there is water in the pipes but it does not move. When the pump is put on, it pushes the water which flows. The power of the pump affects the speed at which the water flows. This analogy is used to explain electrical current. The electrons (water) are already there but they only move when the push (pump) starts.

In the second picture there are two water wheels (shaded squares), the water flows because of the pump and turns the water wheels round. The more water wheels that are placed in the system, the slower the water turns them around. The more bulbs (waterwheels) in an electrical circuit, the dimmer the bulb as there is greater resistance.

Use this with your pupils when you next teach this topic.

- **How useful was this topic?**
- **Did you find any difficulties in using it?**
- **What issues are there with using analogies?**

PRACTICAL TASK PRACTICAL TASK PRACTICAL TASK PRACTICAL TASK PRACTICAL TASK

www.duracell.com/us/northpole/
This site has some interesting Christmas-based activities but is also great for cross-curricular links. Think about how you could use this site to link the topic of electricity at Key Stages 1 or 2 into a cross-curricular topic.

Subject knowledge that underpins the activities in this chapter

Electricity is problematic for most learners as it is seemingly many different things. The effect of electricity is fast, as all the electrons start to move almost instantaneously. Think about the speed at which the light bulb works when the circuit is connected. In fact the electrons themselves move slowly, a few millimetres per minute. Electrical energy can be released from chemical energy in the battery. Batteries become exhausted when the chemicals have reacted but the electrons in conductors are unchanged. There are electrons in the wire at all points and they are not altered in the circuit. Electricity also has many units of measure associated with it: volts (V), amperes (A), watts (W), joules (J), coulombs (C) and ohms (Ω) as well as the current which is referred to by the symbol I.

Volts (v) are the size of the electrical potential and named after the scientist Volta. Watts (w) and amperes (A) are both measurements of the flow rate in a circuit, but they measure two different things.

The amount of charge is measured in coulombs and the number of coulombs flowing per second is the current measured in amperes. So if the water analogy is continued, the litres of water flowing is the coulombs and the flow of the water around the pipes in litres per second is the amperes.

Watts measure the rate of flow of the energy. So watts are the amount of electrical energy flowing per second, and all energy is measured in a unit called the joule. One joule per second is one watt.

Ohms are the measure of resistance, how hard it is for the charge to flow. Ohm's law states that the greater the resistance, the slower the flow for a given potential difference. So if more than one bulb is placed in a circuit with the same battery the bulbs will be dimmer. Primary aged children do not need to know about all these units.

In conductors there are already electrons; they move around in a sea of other electrons, but there are equal numbers of electrons and protons so there is no imbalance. In such a case there is no net charge. In order to get electrical current to flow there must be a potential difference. There is always a balance in terms of numbers, just an imbalance in terms of distribution, i.e. bunching at each side of the cell with positive ions one side and negative ions at the other causing an uneven number of protons and electrons. Charge flows in a circle and batteries 'pump' it and no charge is ever lost. There are four basic ways of creating charge imbalance. These are by:

- **passing a magnet over a conductor – this is how electrical charge is generated in a power station;**
- **putting two different conductors in salt water – this is how a potato clock works;**
- **putting two conductors together and adding light – this is how solar power works;**
- **using friction or motion as in the Van de Graff or other static generators.**

These ways of generating unbalanced charge cause voltage; in the wires, this provides the push that makes the electrons start to move.

Electrical charge is not the same as electrical energy. Electrical energy measured in joules (J) flows from the batteries into the light bulb where it is changed to light and heat. Electrical energy in this case is transformed to the kinetic energy of the electrons which bump into the ions of the metal and cause heating of the high-resistance filament, which causes light when it gets to about 1000°C. Energy-saving bulbs and fluorescent lamps work on a different process altogether. The electron hits a particle in the gas which cannons into a fluorescent material on the side wall and causes photon emission from stimulated electrons dropping back into orbit.

Electrical energy flows very fast, almost at the speed of light. This is because electrons are already there and, just as when you push one end of a stick, the other end moves, so electrical energy flows when the circuit is completed. Electrical energy is invisible but it does exist and electrical energy in the home is paid for by the amount of energy used in kilowatt hours.

If components, e.g. a lamp or motor, are in the circuit, electrical energy is converted to other forms of energy. If you look at an electrical bulb you will notice that the filament is very thin. The electrons move from a thicker wire to thinner wire and this movement, of many electrons, makes the wires hot. The movement energy (kinetic) is transferred to heat and light.

PRACTICAL TASK PRACTICAL TASK PRACTICAL TASK PRACTICAL TASK PRACTICAL TASK

Electrical symbols

In order for scientists and others to communicate with each other and to be able to pass information quickly and accurately, circuit notation has been developed. The symbols are uniform although the symbol for a light bulb may have changed since you were at secondary school. Find the symbols for the components most commonly used in primary schools.

Light bulb (lamp)
Motor
Battery
Cell
Buzzer
Wires

Reflection on the tasks

- **Why do children have problems with circuits?**
- **Will notation help them to understand the topic or is the introduction of notation another aspect that makes this topic even more confusing?**

A SUMMARY OF **KEY POINTS**

Electricity is composed of electrical charge and electrical energy. Electrical charge requires a potential difference; that is an area of unequal charge in order for the current to flow. Electrical charge requires a complete circuit in order for the potential difference to occur. There are many different terms to measure and describe the flow in a circuit. Electrical energy is generated by exciting the particles and requires a complete circuit in order for the energy to be transferred. Electrical energy is pumped in power stations (and batteries) and is measured in Watts (W).

Moving on

The most problematic aspect of this topic in the classroom relates to equipment that will not work and so trouble-shooting skills are useful. Electricity will always take the shortest route, so check to make sure there are no short-circuits (quick pathway) for the energy to follow. If the bulb is not fully screwed into the bulb holder, the bulb will not light. Also whilst bulbs are not affected by the direction of charge, motors are and the direction of turn is dependent on the battery terminal to which they are attached (positive or negative). Buzzers will let energy flow whichever way they are attached but will only make a noise if the red wire is attached to the positive terminal. Bulbs with low voltage often blow, and so 3.5V bulbs are most useful in a classroom. Storing batteries upright will keep them active for longer than putting them into a plastic tub, where they can make complete circuits when in the cupboard. Although there is the same amount of current at any place in the circuit, sometimes some bulbs will appear brighter than others in series circuits. If this happens unscrew the bulb and change its position in the circuit. You will see it is the bulb itself that is brighter, not its position in a circuit. If you leave it, the children will think the electricity is running out as it goes round. If more than one battery is included in a circuit, check the direction of the terminals as they must be connected negative, positive, negative, positive or the components will not work. If too many components are placed in a series circuit only the buzzer or the motor will work and the bulbs will appear not to light. This is related to Ohm's law, where when the push is kept the same but the resistance (the number of things it has to make work) is increased the amount of charge is reduced. If there is less charge there is less friction by the electrons, so – less light.

FURTHER READING FURTHER READING **FURTHER READING** FURTHER READING

Stannard, R. (1998) *Uncle Albert and the Quantum Quest.* London: Faber and Faber

Feynman, R. (1998) *Six Easy Pieces*. London: Penguin Books

Oxford Concise Science Dictionary (1984) Oxford: Oxford University Press

12
Forces and motion

By the end of this chapter you should:

- **be aware of significant subject knowledge that underpins the understanding of forces and motion;**
- **recognise common misconceptions associated with forces and motion;**
- **understand the progression of this topic using some examples of learning activities from 3 to 11 years;**
- **identify specific basic skills, illustrative and investigative opportunities within this topic;**
- **have reflected upon the cross-curricular opportunities presented by this aspect of science.**

Professional Standards for QTS

Q1, Q2, Q4, Q6, Q7a, Q8, Q9, Q10, Q14, Q15, Q17, Q20, Q21a, Q21b, Q22, Q23, Q24, Q25a, Q25b, Q25c, Q25d, Q27, Q28, Q29, Q30, Q31, Q32

Curriculum Guidance for the Foundation Stage and National Curriculum

In the Foundation Stage pupils should:

- **show an interest in why things happen and why things work;**
- **talk about what is seen and what is happening;**
- **ask questions about why things happen and how things work (QCA, 2000, p88).**

At Key Stage 1 pupils should be taught to:

- **find out about, and describe, the movement of familiar things;**
- **that both pushes and pulls are examples of forces;**
- **recognise that when things speed up, slow down or change direction there is a cause (DfEE, 1999 p81).**

At Key Stage 2 pupils should be taught:

- **about the forces of attraction and repulsion between magnets, and about the forces of attraction between magnets and magnetic materials;**
- **that objects are pulled downwards because of the gravitational attraction between them and the Earth;**
- **about friction, including air resistance, as a force that slows moving objects and may prevent objects from starting to move;**
- **that when objects are pushed or pulled, an opposing push or pull can be felt;**
- **how to measure forces and identify the direction in which they act (DfEE, 1999, p88).**

Introduction

Forces are everywhere and are involved in our first moves in the morning even before we wake up. As we rise from bed, dress ourselves, make and eat breakfast, forces continue to affect our lives throughout the day in many different ways. Individuals exert forces on objects and reciprocally, objects exert forces on individuals in ways that are often not even noticed. Forces are generally taken for granted, but wherever there is movement, forces are involved. This is not the whole story because forces are also responsible for keeping everything on the Earth's surface as well as explaining why bridges and container ships withstand heavy loads and even why large buildings like cathedrals do not sink into the Earth.

Essentially, forces are simply pushes and pulls. Difficulty with the topic stems from the forces being invisible whilst their effects are not. At the root of a lack of understanding of science is often the specific vocabulary in science. The topic of forces and motion is especially problematic because its associated words have specific meanings that often conflict with everyday usage of the terms. A force is thought to apply when someone makes you do something you do not want to do, or to be the word for the navy, army and air force. Indeed similar forces are given a variety of names in different contexts. Forces are often counter-intuitive and conflict with our everyday understanding of the world. Nevertheless, working on this topic with young learners, whilst challenging, can be very rewarding.

In reality the basic concepts are not in themselves difficult to understand given an open mind and a little time. Set within a cross-curricular context, the study of forces in the world can provide not only interest, but also the 'awe and wonder' factor so important in providing for curiosity and the motivation to study more about science.

Check your understanding

What do you understand by the following terms? Make a note of your ideas.

Force	Speed
Weight	Mass
Inertia	Density
Pressure	Energy
Upthrust	Friction
Velocity	Acceleration

Check your understanding with the Glossary.

Write down some of the effects of forces.

Forces and motion: some basic ideas

Forces are involved whenever something is pulled, pushed, twisted or bent, lifted, squashed, squeezed, ripped, torn or crumpled. Forces can:

- **change the speed of an object;**
- **change the direction of movement of an object;**
- **change the size or shape of an object.**

Forces also keep objects stationary. The unit of force is the newton (N) and forces can be measured using a spring balance called a newton meter.

Pushes or pulls should be thought about in pairs and scientists consider forces to be an interaction between two bodies. This idea holds true in all cases, for example when a ball is being kicked, where the 'bodies' are a person pushing and the ball being pushed, or the effect of Earth's gravity on the moon; where the bodies are the Earth and the Moon, the Earth's gravity pulling on the Moon and the Moon's gravity pulling on the Earth. You need to be aware of the following common definitions.

- ***Weight*** **is a force. Objects on Earth have weight because of the force of gravity which is the force that pulls everything towards the centre of the Earth.**
- ***Friction*** **is a force that occurs when an object moves over or through a substance. Other names for this force include drag, air resistance or fluid resistance.**
- ***Magnetism*** **is a force that occurs when the domains of, e.g. iron or steel, are lined up in a particular arrangement.**
- ***Upthrust*** **is a force that occurs when an object displaces some liquid when it is fully or partially immersed in it.**
- ***Surface tension*** **is a force that occurs when a thin skin forms on the surface of a liquid. This effect can be observed when a needle can be made to float on water or a water skater or water boatman skims along the surface of a pond.**
- ***Strong and weak*** **forces within molecules hold atoms and molecules in place.**

Children's ideas from research

In the past children have been found to give human attributes to inanimate objects, so a spring uncoils because it wants to get back to its original shape. They often think that forces cause things to move, but that forces are not involved in keeping things still. They think that weight is not a force and that forces hold things in position. They also think of gravity as a single force keeping a car static.

Teaching example 12.1: Foundation Stage

The CGFS does not mention the word 'force' explicitly, but suggests that practitioners should provide collections of objects, e.g. egg whisks and other household items, pulleys and construction kits, for children to play with and talk about including those that work in different ways (QCA, 2000, p89). Doing so will provide regular and different openings for exploration of how objects work but can also introduce and reinforce the idea of pushes and pulls in an everyday context. Pointing out the effects of forces both inside and outside of school, for example, when opening and closing of doors or drawers or observing the wind blowing through trees, can raise the awareness of pupils to forces in action.

Play offers many opportunities for exploring the effect of forces as pupils manipulate objects in their imaginary world. Every time a toy kettle or pan is lifted or a child pretends to sweep up the dust in the home corner, puts on 'dressing up' clothes in the role play area, makes simple models with play dough, kneads bread or stirs cake mixture, builds a bridge or tower with large or small construction equipment, pulls nursery toys on strings or undertakes any one the everyday experiences in a Foundation classroom, the pupils are exploring the effects of forces on objects.

Figure 12.1 Skittles can help young children to explore faces

Of course it is not necessary to intervene in play at every opportunity, but you can draw your children's attention to the effects of force during their everyday explorations. The following provides more structured activities, but you should easily be able to add your own ideas as you become more aware of the openings provided by child-initiated activities.

Feeling weight

Figure 12.2 Which is the heaviest parcel?

Learning intention: To explore the idea of mass and weight at a very simple level

Which container is the hardest to lift?

This is a simple but excellent activity for children to explore the idea that a bigger mass of a material requires a bigger force to lift it. Children are provided with four identical opaque buckets with lids (e.g. old powder paint containers with a handle). Each bucket contains a secret and different amount of sand in it. Pupils are required to lift each bucket in turn and to rank in order the buckets from lightest – the bucket that needs the least force to lift it – to the one that needs the most. This activity involves direct observation and comparison and provides a great opportunity to involve pupils in discussion. This will widen children's understanding of forces and the vocabulary associated with it. Extension play activities could involve children using a big spring to push and pull objects in the classroom. There is an obvious link here with mathematics.

Air resistance
Running into the wind with an open umbrella can be great fun and is a good demonstration of the force of air resistance. Health and safety guidance should be followed.

Water play
Play in the water tray can provide wonderful exploration of forces. There are many water toys including water pumps, wind-up toys and wooden blocks and all involve pushes and pulls.

Figure 12.3 Water play provides a range of opportunities to feel the effect of forces

The upward force of water can easily be felt when a large wooden brick is pushed down under the water. 'Floating and sinking' is always a popular activity. Ideas that heavy things sink and light things float can be challenged by providing a range of objects to test and discuss. Questions to stimulate exploration such as 'Do all light things float?' or 'Do all heavy things sink?' can lead to a clearer understanding of this concept. Challenging children to make an object that floats to sink or an object that sinks, float encourages a creative response in a safe environment. Subsequent activities could involve making plasticine or aluminium boats to be loaded with small objects such as multilink cubes, or compare bears to find out which shape can carry the most weight.

CASE STUDY CASE STUDY **CASE STUDY** CASE STUDY **CASE STUDY** CASE STUDY

Magnets
Michael proudly brought a pair of magnets into school one day to show to the rest of the class. He talked about what he had found out about his magnets and the effect they had on some objects. Michael's teacher suggested that his magnets could provide the start of a display. The response from the other children was excellent. Supplemented with additional magnets, the display became a popular resource for child-initiated exploration. The teacher challenged children to find out what materials they could find that were attracted to a magnet. Other children who were convinced that the biggest magnet would be the strongest were encouraged to think about how they could find out if this was true. The children explored magnets and talked about their findings throughout the whole of the week.

Teaching example 12.2: Key Stage 1

Building on the simple exploration of forces, a range of more structured, activities can follow at Key Stage 1. For example, after ranking heavier and lighter objects in the Foundation Stage, pupils' understanding of weight can be developed by presenting them with a problem-solving, model-making activity at Key Stage 1.

Shopping bags

Children will be familiar with the use of plastic bags for transporting shopping from local shops or supermarkets. This familiar context will add interest to this quite challenging activity that requires children to draw on their understanding of the properties of materials.

Learning intention: To use existing knowledge of the properties of materials to construct a bag strong enough to carry 1kg of vegetables

Question: Can you make a bag strong enough to carry vegetables home from the supermarket?

This activity provides opportunities for children to be creative in their design of the bags for testing. Pupils are provided with a variety of papers and fabrics, glue, string and sticky tape and asked to make a series of bags to be tested for their strength. Testing bags requires pupils to think about not only how to make the testing reliable and the identification of variables (type of materials and size of bag) but also opportunities for planning. Non-standard weights (e.g. small bags of sand of equal weight) could be used. The effects of weight are explored and the essential skills of measuring weight and making simple comparisons of the force exerted on the bags are practised as well as the link between strength and force. Pupils can record results in a simple table using drawings of their bags and the weight of the vegetables it held.

Health and safety: If pupils are to make and test their bags there will be the usual risks and hazards to take account of particularly when the vegetables/other masses are placed in the bag for testing. You will need to ensure that the weights that are used for testing the bags do not land on pupils' feet when the bags are tested.

Investigation

How can we give teddy the longest ride?

This fair test investigation has already been explained in Chapter 2. As well as exploring a number of forces, e.g. friction, movement as a result of gravity, this investigation provides an opportunity for pupils to demonstrate their understanding of a fair test set in a gender-neutral context where there are few discrete variables. It is important to limit pupils to only measuring the distance of Teddy's ride, as trying to measure time taken for the ride can introduce undesirable misconceptions. Measurement of distance travelled can be in arbitrary units (e.g. multilink cubes) or in centimetres. Alternatively, paper strips can be cut to show the distance travelled and can be used to give immediate comparisons on a bar chart. Differentiation for the less able can be achieved by asking for comparison by observation and ranking of the teddy given the longest to the shortest ride, thereby enabling conclusions to be reached about the surface in which the force of friction is the greatest.

Teaching example 12.3: Key Stage 2

Magnets

Pupils will often assume that the biggest magnet is also the strongest. To extend the level of challenge over work in the Foundation Stage this idea can lead to a simple survey investigation. A range of types of magnets and magnetic materials need to be provided. If asked how they might to find out if their idea is correct, a range of methods might be suggested. For example, they might test to find out:

- How many different numbers of layers of paper or material such as aluminium foil or fabric can the magnetic effect work through?

How many paper clips can each magnet pick up?

Strength of materials

Materials that stretch, e.g. springs, elastic bands, strips of elastic or nylon socks can be tested to see what happens to the length of the material as they are stretched. Using simple equipment (see Figure 12.4), weights can be loaded onto a carrier to test the strength of a material.

Here, children can plot, in newtons, the force needed to progressively stretch the tested material to its breaking point. The relative stretchiness of different materials can be compared, graphs can be drawn and conclusions can be reached about the tensile strength of the tested materials.

Figure 12.4 Testing the stretchiness of materials

Observing and investigating the effects of upthrust

Many goods are imported and exported by sea on container ships and by lorry on cross-channel ferries. Children may have seen or been on cross-channel ferries. Alternatively, they may have sailed on a pleasure boat, paddle steamer or pedalo at the seaside.

Building on water play in the nursery, a more serious study of upthrust can be carried out in Key Stage 2. Here pupils can plan and carry out a whole investigation to find out about boat shape and loading weight. A digital camera could be used to produce a record of safe loading of their boats.

Linking to this kind of experience can follow more research, both practical and by using secondary sources, into the idea of safe loading lines. Children could find out about the Plimsoll line, what it is and what it does and about Samuel Plimsoll, who invented it.

Investigating air resistance

Learning intention: To use the term 'air resistance' to explain how to slow a falling object

Children enjoy making and testing parachutes. The investigation can begin by challenging pupils to make a parachute that stays in the air for the longest time. This fair test investigation can make use of a variety of everyday materials such as different sized shopping bags for the canopy, and compare bears as the weight. This activity can be adapted to meet the needs of a wide age and ability.

Following the initial making and trying out of a parachute, a variable scan (see Chapter 2) can be made in discussion with the whole class. Children then can be asked to choose one variable to change whilst keeping all others the same. For example, separate groups might choose to change the size of the parachute, the type of material, the shape of parachute, the number of holes, the weight (size) of the compare bear, the length of string, thickness of string, ways of letting go or the height from which it is dropped. These are the independent variables. The dependent variable is the time taken to hit the ground. Depending on the age and ability of the investigators, parachutes can be compared and ordered by observation and ranking or by counting the time of fall in seconds. Older pupils might choose to use a stop-watch to help them to collect data. Use of shopping bags of different sizes works well. The bears can be attached to the bag with an elastic band around their body with strings tied onto them. Strings can be knotted onto the corners of the bag or attached with masking tape but for health and safety reasons, supervision is needed here, especially when the parachutes are tested.

Learning intentions:

- To be able take a range of readings suitable for the task;
- To be able to explain what is found using simple scientific vocabulary.

Which spinner will stay in the air for the longest time?

This simple activity can be undertaken at a number of different key stages. The level of challenge comes not with the activity itself, but with demands made at the planning, recording and interpretation stages. There are many possible independent variables. The dependent variables are the time taken to fall, number of spins, observation and ranking. With a Year 6 class the possibilities are endless. This makes a good investigation to practise skills. Make sure that you provide a template so that only one factor is changed each time otherwise this becomes a design technology activity and no trends and patterns can be developed with the class. It is vital that the children and the teacher also observe the way the spinner falls through the air. Observations of how the spinner falls should also be made and the result table should also include an area for the children to make a record of these observations. If it spins, this should be recorded along with whether it floated or plummeted to the ground. Using a digital camera to record the falling spinner to use later is also useful. The beauty of this activity is that the results are often not what the children expected, therefore making this an ideal activity for the opportunity for explanation of results and communication of findings. This is because the answer is to do with surface area, not the mass.

PRACTICAL TASK PRACTICAL TASK PRACTICAL TASK PRACTICAL TASK PRACTICAL TASK

See if you can find out which tube travels the furthest.

If a number of tubes with seals, or empty cylinder-shaped washing-up bottles are filled with different amounts of dry sand and water and then placed at the top of a ramp and released, the distance travelled by each tube can be compared or measured. The fascinating thing is that the results can be unexpected and are very different for sand and water. These can provide some excellent themes for discussion such as the movement of different materials linked to movement as a result of the pull of gravity.

PRACTICAL TASK PRACTICAL TASK PRACTICAL TASK PRACTICAL TASK PRACTICAL TASK

Cross-curricular opportunities

Here are a few suggestions for consideration when you next plan to develop pupils' understanding of forces and motion in a cross-curricular context.

- **Local history study, e.g. village pump.**
- **Brunel's SS *Great Britain* – heavy metal ship that some said was too heavy to float immediately before its launch.**
- **Coracles on the River Teifi – a lightweight boat with a skeleton made from ash contrasts well with the SS *Great Britain* – great as a starting point for exploring floating and sinking at the top end of Key Stage 2.**
- **Plimsoll lines – safe loading lines for sailing the oceans worldwide.**
- **Rope-making at Chatham Historic Dockyard (link to historic sailing vessels and modern yachts, pulleys and movement of heavy equipment).**
- **Clifton suspension bridge at Bristol, Millau Bridge in France (link to PMFL), Menai Strait bridge; link to mathematics using the designs on coins as a starting point.**

- **Castles and siege engines at, e.g. Dover Castle, Conway or Carcassonne in France,**
- **Flying buttresses on churches and cathedrals – cathedrals and other large holy buildings are widespread in all countries in Europe, e.g. Evreux and Lyon in France, Gerona, Barcelona and Malaga in mainland Spain, Palma in the Balearics, Genoa and Milan in Italy, etc.**
- **Towers, e.g. English keeps and the Leaning Tower of Pisa.**
- **Hydroelectricity in, e.g. Conwy Valley, windmills and water mills where the turning of wind or watermills are used in the milling of flour for the baking of bread.**
- **Birds in flight, aeroplanes, kites and parachutes.**
- **Machines using forces to squeeze out the juice from cider apples or perry pears in presses.**
- **The movement of water that turns turbines in the hydroelectric power stations in North Wales.**
- **Shaduf water system in Egypt.**

Further starting points include the amazing feats of the past such as when the stones were moved for building castles, cathedrals, stone-circles like Stonehenge or the building of the pyramids. Just how were those stones cut from the earth, moved from their source to the final location and erected in place? This provides many opportunities for research, problem-solving, applying ideas and model-making.

PRACTICAL TASK PRACTICAL TASK PRACTICAL TASK PRACTICAL TASK PRACTICAL TASK

Find out about the industries past or present in your local area or about a feature in your local environment; for example, a village pump, a local bridge, a church or cathedral. You might want to use a ship like HMS *Victory*, SS *Great Britain*, or the *Mary Rose* as a focus. Choose one or more interesting resources to research further the opportunities for studying forces in action in the environment.

Identify specifically where pushes and pulls are involved in creating motion or keeping things still.

How could you use your identified focus to develop your pupils' understanding of forces and motion?

How could your ideas be incorporated into a cross-curricular scheme of work?

Subject knowledge that underpins the activities in this chapter

The activities in this chapter are essentially concerned with how primary children can become aware of forces and the action of forces in their environment. Essentially, forces act in pairs and many of the suggested activities allow children to feel the forces, for example when magnets are brought together, the force of repulsion or attraction can be felt quite easily. When lifting things, the heavier the object, the greater the force needed to lift it. Investigating how Teddy can be given the longest ride provides concrete experience of friction and how different surfaces can inhibit movement.

A study of static objects such as bridges, castles or cathedrals can help children to appreciate that massive objects require large forces to support them and that flying buttresses can support the weight of the cathedral walls transmitting the force down into the ground.

Floating and sinking

Simple water play in the Nursery or Reception class provides many opportunities for young children to feel the upthrust, or the upward force of water acting on objects immersed or partially immersed in water. Upthrust enables both light and heavy objects to float. Initially pupils will state that heavy objects will sink and light objects will float, when the essential point here is that it is the density of an object. Density is the ratio between the volume and mass of an object and if the object has a greater density than water it will sink, if placed in water. So heavy things do not always sink: it depends on whether they are heavy for their size. Boats come in many shapes and sizes and are made of different materials.

Friction and air resistance

Friction occurs when one object moves over another object. Friction acts to stop this movement and always opposes the direction of movement of an object. You can feel the force of friction if you rub your hands together. In this case, you will also feel heat as some of the kinetic (movement) energy is converted into heat energy. Another example is when you brake hard when on a bicycle; if you touch the brakes, heat can be felt. This effect of heat being generated in moving machines reduces the efficiency of the machines and is why machines need oil to help reduce the effect of friction. Health and safety: ensure that children do not touch hot brakes or moving parts of a machine whilst they are moving.

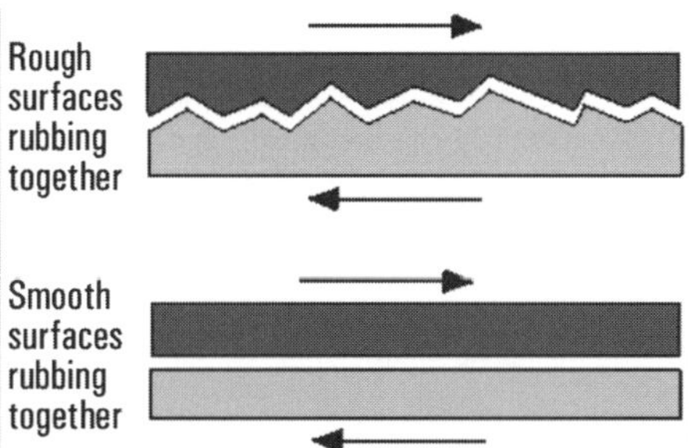

Try rubbing a little oil or cream onto your hands and rub them together. What do you notice? Friction between other surfaces is sometimes reduced by separating the surfaces by air. Rolling a cylinder along a table creates less friction than pushing it on its end. Other objects are streamlined to reduce fiction between the object and the air. There is also friction when an object such as a boat or an animal travels through water. In the same way, streamlined shapes can reduce the friction between themselves and water and are able to travel more quickly. This idea can be explored in the classroom using different shaped pieces of plasticine and a viscous liquid such as washing-up liquid contained in a large plastic bottle with the neck removed.

Air resistance is a force that is produced when a solid object like a parachute, a plane or a balloon travels through the air. A sky diver relies on air resistance to slow his fall. If there was no air resistance, a parachutist would hurtle to the ground with an acceleration of 9.8 metres per second per second – the acceleration due to gravity.

Gravity is a force that pulls down on objects on the Earth. A ball thrown into the air slows down, stops in the air and then falls back to the ground under the force of gravity. It accelerates downwards. If there was no air resitance, then all objects would fall at the same rate. Although this is disputed, Galileo is said to have dropped heavy and light cannon balls together from the Leaning Tower of Pisa to test out his ideas about objects falling under gravity. Both landed together because they accelerated at the same rate. He then stated that it was not the mass but the size of an object that affected its fall when there is air resistance. Famously, astronauts tested out this theory on the Moon with a hammer and a feather. They both landed at the same time as there is no air on the Moon.

On Earth there usually is air resistance slowing down falling objects. As a result, an object falling from the sky initially accelerates towards the Earth. At the same time, it is slowed down by air resistance acting in the opposite direction. These two opposing forces result in the object achieving a terminal velocity when the two forces are balanced. In this way a parachute reduces the terminal velocity of a skydiver by increasing the effect of the air resistance on the person making the jump. This is an example of Newton's First Law.

Friction is caused when two materials 'stick' together. Using a digital microscope can help children see that materials like wood are rough at a microscopic level. Some materials are visibly rough, like sandpaper, but others might seem smooth. If a glass is placed on a glass ramp it will show impressive friction. The particles fit together almost like Velcro (or a lock and a key) and the glass will require a great deal of force to make it move. This activity is not suitable for most schools as glass is a material that is banned.

Essentially, although it is not appropriate for you to teach specifically about Newton's three laws of motion, all the activities in this chapter illustrate the current view of scientists in relation forces and motion, in particular Newton's First and Third Laws.

Newton's First Law

An object continues in a state of rest or in uniform motion in a straight line unless acted upon by some external force. This law explains why an elastic band does not stretch unless we pull it between our fingers or hang weights from it or why Teddy, as he moves down the slope is stopped by the force of friction acting between the bottom surface of the sledge and the surface of the ramp, or why air resistance acting between the parachute and the air in contact with it slows down the parachute.

Newton's Second Law relates to situations when the forces on an object are unbalanced and there is an unbalanced force, e.g. when objects are thrown into the air. The acceleration of an object is dependent upon two variables: the force upon the object and the mass of the object. However, this aspect of physics is not normally explored formally at the primary level.

Newton's Third Law

For every action there is an equal and opposite reaction. This explains why some objects float; when the downward force of gravity on a boat is exactly balanced by the upthrust of water on the boat, or why a ladder is supported against the wall of a house because the force of the ladder pushing against the object is exactly matched by the force of the wall pushing against the ladder. The forces are balanced, equal and opposite.

In the elastic band example two forces are in action, i.e. the force of gravity acting on the weight that acts downwards on the elastic band that exerts an equal and opposite upwards force on the weight.

PRACTICAL TASK PRACTICAL TASK **PRACTICAL TASK** PRACTICAL TASK **PRACTICAL TASK**

Watch the Teachers TV programme on Forces **www.teachers.tv/video/1452.**

This programme shows a young trainee teaching about gravity, mass and weight to a mixed-gender class of Year 6 pupils. You will probably need to watch the programme a number of times. Whilst watching:

- **compare the content of the lesson with the National Curriculum requirements at Key Stage 2;**
- **identify aspects of 'good practice' in teaching science;**
- **note the deployment of the teaching assistant during the lesson.**

Record any aspects of particular use for your future teaching.

A SUMMARY OF **KEY POINTS**

The focus of the work in this chapter was on the activities to help learners understand more about forces and motion. In particular it has:

> **presented a number of activities on the theme of forces and motion, showing how learners' understanding of the basic ideas of materials can be developed over the primary age range;**

> **explored the cross-curricular links presented by a range of topics that can provide opportunities for pupils to learn about forces and motion in a science-in-action context;**

> **clarified particular meanings of a range of words associated with force and motion;**

> **made the link between force and energy;**

> **emphasised the need for practical exploration and discussion of ideas within this topic.**

Moving on

Energy is closely associated with forces and movement. When anything moves, energy changes are involved. Forces transfer energy from one object to another; when you drive a car, food energy in your body is transferred to kinetic energy when you press the accelerator and this force leads to the transfer of energy in various ways within the car, leading to movement of the car. However, although it is often confused, force is not the same as energy. Forces are pushes or pulls. Energy can neither be created nor destroyed, but it can be changed from one form to another and there are many forms of energy.

You may have noticed that throughout this book, references are made to energy changes. For example, in Chapter 5 energy is involved in photosynthesis in plants and in Chapter 10 chemical changes involve changes of energy when mixtures of materials are said to react. In this chapter, the application of a force often leads to movement and energy changes.

Although energy is an important concept in science, it is not dealt with explicitly within the National Curriculum until Key Stage 3. However, it is important that you have a clear understanding of the link between force and energy and of the different forms of energy.

Read the following:

Peacock, G., Sharp, J., Johnsey, R. and Wright, D. (2007) Energy, Chapter 9 in *Primary Science: Knowledge and Understanding*. 3rd edition. Exeter: Learning Matters

You may want to explore your understanding of energy.

- **Scrutinise a scheme of work and lesson plans of a science topic you are about to teach.**

Identify where energy changes are involved in this topic.

FURTHER READING FURTHER READING FURTHER READING FURTHER READING

Peacock, G., Sharp, J., Johnsey, R. and Wright, D. (2007) Materials, Chapter 6 in *Primary Science: Knowledge and Understanding*, 3rd edition. Exeter: Learning Matters

13
Light

By the end of this chapter you should:

- **be aware of significant subject knowledge that underpins the understanding of light;**
- **recognise common misconceptions associated with light;**
- **understand the progression of this topic using some examples of learning activities from 3 to 11 years;**
- **identify specific basic skills, illustrative and investigative opportunities within this topic;**
- **have recognised the need to listen to what pupils say as a key to their understanding;**
- **have reflected upon the way children explain the effects of observable phenomena.**

Professional Standards for QTS

Q1, Q2, Q4, Q7a, Q8, Q9, Q10, Q14, Q15, Q17, Q18, Q19, Q21a, Q21b, Q22, Q23, Q25a, Q25b, Q25c, Q25d, Q26b, Q27, Q28, Q29, Q30, Q31

Curriculum Guidance for the Foundation Stage and National Curriculum

In the Foundation Stage pupils should:

- **show curiosity, observe and manipulate objects;**
- **examine objects to find out more about them (QCA, 2000, p86).**

At Key Stage 1 pupils should be taught:

- **that light comes from a variety of sources including the Sun;**
- **that darkness is the absence of light (DfEE, 1999, p81).**

At Key Stage 2 pupils should be taught:

- **that light travels from a source;**
- **that light cannot pass through some materials and this leads to the formation of shadows;**
- **that light can be reflected from some surfaces e.g. mirrors and polished metals;**
- **that we see light sources e.g. light bulbs, candles, because light from them enters our eyes (DfEE, 1999, p88).**

Introduction

Unlike sound, which needs a medium for the energy to be passed from particle to particle, light can travel through a vacuum. Light travels at a speed of about 300,000 kilometres per second. Nothing known can travel faster. Light from the Sun takes about 8 minutes to travel the 93,000,000 miles to the Earth. Visible light is part of the electromagnetic spectrum, but only the part that is visible is called light. This chapter will focus on learning about light;

however, the activities will focus on making children think to explain observable features where they do not need to work out why things happen, but just make links, ask questions and think of new things to try to see if they find the same patterns.

Check your understanding
What do you understand by the following terms? Make a note of your ideas.

Light	Luminous
Reflection	Transparent
Shadow	Opaque
Refraction	Translucent
Shiny	Seeing
Non-luminous	Colour
See-through	Scattering
Image	Electromagnetic spectrum

Check your understanding with the Glossary.

Write down or draw a diagram to show how you think shadows are formed.

Light: some basic ideas

Light is a form of energy, so the transmission of light is the transmission of energy. It enables us to see and provides information about the world around us. A **luminous** body is one which gives off its own light. The Sun is a luminous body. A **non-luminous** body is one which reflects light given by a luminous body. The Moon is a non-luminous body. Scientists over time have not always agreed with each other about the nature of light.

In the early seventeenth century a Dutch scientist called Huygens proposed that light travels as waves. However, Isaac Newton suggested that light was really composed of tiny particles emitted by luminous bodies. The debate was won by Newton because he had more credibility at the time; however, in the nineteenth century wave theory again dominated when it became clear that light was composed of many colours and wave theory was the only one that could explain this phenomenon in a satisfactory way.

When it was realised that light was part of the electromagnetic spectrum a new theory called quantum theory was created. This theory uses elements of both the particle and wave theory to explain what light is and how it travels. Einstein was the scientist who identified that light is both wave- and particle-like in nature. This dual explanation exists today because some properties of light can only be explained by one or other theory. Whilst this may cause some confusion it also demonstrates the complexity of scientific phenomena and the theories that explain them.

White light, known as 'light' in everyday terms, is composed of light of different wavelengths, or otherwise 'all the colours of the rainbow'. Light is part of the **electromagnetic spectrum**, but only a small range of this is visible to the human eye. This small visible section has a frequency of between about 350 nanometres (nm) and 750nm. Infrared radiation has a shorter frequency than light and ultraviolet or black light has frequency greater than visible light. Light transmitted from an object to the eye stimulates the different colour cones of the retina, thus making it possible for people to perceive different coloured objects.

Seeing is not an active process. Sight occurs when light from an object is reflected into the eye. However, not all light that falls on all objects is reflected. Generally, some is reflected and some is absorbed. Reflected light enters the eye, hits the retina and the brain then makes sense of what is seen. If the surface of the object struck by light is very smooth then the light is reflected into the eye without any alteration. If the surface is very, very smooth, the light will be bounced at a 90° angle and a reflection will be seen. If however the light strikes an irregular, bumpy surface the light will be bounced, scattered in different directions. Some will enter the eye but it will not carry a perfect reflection and the information received will be in a distorted way.

When light passes through different materials, the constituent parts of white light travel at different speeds through the materials. Red light has the longest wavelength and will therefore travel the quickest. Violet light has the shortest wavelength and will travel the slowest. The speeds of the other colours of light fall between those of red and violet. When light hits an object the colour of this object depends on the wavelengths of light that the object absorbs. A black object absorbs nearly all wavelengths and reflects little light. Contrastingly, a white object transmits all wavelengths, absorbing very few. A green object is seen to be green as this is the wavelength of light that it does not absorb but reflects. Green plants are green because green light is reflected away from the plant; it is not needed by the plant.

In the model used to explain how light travels, it is stated that light travels in straight lines. This fact can then be used to explain shadows. If an opaque object is placed in the pathway of the light, the object blocks the path of the light and the area behind the object is in darkness. This is called a shadow. A definition of a shadow is: where light is blocked.

Children's ideas from research

Light is an everyday phenomenon and children expect it to be there. The NCC (1992) reported that most three-year-olds recognise that they see with their eyes and know that they can't see an object if a barrier is placed between them and an object. Children know the limitations of the process of seeing rather than offering an explanation of it. Young children use the terms 'reflection' and 'shadow' interchangeably.

The programme of study at Key Stage 1 states that children have to know that darkness is the absence of light. This is problematic because rarely today is total darkness achievable because of the high incidence of light pollution in the UK. When asked what they can see in the dark, many children reply that their 'eyes cannot see to start with but that if you wait a bit your eyes get used to it and yes you can see in the dark'. One four-year-old child was certain that you turned darkness on when the light was switched off. This is a common view held by small children.

SPACE (Scientific Processes and Concept Exploration) research in the 1990s found that children gave many examples of non-luminous bodies when asked for things that gave light. Examples included the Moon and mirrors. So, your pupils may not appreciate that light has a source and they may find the difference between light sources and reflectors difficult. Key Stages 1 and 2 children often think that the Moon is a light source and they do not find it obvious that light enables objects to be seen. Shadows too are problematic because children may not understand these as an absence of light.

PRACTICAL TASK PRACTICAL TASK PRACTICAL TASK PRACTICAL TASK PRACTICAL TASK

Find out what ideas your class have about light.

- **How do these ideas compare with those above?**
- **What activities might you provide to move your children's ideas on?**
- **Make a note of these ideas for future reference.**

Teaching example 13.1: Foundation Stage

Aspects of light should be addressed in a number of ways at the Foundation Stage using a range of activities. Light and dark are concepts well understood by young children since their lives revolve around a pattern of life dominated by night and day. At this stage you should provide children with a range of toys and torches that emit light, to stimulate their curiosity.

Build a dark place

Learning intention: To be able to talk about light and dark

Success criteria: To make a dark place with as little light in it as possible

Context: Role-play area/home corner

Using the role-play area, a clothes airer or large cardboard boxes and blankets, children can to try to make a dark place for themselves. Provide a range of cushions and soft toys and other 'comfort' materials as young children often associate darkness with unpleasantness. To help them think about what to do to make a dark area, ask questions such as:

- How can we make a dark area?
- What is the dark like?
- What can you see in the dark?

After their first attempt, if there is still light, ask, e.g.:

- Where does the light still come from?
- How can we make our dark area darker?
- How could we make our dark area lighter?
- What could we use to light our dark area safely to read stories about the dark, e.g. *The owl that was afraid of the dark*?

When the dark area is ready give the children a range of different articles of different colours, different paper, coloured card, and ask them if they can see these well in the dark area. Young children associate light as a normal occurrence so may not have thought about whether it is possible to see their image in a mirror in the dark place, so include a mirror and ask them to find out if they can see themselves in the dark area. Simple explorations like these can lead to simple investigations to find out, e.g. which materials are seen more clearly when there is little light, which colour is more/less visible? Can we see anything in the dark? What have we found out about the dark?

Reflecting light

Particularly at Christmas time it is nice to investigate shiny things. Children love baubles, so make a collection of Christmas bells and balls of different colours. A fun activity for very young children is to look at their reflection using a selection of shiny objects. If possible include a shaving or make-up mirror with a magnifying lens. Mirror board can provide larger shiny surfaces that can be bent to produce the kinds of distorted images that children might have seen at the fun-fair. Similar effects can be seen by looking at themselves in both sides of a shiny spoon. Simple recordings can be made:

Draw your image:

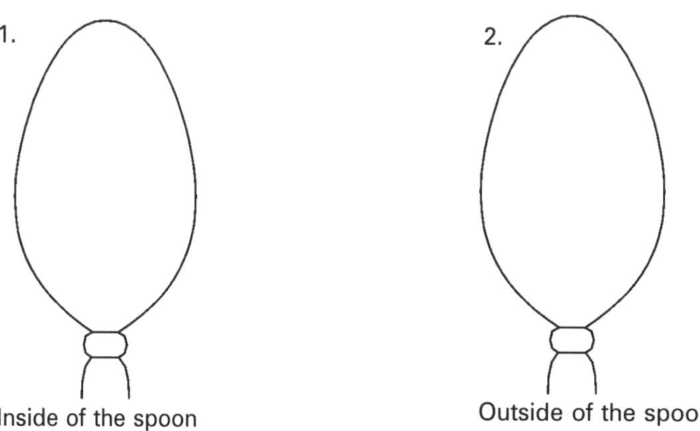

Figure 13.1 Looking in spoons

Set up a display table with items that will reflect light

Add labels to reinforce simple terms related to light, shiny things and reflection. Simple sorting of shiny and dull objects can follow. Challenge children to reflect light from the window onto the ceiling. Introduce a prism and ask if light can be reflected. Do they notice anything special? Where have they seen something like this before?

Beware of health and safety:

- Even sunlight reflected with a mirror can be harmful.
- Glass and breakables may be dangerous in the reach of young children.

Blowing bubbles

Bubble-blowing, like looking through prisms, is a good opportunity to look at light and colour. Provide a bubble mix and ask children to blow a bubble that has more than one colour in it. What colours can they see? Using a large lorry tyre cut in half (obtainable from tyre fitters) as a place to put bubble mix, and a PE hoop, make a bubble big enough for children to stand in. Make a bubble through which the children can see the world. What does it look like? Using large bubble-blowers and bubble machines is also an excellent way of enabling children to observe bubbles and colour.

Teaching example 13.2: Key Stage 1

Making a dark cylinder

Learning intention: To know that darkness is the absence of light

Success criteria: To be able to communicate observations in drawings.

Using an A3 sheet of black sugar paper, ask the children to make a cylinder shape the size of their face, so that when they place their face into the top of the cylinder it just fits. Attach this cylinder firmly to a piece of black paper. Ask the children to look down the cylinder and using masking tape seal the bottom down so there is no light getting in. (Making cuts in the bottom of the cylinder can help to make a good seal.)

Figure 13.2 The black cylinder

Once the children are happy that it is dark in their cylinder, provide a range of materials to drop one by one into the cylinder and ask if they can still be seen. Ask the children why they think the items cannot be seen. Then encourage them to make holes in the cylinder, one at a time, to see how big the holes have to be or what shape they need to be in order for the object to be seen. Sometimes a by-product of this activity is that the light is seen clearly to be travelling in straight lines.

Making a coat to keep a toy safe in the dark

Provide the children with a range of small strips of materials, some of which are reflective, some of which are shiny, some dark in colour, some light and some of everyday fabrics. Ask your children to think about the doll on its way home in the dark. What would the doll need to be seen in the dark? Ask the children what coat they think might make a difference to keeping the doll safe. Encourage them to think about either the types of material or the amount of light. Provide them with a small doll-shaped coat template made of white card that has paperclips at the top for holding on the strips of material. Put the doll shape in a dark place and shine a light on the coats. Using a star chart as an arbitrary scale, give each coat a score for brightness. Encourage the children to talk about which material was the one that was the easiest to see.

ICT task

Visit the *Be safe, be seen* website **www.hedgehogs.gov.uk**

- What can this offer to children's learning here?

Shadows

Looking at and chasing shadows in the playground is a fun way to raise awareness of shadows and to introduce how they are formed. You can ask your youngest children if they can catch their shadow, if they can make their shadow shorter or longer, or, e.g. what happens to their shadow if they spread out their arms and legs or curl up tight. Digital photographs could capture the objects and their shadows for later comparisons. Back in the classroom, children could draw themselves and their shadows and these could later provide you with an assessment opportunity to give an idea of their early understanding of basic concepts. You might find, for example, that children will record their shadow as a reflection, putting clothes and faces on their shadows and colouring in their shadow. They might also leave a gap between their feet on their picture and their shadow, providing you with an almost instant opportunity to challenge such ideas, weather permitting, by taking your children out to look again.

Outside in the sunshine, or inside using an anglepoise lamp, working in pairs, pupils could draw around each other's shadow on large pieces of paper to help them to notice more about shadows. Overhead projectors (OHPs) can be used to draw an outline of a shadow on a large piece of paper around the shadow produced when a child stands between a lit OHP and the paper. Later, pupils can try to match the profile with the child.

Teaching example 13: Key Stage 2

Learning intention: To know that light travels from an object and enters the eye

Success criteria: To read a hidden message using mirrors

Context: Secret messages

Children at Key Stage 2 need to know that light travels from an object and that light enters the eye, not the other way around. Start by asking the children to place a sticky note with a nice message written on it on their friend's back. Ask for their ideas about how the friend might read it without taking the message off. Provide two mirrors and help them to read what is written. Where do they need to stand and to hold the mirrors to read the message?

Once the pathway is made, ask one child to reverse their mirror. Can they still see the message? Why can they no longer see the message? Next, use two cardboard tubes and a torch. Shine the torch down the tube until the light is seen at the end; now use a mirror to reflect this light down another tube. When the light is bounced out of the end, make sure the tubes remain still. Now place a message at one end of one cylinder and ask the children to look down the end of the other cylinder and read the note. Can you see the light? Why do you think light cannot travel round corners?

A complete investigation of the size of the shadow can be undertaken. Children could make their own shapes from card attached to plastic straws by masking tape to block light to add interest. The variables or factors to change could include the light source, the position of the light source, and the position of the object, the type of object or the colour of the screen. The factors to measure could be the size of the shadow or the density of the shadow. Using a light meter can help children to measure the amount of light in lux. Whilst the scales are often problematic, comparisons of brightness or amount of light can be made.

Shadows can be investigated further by asking children to make a simple shadow puppet out of thin card with a straw attached with masking tape then placing it in the path of light from an OHP or other light source and noticing what happens to the size and definition of the shadow when the puppet is moved between the light source and the screen. Most children like to make and to play with simple puppets and, even better, if they can use their puppets in a shadow theatre.

An alternative investigation could be undertaken taking the context of rose-coloured glasses. Does the world really look better wearing such things? What happens to light through coloured acetate? Your children might be able to investigate to find any patterns and trends using coloured acetates placed over the ends of torches to mix colours together. Could they make white light?

Challenge to make your pupils think
Ask one child to place a coin on the bottom of a bowl using BluTack then to step back until the coin is just out of sight. Next, ask another child to pour water into the basin to cover the coin after asking the first child to stay put. Ask if anything has happened – the child should now be able to see the coin. Ask them to explain what they think might have happened.

Cross-curricular link
Linked to design technology and problem-solving, encourage your children to grow plants individually in 2 litre plastic bottles. After a week, or when you believe the plants are well established, suggest they could find out what happens when the bottles are covered with different coloured acetate sheets. Use green, red and blue acetates on separate plants. Leave for three weeks, watering, but do not leave on a windowsill as this may be too hot during the day and too cold at night. Ask your children if they think the colour of acetate will influence the way a plant grows. After a few weeks, compare the plants. Is there any difference between the plants grown in different coloured bottles?

Subject knowledge that underpins the activities in this chapter

Light travels in straight lines and is reflected uniformly off shiny surfaces and irregularly off matt surfaces. We see objects because of the light that is reflected off them. In total darkness, i.e. where there is no light at all, objects cannot be seen. Reflection occurs where light from a light source like the Sun or a torch first strikes then is bounced (reflected) from an object, which enables it to be seen.

Transparent materials allow light to pass through them uninterrupted, e.g. air or glass. Translucent materials will allow light to travel through, but not in straight lines, e.g. frosted glass or very fine fabrics. Opaque materials do not allow light to pass through: they block light. Shadows form where light is blocked by an object. If an object is closer to the source of the light, more of the light will be blocked and the shadow will be bigger. If the light source is further away then more light will be able to pass around the object and the shadow will be smaller. If light is passed through a coloured acetate sheet, a coloured image will be seen; this is not really a total shadow as not all the light was blocked. The object absorbs all the colours except one which it lets through.

Light rays are bent when they enter glass or water and bent again on leaving. This is called refraction. Although light waves can travel through transparent things, their speed is reduced. The speed here depends on the density of the medium through which it is passing. The speed of light is reduced by 25 per cent in water and 35 per cent in glass, which explains why the coin on the bottom of the water-filled bowl can be seen when in the empty bowl it could not. The light rays reflected by the coin are bent as they pass through the water and out into the air before entering the eye.

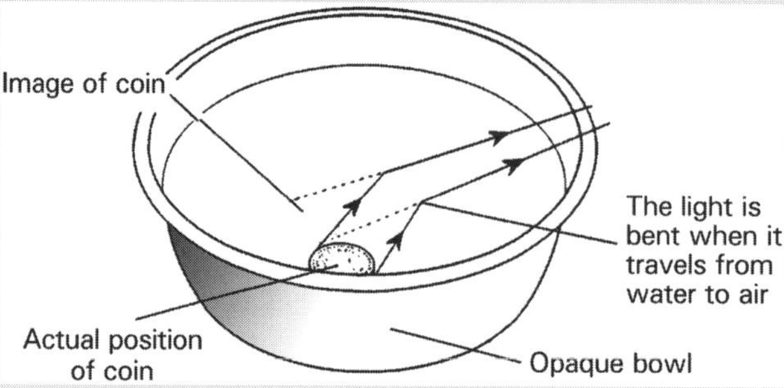

Figure 13.3 Magic coin trick

Coloured filters do not colour light; instead, they remove colours from the incident light, e.g. a red filter will allow only red light to pass through it. A green filter will absorb all colours except green. Our eyes contain just three types of sensors – one responds to red light, one to green and the third to blue. If red, green and blue are received by the eyes simultaneously, this is seen as white light. The plant in the green bottle should not grow well as it will not be able to use the green light necessary for it to make food. Sometimes this activity is not completely successful when cheap coloured acetate is used. This is because there will always be some light of other colours that also get through, but the effect should be enough to show the effect of coloured light on growth.

The current understanding of light is in terms of photons; these are bundles of energy which act in both a wave and particulate way. This however is still only a model to explain how the world works. In all models physicists do not explain why things happen, only how they happen. Physics explains how nature works but cannot explain why it works. 'Nature is so strange' (Feynman, 1998).

PRACTICAL TASK PRACTICAL TASK PRACTICAL TASK PRACTICAL TASK PRACTICAL TASK

Activity to make you think

Cover a torch with different coloured acetate and then shine the coloured light on objects of different colours from white through to black. Decide what colour the object will be under red light. Record and then see if you were right. What happens if you change the acetate to blue: will any of the objects change colour? Did they change colour or did they appear to?

What have you learnt about light as a result?

REFLECTIVE TASK

Look back at your findings related to children's understanding of light. Consider each explanation carefully. Compare them with the following ideas:

- **Can you identify some ideas that are merely simple observations?**
- **Are some ideas more sophisticated? If so, which?**

How do children's ideas differ in complexity?

A SUMMARY OF **KEY POINTS**

- **Light travels in straight lines;**
- **Light is both particulate and wave-like in nature;**
- **Light can travel in a vacuum;**
- **Nothing travels faster than light;**
- **Children need to be presented with challenges.**

The focus of the work in this chapter was on activities to help learners understand more about light. In particular it has:

- **presented a number of activities on the theme of thinking tasks showing how learners' understanding of the basic ideas of light can be developed over the primary age range.**

Moving on

In order for children to make sense of their observations and the phenomena they see, they need the opportunity to think about and explain their ideas. Scientists through the ages have made observations, tried to explain their observations and have sometimes put their ideas forward only to find them challenged by others who are also trying to make sense of the same thing. This is how science progresses. In terms of the theories associated with light, there has been much disagreement in the past, some scientists arguing that light travelled in waves, others as packets of energy. After much debate and argument, light is now known to travel as packets of light called photons.

When children meet ideas that are new to them, they go through the same process as scientists: they need time to make observations, and crucially, they need the opportunity to explain their ideas to others. Sometimes their ideas concur with the accepted idea, but sometimes they don't. You need to listen to your pupils' ideas. You can challenge them, sometimes providing some background information, or the opportunity to research other people's ideas before they will understand, accept and remember what they have learned.

Do some research of your own into what other activities you could provide for your children to help them to understand the ideas presented within this chapter.

Listen to your children. Record the explanations they put forward to explain, e.g. the coin activity. Collect their ideas on a whiteboard. Share the different ideas with the class. Which do they think are correct and why?

REFERENCES REFERENCES REFERENCES REFERENCES REFERENCES REFERENCES

NCC (1992) *Teaching Science at Key Stages 1 and 2*. London: HMSO

FURTHER READING FURTHER READING FURTHER READING FURTHER READING

Burton, N. (2000) Light, pp94–120 in *Pocket Guides to the Primary Curriculum: Science Physical Processes*. Leamington Spa: Scholastic

Feynman, R. (1998) *Six Easy Pieces*. London: Penguin Books

Peacock, G., Sharp, J., Johnsey, R. and Wright, D. (2007) Light, Chapter 11 in *Primary Science: Knowledge and Understanding*, 3rd edition. Exeter: Learning Matters

Newton, D.P., (2002) *Talking Sense in Science. Helping Children to Understand Through Talk*. Abingdon: RoutledgeFalmer

14
Sound

By the end of this chapter you should:

- **be aware of some of the significant subject knowledge that underpins the understanding of sound;**
- **recognise some of the common problems associated with understanding the progression of this topic using some examples of learning activities from 3 to 11 years;**
- **identify specific basic skills, illustrative and investigative opportunities within this topic;**
- **recognise how pupils can record in different ways some of their activities within this topic;**
- **have reflected upon the importance of progression within this aspect.**

Professional Standards for QTS

Q1, Q2, Q4, Q7a, Q8, Q9, Q10, Q14, Q15, Q17, Q18, Q19, Q21a, Q21b, Q22, Q23, Q25a, Q25b, Q25c, Q25d, Q26b, Q27, Q28, Q29, Q30, Q31

Curriculum Guidance for the Foundation Stage and National Curriculum

In the Foundation Stage pupils should:

- **examine objects and living things to find out more about them;**
- **investigate objects by using all of their senses as appropriate (CGFS, p86);**
- **be given opportunities, some adult directed, some child initiated, to investigate, using a range of techniques and senses (CGFS, p87).**

At Key Stage 1 pupils should be taught:

- **that there are many kinds of sound and sources of sound;**
- **that sounds travel away from sources, getting fainter as they do so, and that they are heard when they enter the ear (DfEE, 1999, p81).**

At Key Stage 2 pupils should be taught:

- **that sounds are made when objects vibrate but that vibrations are not always directly visible;**
- **how to change the pitch and loudness of sounds produced by some vibrating objects;**
- **that vibrations from sound sources require a medium through which to travel to the ear (DfEE, 1999, p88).**

Introduction

Sound is a form of energy, like light, but unlike light it requires a medium in order to travel. Sounds are made when objects vibrate. If there is no vibrating object then there is no sound. If there is a vibrating object but no medium (i.e. solid, liquid or gas) for the sound to travel through then there is no sound. Sound is thought of as having two aspects; as a type of energy and as the process of hearing.

Light travels at a speed of 229,792,458 metres per second in a vacuum; sound will not travel in a vacuum and travels at different speeds dependent upon the medium it travels through. Sound travels about 344 metres per second in dry air at sea level. Sounds travel much slower than light (about 870,000 times slower) which is why, unless you are hit by lightning, you see the light flash before you hear the rumble of thunder.

Although humans are adapted to hear most efficiently through air, sound energy travels better through solid materials. Sound travels at 1482m/s through water at 20°C and 6420m/s through aluminium. Sound can be changed according to pitch, loudness and timbre. In the primary classroom 'sound' is most effectively taught alongside music and there are obvious links here with the development of listening skills in literacy. This is an area of science where you can include many fun activities to help children to understand the science principles that underpin practical activities.

Check your understanding

What do you understand by the following terms? Make a note of your ideas.

Vibration	Loudness	Compression
Sound wave	Volume	Rarefaction
Pitch	Amplitude	Timbre

Check your understanding with the Glossary.

Sound: some basic ideas

Sound energy travels by transferring energy through the particles of a material that transmit sound as a wave. When a ball is thrown, it is the ball, the matter itself, that moves. With sound, energy is transferred by the particles of the material, not as a packet of sound that leaves the source and travels to your ears, but as energy that moves through particles between the source and your ears. This is what happens in waves: the wave moves, but the medium through which it travels does not. You will be familiar with a Mexican wave in a sports stadium when spectators move in a synchronised way. This idea can be used as a model to explain how sound can travel. A Mexican wave is set up when spectators in a stadium stand up from their seats and then sit down. Here the wave moves around the stadium but the spectators only move on the spot. Individuals are temporarily displaced, but then return to their original positions. In the same way, when sound energy is passed through a material, particles are temporarily displaced, the energy is transferred and the particles return to their starting points. If there are no particles, for example in a vacuum or outer space, sound waves will not travel, as there is nothing to transfer the energy.

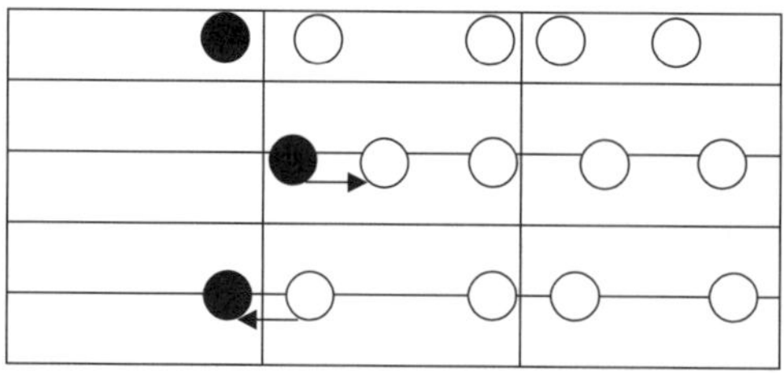

Figure 14.1 Particles moving on the spot and sound travelling

In Figure 14.1, the object (black dot) that vibrates moves backwards and forwards, knocking the air particles near to it. These air particles also move and then return to their original places, like in the Mexican wave. In this way the sound energy travels away from the source. The vibrations that make the particles move transfer the energy from one particle to another. However, during this process, some energy is also transferred as heat so that over a distance the movement of particles becomes less pronounced and eventually stops. One thing to remember is that, unlike in this model, sound radiates out from a source in all directions, rather like when a raindrop falls into a puddle a circular wave pattern is seen to move outwards on the surface of the water.

Sound energy is always greater near the source and diminishes with distance so sounds are louder nearer their source. The closer the particles are together, the louder the sound, which means sound is heard better when it travels through solids than liquids and better in liquids than gases. This idea seems strange to us as animals that are adapted to hearing in air, but is nevertheless true. You can test this idea out at home when you take a bath. Gently knock together two spoons under the water or let a tap drip slowly into the bath. If your ears are under the water you will hear the sounds of the spoons bashing together, or the dripping droplets hitting the water, very loudly and clearly.

Sounds can be loud or quiet; this should not be called 'volume' as in the everyday use of the term, but loudness. Volume in science is a measure of capacity and the term 'volume' should not be used in this topic. In order to make a louder sound the object needs to be made to vibrate more. Often the vibrations are so quick that the eye does not perceive them. If a middle C tuning fork is hit it will vibrate at a speed of 256 times per second. This is very fast. The amplitude, which is the size of the vibration, determines the loudness of the sound. The greater the number of particles made to vibrate, the louder the sound. This is why when an object is hit with more force the energy produced is enough to enable many more particles to vibrate and the sound will be louder. If a tuning fork is placed on a solid surface the sound will be louder. Here a louder sound is heard because in addition to the vibration in the fork, the wood is also made to vibrate so more sound is heard because more particles are vibrating. Loudness is measured as decibels.

The number of times an object vibrates per second is a measure of **frequency** measured in hertz (Hz). The pitch of the sound can be changed according to the length of the vibrating object; if it is a small object then the same amount of energy will make it vibrate faster; this will make a higher-pitched sound. A large object will vibrate more slowly and thus gives a lower-pitched sound, e.g. small bells produce high-pitched sounds while large bells produce low-pitched sounds; similarly for short and long guitar strings, small and large empty patio flowerpots, small and large chime bars and organ pipes, etc.

REFLECTIVE TASK

Consider an old philosophical question: 'If a tree fell down in a desert, where there were no people or animals, would it make a noise?' (See Appendix 4 for an answer and an explanation.)

Children's ideas from research

The SPACE project (Science Processes and Concepts Exploration 1990 onwards) reported that children often have their own ideas about how sound travels. These tend to be limited, but often very creative, e.g. 'tunes are very small and they can get through the gaps in the doors' (Nuffield Primary Science, 1997). Children have no problem in drawing pictures about their ideas of how sounds travel, but this often bears little resemblance to the accepted model. Young children do not associate sounds with vibrations; even Year 3 children need to have 'vibrations' pointed out to them. Children know that if an object is hit harder the sound will be louder. However, children often only make the link between the hitting of the object and the sound and do not see the vibrations that are caused because of the speed of the vibrations.

Some children seem to have a major and persistent problem with identifying the difference between pitch and loudness. Recently, it was found that some six-year-old children in a school in Dover were not able to distinguish between notes of different pitch. The children were asked to listen to single notes with their eyes closed. They were then asked to state whether the sounds they heard were high notes (indicated by raising their hands high) or low notes (indicating by lowering their hands). Out of 19 children, none identified more than one sound appropriately.

PRACTICAL TASK PRACTICAL TASK PRACTICAL TASK PRACTICAL TASK PRACTICAL TASK

The children in the above example had had limited exposure to music lessons. They could recognise loudness and could show whether a sound was loud by making their hands stretch further apart or quiet, shown by putting their hands together.

- **What experiences would you provide children to help with this issue?**

Using a group of children and an instrument like a xylophone or chime bars, ask children to identify whether a note is higher or lower than a previous one.

- **Compare your experience with that recorded above and reflect on your findings.**
- **How successful were you in moving your children's learning on in relation to this idea?**

REFLECTIVE TASK

Read the following and undertake the suggested activities:

'The phenomenon of sound can be totally understood as the motion of atoms in the air' (Feynman, 1998).

Activities
To help young children to associate sounds with vibrations, you need to set up situations to focus their observations.

Fill a balloon with air and ask a friend to talk to you from the other side while you hold the balloon between your hands. What can you feel when they talk quietly or softly?

Use a tuning fork, hit it on the table and then place it into a tub or saucer of water. What do you see? Hit a tuning fork and then place it on the end of your nose, your chin and your ear lobe. It is also fun to place it on your bottom lip and your fingernail. What do you feel?

Reflection on the activities

The above situations all allow you to feel or see vibrations. The harder you hit the object, the more it vibrates. This gives us a measure of loudness. Think about the following statements. How can you use them to explain the sound activity above?

- **Energy can be transferred but it is never lost or destroyed.**
- **Particles in solids are closer together than in liquids.**
- **Sound is a type of energy.**
- **Energy cannot be destroyed, just changed into another form, which might not be as useful.**

Teaching example 14.1: Foundation Stage

Asking children to close their eyes and to listen to the sounds around them can help them to develop their awareness and ability to distinguish between and to identify individual sounds. A 'sound walk' around the school grounds or local area can extend their understanding further. If this is undertaken at different times of the year, children can come to conclude that sounds travel further within a wood in the winter than in summer and that the reduction of sound energy is related to the more abundant foliage in the summer than in the winter. Taking digital photographs 'en route' of familiar locations can then be used in other ways when back in the classroom.

Play bingo

Use a digital camera to take pictures of different places in the school and school grounds. Use these to make a range of different bingo cards each with different places marked on them for children to use in groups. Provide each group with counters. Using a pre-recorded set of previously heard sounds from around the school – noises of animals or home noises like a telephone – ask the children to first identify and then cover up the sounds with a counter if they have them on their card. This activity should help children to understand that there are many different types of sound. Small groups of children could then, with suitable supervision, tape their own chosen sounds and photographs to make games for other children to use.

Scenario

Children sat on the carpet listening to music. The teacher, in turn, turned the sound level up and down to reinforce the idea of loud and quiet. Later discussion focused on high and low notes. Children sang some familiar songs and had to decide which notes were high and which low. A cushion was placed over the radio and lifted from time to time to explore how some materials can make sounds quieter. Then children, in pairs, were given a word on a piece of card, e.g. loud, quiet, high, low. Junk materials were available. The task was for each group to represent the word on their card using available items. One group of children given 'loud' put some small pebbles into an empty plastic bottle with a lid and shook the bottle; similarly, another group put feathers into bottle to represent a quiet sound.

Teaching example 14.2 Foundation Stage

Learning intention: To communicate observations

Success criteria

- To make a musical instrument.
- To talk about the musical instrument.
- To use some sound words.

Context: Making musical instruments using pots and ingredients from the kitchen cupboard.

Children were provided with clean empty yogurt pots, greaseproof paper and elastic bands. They were encouraged to put different dried materials into the clean, empty yogurt pots and cover them with the greaseproof paper and shake them to see what sounds could be made. Different types of pastas in different shaped and sized pots made different sounds. Children were given split peas to compared with couscous. The teacher encouraged the children to talk about the noises and to think about an imaginary animal that might make each sound by asking questions such as, 'Could their feet have made the sound?' or 'Was it the noise they made when they talked?' Once the children had experimented with dried materials and made shakers, they were introduced to the idea of making an instrument using an old tissue box and elastic bands of different thicknesses. When they had made these instruments, they were asked if they could find a pattern that related the thickness of the different elastic bands to the pitch of the sound produced when the band was plucked.

Musical noises in the water tray

The children played with a commercial bath toy that made different noises depending on the amount of water contained in the tubes. The children were challenged to find out how to change the sound and to make a set of sounds to accompany the plastic animals moving in the water tray.

Teaching example 14.3: Key Stage 1

Learning intention: To know that sounds travel from the source, getting quieter as they do so

Context: A listening game, e.g. 'What time is it, Mr Wolf?'

Success criteria

- To be able to communicate observations.
- To know sounds travel.
- To know that sounds get fainter the further away from the source.

The teacher stands in the centre of a circle of children who are facing outwards. The teacher should make a quiet sound, e.g. dropping an inflated balloon on the floor. If the children hear the sound they should take one step away. The process is repeated systematically until, when dropped, they can no longer hear the sound and move no further. When a point is reached that all children are unable to hear the sound, each child turns inward and counts the number of steps back to their starting point. This can be recorded using pictures and words.

Investigation

How can sound be changed?

In this investigation, the variables available to be changed include the object that is dropped, the surface on which it is dropped, the height of the drop, the force of the drop and the type of object. The variables that can be measured are the loudness of the sound, measured with a datalogger, or by using an arbitrary scale, e.g. with 5 being loud and zero being quiet. Ask the children to select a variable to change and to decide how they will measure the effect. They can record their results in tables or charts.

No breakable objects should be used and the drop should be from the hand with the force kept the same, for health and safety reasons. Children will find out about the different sounds made by different objects, the material of the object and how the materials of the surface affect the sound generated. For example, a very different sound will be produced if a ball bearing is dropped on a hard surface compared with if it is dropped in sand.

Teaching example 14.4: Key Stage 2

To know that sounds are made when objects vibrate

Children find it difficult to make the link between the force that causes an object to vibrate and the object vibrating, e.g. when a drum is hit when it has rice on it. Children think the rice moves because the drum was hit. This activity can be good to show the principle of vibration, but not if the children do not make the correct connection because the objective is not met. It is useful, however, to use the drum and the rice in a different way. Place the rice on a piece of paper or plastic film above a drum or plastic bowl. Make sure there is a visible space between the surface of the drum and the paper with the rice on. Now hit the drum or plastic bowl underneath. This will make a vibration which will move the air and the rice will jump on the paper (see Figure 14.2).

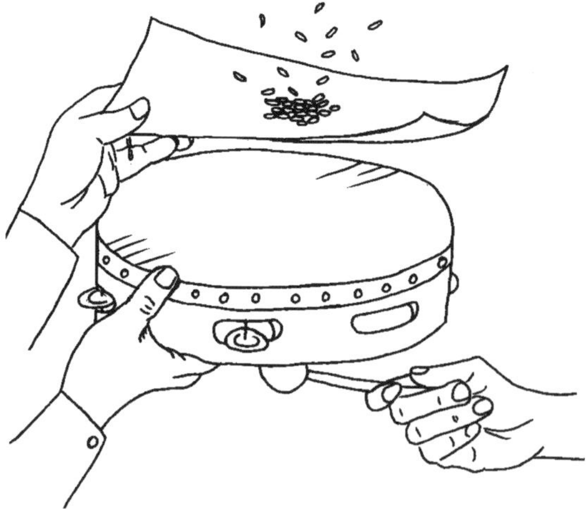

Figure 14.2 Rice vibrating as a result of sound travelling from a source

Another associated activity is to use a simple air movement generator by cutting the bottom off a plastic bottle and covering the cut end with plastic or rubber cut from a balloon and stretched over the cut end of the bottle (see Figure 14.3). This should be held onto the bottom of the bottle tightly. Keep the top of the bottle open at the neck.

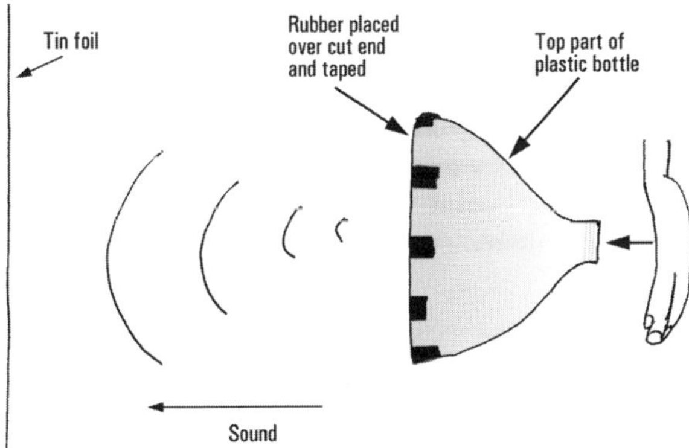

Figure 14.3 Simple air movement generator

Hang a piece of aluminium tinfoil from the ceiling then hit the air generator on the bottom with the neck facing the tin foil at a distance of about 20cm from the foil. The tinfoil will bounce with a lovely sound when you point the bottle neck at it. If you have an 'airzooka' you can make a child's hair move in a similar way. Fill with perfume to send smells around the classroom at the speed of sound, or make the tinfoil wobble with a resounding 'phwlat' noise.

Figure 14.4 An 'airzooka'

Learning intention: To know that sounds will travel through different materials

Success criteria:

- To talk about the loudness of the sound.
- To discuss sound travelling in different media.

Use a waterproof radio and a bucket of water to allow children to discover for themselves that sounds travel through water better than through air. Place a bucket of water in the classroom and turn on the waterproof radio. Place the waterproof radio in the bucket of water. Ask the children, one at a time, to place their ear into the water and to listen. Children will get wet, but will be delighted with the unforgettable experience of hearing very loud music in the water. If you can protect a sound sensor with a plastic bag with all the air removed, you can also record the amount of sound in water and in air.

Health and safety

Before you start on an activity like this, you need to consider that the sound will be very loud in the water and set the radio on low.

Teaching example 14.5: Key Stage 2

Learning intention:

- To be able to show that sounds travel better through some materials.
- To understand and explain why this is.

Success criteria

- To test at least four different materials.
- To discuss findings.
- To make a simple explanation for results.

Share the following poem 'The Sound Collector', with your class:

'The Sound Collector' (Roger McGough)

A stranger called this morning
Dressed all in black and grey
Put every sound into a bag
And carried it away

The whistling of the kettle
The turning of the lock
The purring of the kitten
The ticking of the clock

The popping of the toaster
The crunching of the flakes
When you spread the marmalade
The scraping noise it makes

The hissing of the frying pan
The ticking of the grill
The bubbling of the bath tub
As it starts to fill

The drumming of the raindrops
On the window pane
When you do the washing up
The gurgle of the drain

The crying of the baby
The squeaking of the chair
The swishing of the curtain
The creaking of the stair

A stranger called this morning
He didn't leave his name
Left us only silence
Life will never be the same.

Allow time for the children to think about and then discuss what the Sound Collector does. Set the problem for pairs of children to decide what material the Sound Collector's bag should be made of to ensure that he does not get caught stealing the sound. Which material will muffle the sound most effectively? Ask the children to measure and record the sound in decibels if sound sensors are available. Alternatively, a hand-held decimeter might be used. Failing this, ask your children to devise their own arbitrary scale.

PRACTICAL TASK PRACTICAL TASK **PRACTICAL TASK** PRACTICAL TASK **PRACTICAL TASK**

Thinking about one of the activities explored above:

- **How could you encourage children's explanations?**
- **What vocabulary could be reinforced?**
- **What other simple activities could you set for your pupils to extend their learning of this aspect of science?**

PRACTICAL TASK PRACTICAL TASK **PRACTICAL TASK** PRACTICAL TASK **PRACTICAL TASK**

Look at websites **http://library.thinkquest.org/19537/Physics4.html**
http://starryskies.com/articles/dln/9-97/sound.html

Subject knowledge that underpins the activities in this chapter

The activities in this chapter are essentially concerned with the generation and transmission of sound. Sounds travel as waves and requires particles in order to do so. The movement of the particles from their starting point returning to their starting point gives information about the loudness and pitch of the sound. If the sound wave was travelling in air, the particles would be compressed and then would move back to their starting point and then be compressed as the next vibration passed through. This would look like Figure 14.5. When the particles are moved by the energy they are compressed and then when they pass that energy on to the next particle it is called rarefactions. The particles then return to their original starting point.

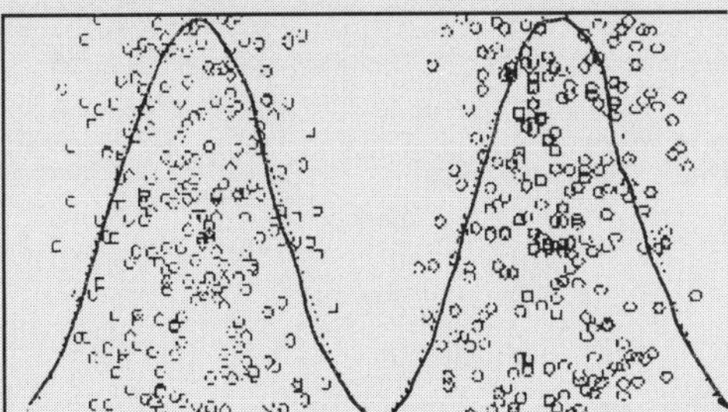

Figure 14.5 Pictorial representation of particles being compressed as sound energy passes

If the areas of compression and rarefaction are drawn using lines rather than the particles, it becomes easier to see the wave travelling. This can be explained by thinking again of the Mexican wave, the people first standing up then sitting down as the energy is passed. This movement can be seen from the other side of a stadium as a wave. If a pebble is thrown into a puddle, a ripple will start and moves outward; it is the ripple that moves though the water. The water is disturbed but returns to the original starting point. If a stick were floating on the water it would just bob up and down as the wave passed. This wave gives peaks and troughs. A scientist would draw a line between the top of the peak and the bottom, ensuring equidistance between the top and bottom. See Figure 14.5. Returning to the Mexican wave example, the line would be drawn halfway between the seat and the full height of the standing person. Picture individual people off their seat, but with their knees bent. If small children were undertaking the Mexican wave rather than six-foot Mexicans, there would be a smaller distance between the peak (i.e. when standing up) and the seat, which we could describe as the trough.

The difference between the peaks and the troughs in the movement of sound energy provides information about the loudness of the sound. The greater the difference, the louder the sound. The smaller the distance the quieter the sound. Therefore, in our Mexican wave model, children would be quiet sounds and adults loud sounds. The height of the wave is called the amplitude of the sound. Amplitude is measured in decibels.

In Figure 14.5, the peaks and troughs are not very high or low. This represents a quiet sound with small amplitude. In this case, the vibration only makes the particles move slightly. The energy to make the particles move was less than the sound produced in Figure 14.6. In this case the vibration had a lot of energy and the peaks and troughs are greater – a louder sound with a bigger amplitude. The arrow demonstrates amplitude.

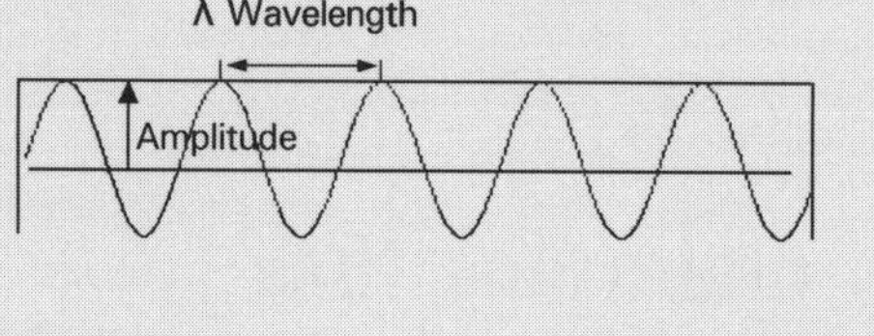

Figure 14.6 Quiet sound with small amplitude

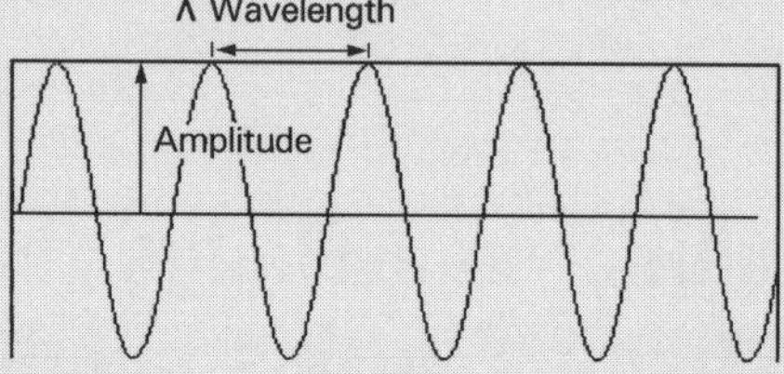

Figure 14.7 Loud sound with large amplitude

The distance from the centre of one peak to the next or from one trough to the next indicates the pitch of the sound. The nearer the peaks or troughs, the higher the sound. The further away, the lower the sound. This is the called the wavelength of the sound. The wavelength in Figure 14.7 is much longer than the wavelength in Figure 14.8. So the pitch of the sound in Figure 14.7 is lower than the pitch is Figure 14.8. The only way to change the pitch of a vibrating object is to change its length. The shorter the object, the higher the pitch. This is because the energy can make the particles vibrate quicker as there are fewer of them in a shorter object. As you will know, the material itself will also affect the sound.

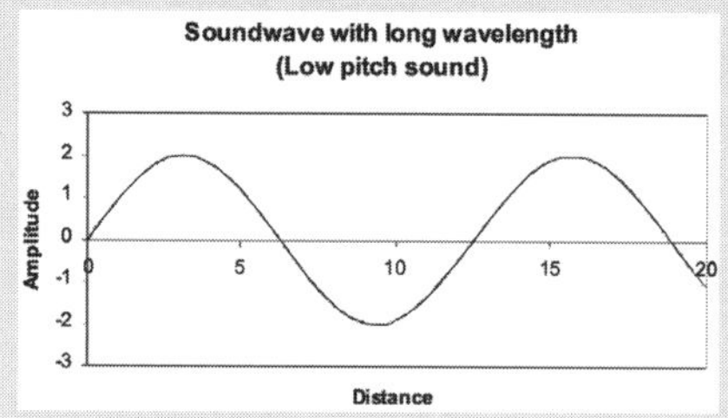

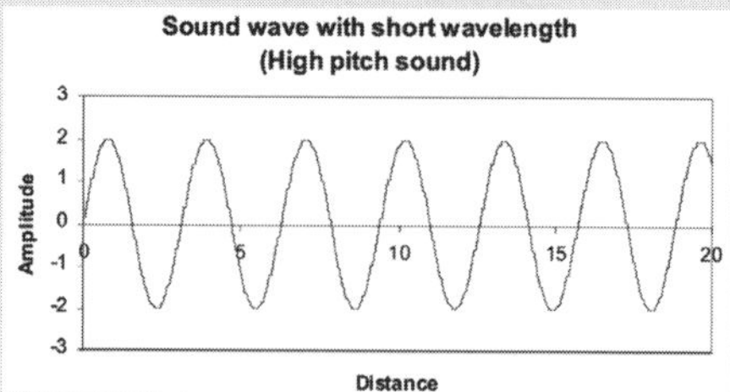

Figures 14.8 and 14.9 Sound waves

Some materials are good conductors of sound. Similar to the way that the structure of atoms enables heat to be transferred, good conductors of sound have particles organised in such a way that allows the energy to pass through easily. If atoms are able to move, this allows the sound energy to be transmitted easily and the material is a good conductor. Some materials deaden sound as their particles do not let the sound energy move them from their position. In our model, they are stuck in their seat and do not join in the Mexican wave.

Unlike light and radio waves, sounds are not part of the electromagnetic spectrum because sound is a vibration of matter. All elements of the electromagnetic spectrum are parcels of energy called photons.

They have different wavelengths. Radio waves need to be converted to sound for us to hear them. This is what a radio does.

Sounds travel most effectively in solids rather than liquids or gases because the particles are closer together and this make the transfer of energy from one particle to the next easier. However, if a sound starts in air, shutting a door will reduce the sound that reaches the corridor. This is because the door will absorb some of the sound energy, some of it will travel through the door and some will be reflected back into the room. For sounds to travel well in a solid the sound wave must start in that material, rather than move from one medium to another.

If the same tune is played on a piano and a violin, although the notes are the same the sound is different. This property of music is called the timbre and is a result of the different materials' ability to let sounds travel. Burton (2000) states that in music, timbre is the 'collection of secondary notes that accompany the main notes that add richness to the sound' (p127). Sound in science is about the movement of the energy; sound in music is also about its aesthetic qualities.

A SUMMARY OF **KEY POINTS**

Sound is a type of energy. Sound waves travel but the particles only transmit the energy. They pass on the sound and then return to their original position. Sounds travel better through solids, as the particles are closer together to make the transmission of sound easier. Sound has three aspects: the way it is generated, the way it is transmitted and the way it is heard. The National Curriculum does not expect primary age children to understand how the ear functions; this is developed in Key Stage 3.

Moving on

Think about how the ear works and the role of ears and hearing in different animals. Some animals do not hear sounds in the same range as humans. Dog whistles are not heard by humans because they are of a higher pitch, outside our range of hearing. Bats use ultrasound to help them position themselves in the darkness.

How could the ears and the position of ears on different animals be used to help children understand that they funnel sounds? Do elephants have big ears because they have problems hearing? Why don't fish have external ears? Are they deaf? Do we have external ears?

- **Develop some ways in which your pupils could explore some of these ideas practically.**

REFERENCES REFERENCES REFERENCES REFERENCES REFERENCES REFERENCES

Burton, N. (2000) *Pocket Guides to the Primary Curriculum: Physical Processes*. Leamington Spa: Scholastic

Feynman, R. (1998) *Six Easy Pieces*. London: Penguin Books

Nuffield Primary Science (1997) *Science Process and Concept Exploration: Understanding Scientific Ideas*. London: Collins.

FURTHER READING FURTHER READING FURTHER READING FURTHER READING

Peacock, G., Sharp, J., Johnsey, J. and Wright, D. (2007) Sound, Chapter 12 in *Primary Science: Knowledge and Understanding*, 3rd edition. Exeter: Learning Matters

Watt, D. and Russell, T. (1990) *Science Processes and Concept Exploration Report: Sound.* Liverpool: Liverpool University Press

15
The Earth and beyond

By the end of this chapter you should:

- **be aware of the significant subject knowledge that underpins the understanding of the Earth and beyond;**
- **recognise common misconceptions associated with the Earth and beyond;**
- **understand the progression of this topic using some examples of learning activities from 3 to 11 years;**
- **identify specific basic skills, illustrative and investigative opportunities within this topic;**
- **have considered the use of models and role play to support learning in this aspect of science;**
- **have reflected upon the opportunities for homework and parental involvement in children's learning about the Earth and beyond.**

Professional Standards for QTS

Q1, Q2, Q3b, Q4, Q5, Q6, Q7a, Q8, Q9, Q10, Q14, Q15, Q17, Q19, Q21a, Q21b, Q22, Q23, Q24, Q25a, Q25b, Q25c, Q25d, Q26a, Q27, Q28, Q29, Q30, Q31

Curriculum Guidance for the Foundation Stage and National Curriculum

There is no statutory requirement related to 'The Earth and beyond' in the Foundation Stage or Key Stage 1.

At Key Stage 2 pupils should be taught:

- **that science is about thinking creatively to try to explain how non-living things work and to establish links between cause and effects;**
- **that it is important to test ideas using evidence from observation and measurement;**
- **that the Sun, Moon and Earth are approximately spherical;**
- **how the position of the Sun appears to change during the day, and how shadows change as this happens;**
- **how day and night are related to the spin of the Earth on its own axis;**
- **that the Earth orbits the sun once each year, and that the Moon takes approximately 28 days to orbit the Earth (DfES, 1999, p89).**

Introduction

Given the centrality of aspects of the Earth and beyond in all our lives it should take centre stage in science teaching. This area has close association with other areas of science, particularly light, forces and energy, and ultimately the Sun provides the energy supporting all life on Earth. Since they first walked on the Earth, humans have looked at the stars, watched the apparent movement of the Sun across the sky and observed the changes in the Moon. In the northern and southern hemispheres there were also environment changes caused by changing patterns of day and night and the seasons. To ancient peoples, these changes were important because they significantly affected the pattern of their lives and those of other animals on which they depended for food.

Whilst seasonal change does not significantly determine human activity today as it did in the past, men, women and children are interested in and fascinated by some aspects of the Earth and beyond. Popular media interest is shown every time there is an eclipse of the Sun or Moon or when a shuttle or rocket is launched into space. Millions of people watching television saw Man's first steps on the Moon in July 1969 and there is still much expenditure on research into space. Nevertheless, some people have never accepted the idea that the Earth is spherical. Indeed, even today the Flat Earth Society flourishes and some believe that the Moon landing by Neil Armstrong in 1969 was a theatrical stunt.

The stars form recognisable patterns in the night sky. These were used by ancient mariners as they explored the original unknown 'space' on Earth: the oceans. In doing so, they discovered 'new worlds' as they navigated using star charts. Later, merchants traded commercially with exotic countries around the world. Planets however, were seen to wander across the sky. Today, the planet Venus, known both as the morning and the evening star, is seen particularly in winter where it appears bright and beautiful in the eastern sky just before sunrise and in the western sky just after sunset. Comets too are fascinating, evoking an air of mystery. Made of rock, dust and ice, they have sometimes been viewed with fear and dread. Some believe that Halley's Comet was the Star of Bethlehem reported in the Christian Bible; it is known to have appeared in 1066 when the Saxons in England viewed it as a warning of the Norman invasion; and it has reappeared cyclically every 76 years since. You may remember Hale-Bopp, the comet that made a spectacular appearance in the night sky towards the end of the twentieth century.

Although it is difficult to provide 'first-hand' activities in the usual sense of the term, it is possible for children to make systematic studies of observations related to this topic and for you to provide alternative experiences to reinforce basic ideas. The School of Physics and Astronomy at the University of Southampton (**www.phys.soton.ac.uk**) points out that although the basic facts involved may seem obvious to us, children need to use a lot of imagination to understand them. So, just like the early scientists, your pupils need time to think about and assimilate the abstract ideas, to research using secondary sources, including the internet, and to consider ideas and the evidence for themselves. Taking part in visual activities using models and role play can enable them to begin to understand the complexities of the Earth and beyond that otherwise might be too difficult. In approaching this topic in a creative way, you will make it exciting and stimulating for your young scientists.

Check your understanding

What do you understand by the following terms? Make a note of your ideas.

Solar system	Planet
Satellite	Galaxy
Star	Universe
Axis	Orbit
Eclipse	Centrifugal force
Comet	

Check your understanding with the Glossary.

The Earth and beyond: some basic ideas

Although many religious people believe in the account of creation recorded in the Bible, astronomers generally believe that about 12 billion years ago a 'big bang' caused the formation of the universe, which has been expanding and cooling ever since. The universe is all the matter, energy and space that exists from the micro level, the incredibly small particles within atoms and molecules, to the macro level within and between stars and galaxies.

The Sun, our nearest star, is at the centre of our universe. The Sun and its 'family' of nine known planets are located in the galaxy called the Milky Way. The number of planets and whether Pluto is still included will be returned to at the end of this chapter. Although the Sun is very important to life on Earth it is only one small star in a continuously expanding universe of about 100 billion other stars located in many other different galaxies. The Sun is not the only star we see in the sky, but others are so far away that they look like tiny pin-pricks in the night sky. Starlight is caused by chemical reactions on the surface of the star which travels through the vast vacuum of space outwards into space in all directions. This energy in the form of light and heat penetrates the Earth's atmosphere. The amount of heat and light provided on the Earth by very distant stars is negligible, but that from the Sun, because it is relatively near, provides all the heat and light necessary for life on Earth. The Sun is present in the sky during the day, even when cloud cover obscures it. What is less obvious is that other stars are also present during the day, but cannot be seen because the relative brightness of the Sun makes the lesser light from the other stars invisible. In the same way, having the headlights of your car on a sunny day makes little visual difference to your driving and even on full beam will not blind other motorists.

The Sun appears much bigger than other stars in the sky. This does not necessarily mean that it is bigger than other visible stars, it is just nearer. Planets including the Earth are basically spherical and spin in regular, but different, orbits around the Sun in our solar system. These, along with their natural satellites or moons and other bodies like comets, meteors and asteroids all travel around the Sun like points on a spinning top. Unlike a spinning top, however, their orbits are elliptical and held in position around the Sun by the massive forces of gravity that exist between the Sun and each of the planets. Although gravity is often thought of as simply a force that attracts things to the centre of the Earth, and despite being a force not yet fully understood by scientists, its influence in the universe is fundamental.

Although the planets are often described as spherical, they are more accurately oblate spheroids. An oblate spheroid is a sphere flattened by a very large centrifugal force around its equator caused by the planet's massive size, its speed of spin and the state of the material of which it is formed. The centrifugal force is the force that attempts to fling everything off the surface of any spinning body in a straight line. This is the same kind of force you can feel when you are spinning on a playground roundabout: when you step off the roundabout you leave it at a tangent to its circumference. Centrifugal force in the case of planets causes a fattening, a bulging at their equators, and a flattening at their poles.

Unlike stars, planets do not produce their own light. Instead, planets reflect light from the Sun. Each planet in the solar system is unique. The size of a planet and its distance from the Sun determines its characteristics, e.g. the length of day and night and the temperature of its surface. Earth is the only planet currently known to support life. The fact that it does so is amazing. Put simply, life evolved because of Earth's unique position in the order of the planets orbiting the Sun and this created particular atmospheric and weather patterns that provided an opportunity for life to develop on Earth.

The Moon is the Earth's only natural satellite and appears large in the sky. Although its appearance is associated with night, the Moon can often be seen in the sky during the day. Like the planets, the Moon can be seen from the Earth because it reflects light from the Sun. Evidence for this is provided by the waxing and waning of the Moon as it orbits the Earth over approximately 28 days.

RESEARCH SUMMARY RESEARCH SUMMARY **RESEARCH SUMMARY** RESEARCH SUMMARY

Many children start school with ideas about the shape of the Earth. Some think it is hollow and covered with a dome-like sky. Others think there are two Earths: one they live on and one they hear talked about. The SPACE (Science Processes and Concepts Exploration) research in the 1990s found that Key Stage 1 children could understand basic associated concepts when they had grasped that the Earth, the Sun and the Moon exist as separate spherical bodies. Similarly, older children appeared to better understand basic ideas about the Earth–Sun–Moon system when they understood ideas about the solar system. Some children think the Sun and the Moon orbit the Earth and that day and night are caused by the Sun 'going down' so that people can get to sleep. A popular idea is that seasons are caused by the Sun heating up or cooling down. Another common misconception is that the Earth moves closer to the Sun in summer and further away in winter and this accounts for differences between seasons. Children often think that the Moon produces its own light. Clouds are often said to cause the Moon's phases.

PRACTICAL TASK PRACTICAL TASK **PRACTICAL TASK** PRACTICAL TASK **PRACTICAL TASK**

Find out whether the children's ideas reported above are held by your pupils today.

- **Explore children's ideas about the Earth, Sun and Moon at different stages in school.**
- **Ask the children why they hold these ideas and where the ideas have come from.**
- **Ask what they would like to learn about the Earth and beyond.**

To what extent do they concur with those reported above?

- **Compare the children's interest in Earth and beyond with the requirements of the National Curriculum links.**

What are the implications of your findings?

Johnsey et al. (2007) argue that there is a case for teaching about the solar system before or alongside such things as day or night, the seasons and the phases of the Moon.

- **What do you think?**

Teaching example 15.1: Foundation Stage

The Earth and beyond does not feature in the Curriculum Guidance for the Foundation Stage or the National Curriculum at Key Stage 1. Challenging this position within a cross-curricular context, Howe et al. (2005) ask:

> '[D]o children only start gazing up into the sky as they leave KS1? Surely the concept of day and night is highly relevant to the youngest of nursery children . . . Our whole

notion of passing time is so closely related to the periods of rotation and orbit of the Earth around the sun that no study of 'Ourselves' or 'Autumn' is complete without some link to these concepts. (Howe et al., 2005, p125)

Children begin to learn the basics about the Earth and beyond from a very young age. Nursery rhymes such as 'Twinkle, twinkle little star' pose questions when the rhyme continues 'how I wonder what you are, up above the world so high, like a diamond in the sky' and introduce ideas that reflect the observations made over time.

Many popular children's books refer to night and day in everyday contexts, but others use space, spacemen and aliens which may, unintentionally, introduce misconceptions. As a teacher, you need to be aware of possible misconceptions and make use of the ideas presented to challenge the unwanted ideas. Stories such as *The owl that was afraid of the dark* by Jill Tomlinson (2004) and *Good night, little bear* by Patricia and Richard Scarry (2004) are suitable stories to reinforce the idea of day and night and provide opportunities to look into the sky on a clear night to see the stars and their patterns in the sky and for children to begin to understand the vastness of space. Be aware that even these books can include some misconceptions.

Teaching example 15.2: Key Stage 1

Many schools now take pupils out of school regularly during the year to familiarise them with and note the changes that take place in the environment as the seasons change. As part of this, you can draw your pupils' attention to the changing length of their shadow at various times of the day. Chasing their shadows is also a fun thing to do. See also the shadow activities in Chapter 13 that are also relevant here.

Day and night

Teaching example 15.3: Key Stage 2

Although teachers like to teach about the planets and their position in the solar system, there is no statutory requirement to do so at Key Stage 2. Instead pupils need to understand the relatively difficult abstract concepts concerned with the Earth, the Moon and the Sun such as the ideas of night and day, the phases of the Moon and the changes of the seasons.

Whilst this topic does not lend itself to investigation of the fair test variety, it can offer opportunities for systematic observation of change over time, model-making and role play. It also provides opportunities for cross-curricular links with design technology and literacy which can aid understanding in this topic.

Shadows

Learning intention: To systematically record the changing length of children's shadows over time

Building on work at Key Stage 1, and linked to work in light, older pupils can record the length of their shadows on a sunny day. If this is repeated over time pupils will be able to compare their own measurements and arrive at their own conclusions based upon their own evidence. More able pupils could devise their own way of recording their data during the day. They would need to show the apparent changing of position of the Sun in relation to the ground and to record measurements of a static object in an unobstructed position in the school grounds. The position of the object needs to be chosen carefully prior to the investigation.

Children could undertake some initial observations to find out which parts of the school would be in the sunshine all day. If your pupils are less experienced, you might offer them more support. Importantly, a visual record like the one below, indicating the relative height of the Sun in the sky over time coupled with measurements of the shadow of themselves or a standard object, will not only help your children to understand the concept, but will also make the explaining and the communication of their findings easier.

Figure 15.3 Recording length of shadows

The Earth, Sun and Moon

Learning Intention: To make an orrery to show the relative positions of the Earth, the Moon and the Sun. There are many simple kits available that can be used by children to model the positions of the Sun, the Moon and the Earth.

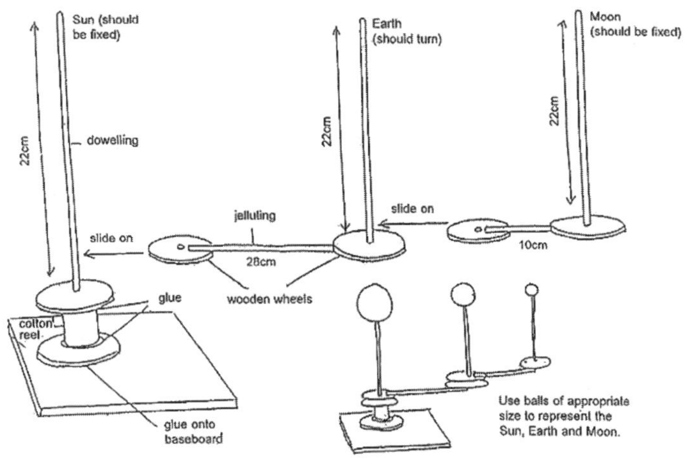

Figure 15.4 Simple model of Sun, Earth and Moon

Children should also be encouraged to act out the movement of the Moon around the Earth to understand the phases of the Moon. The Sun should be included in the model.

Exploring the idea of day and night

For this activity you need a white polystyrene ball with a knitting needle inserted through the middle of it to represent the Earth and an angled lamp to represent the Sun. In a darkened room, the Earth can be rotated in the light of the Sun. Questioning children about which parts of the ball are in the light and then in the dark can reinforce the idea of night and day.

Again using the polystyrene ball or alternatively a blow-up model of the Earth, it is also possible to demonstrate summer and winter. The model will have the advantage of having the countries marked on it so that pupils can see easily how the position of the northern and southern hemispheres moves in relation to Sun which can be represented by a fixed object. Tilting the Earth at an angle of about 23°, a pupil can walk around the Sun. Twelve other pupils, each labelled with the name of one month of the year, can spread themselves out around the orbit of the Earth to represent the passing year.

Other ideas

Ask your children to collect photographs including shadows. Can they work out at what time of day the photograph was taken? Ask them to sequence these pictures and provide evidence for their ideas.

Look at a sundial. How did people in the past tell the time using shadow sticks?

Figure 15.5 Sundials

Watching the rising of the Sun at daybreak or the setting of the Sun at dusk can provide a wonderful experience as the light changes as the Sun's rays creep progressively over or retreat from the landscape. The popular French impressionist artist Monet was well known to have been fascinated by the changes in the light and its effect on aspects of the landscape. Here is a good way to link science to art. Monet created a series of paintings related to the changing light on haystacks, including shadows. Many artists since, inspired by the work of Monet, have used the theme of shadows, particularly in relation to hay bales. Linking science to art in this way can extend children's understanding of shadows and the changing light over time.

Time travel

During the twentieth century, Man explored space, but only in films is Man able to travel in time. In 1960, rockets were successfully launched into space, but it was to be another nine years before a manned craft landed on the Moon. Those responsible based their work on mathematical problems using the information about what was then known about, e.g. gravity in the Earth and Moon, the distance of the Moon from the Earth, etc. They had to calculate what was termed the 'escape velocity', that is, the speed needed for a rocket to escape from the Earth's atmosphere to reach the relative emptiness of space. Such calculations informed launchings during the 1950s and 1960s. In 1960, children interested in space did not learn about the Moon landings, the space shuttle and about Man's other adventures into space.

Links to literacy: Ask your pupils first to research and then to imagine they are time travellers transported back to 1960 where they meet some children of their own age. What would they say to them? How would they explain the developments in space exploration and what has been discovered since then to their peers of almost 50 years ago?

PRACTICAL TASK PRACTICAL TASK **PRACTICAL TASK** PRACTICAL TASK **PRACTICAL TASK**

Knowledge and understanding in science are not static. People sometimes don't understand that scientific ideas and understanding change over time. The need for ideas to be supported by evidence is one that is fundamental to science education.

Theories accepted today came about through much thought, the linking and testing of ideas through considering and presenting evidence, thereby arriving at reliable conclusions based on sound evidence. Research shows that changing children's ideas, just like trying to change the ideas of scientists in the past, can be difficult and sometimes painful. This topic provides excellent opportunities to demonstrate these ideas through consideration of the changing ideas about the Earth and beyond through study of the scientists involved and their ideas.

Find out more about the ideas of Aristotle and Gallileo, and how their ideas influenced and revolutionised thinking about the Earth and beyond.

- **Thinking creatively, how could you incorporate a study of this kind into your teaching?**
- **Could the children act out the famous debates about the position of the Sun in the solar system over time?**

PRACTICAL TASK PRACTICAL TASK **PRACTICAL TASK** PRACTICAL TASK **PRACTICAL TASK**

Websites

Visit the site **www.worldtimezone.com**, which potentially offers some excellent activities enabling your pupils to explore time zones around the world. How could you use this website in your teaching?

Southampton University provides a number of informative websites to help the understanding of this topic. Visit and critique the following website that provides useful ideas for parents to assist in their children's learning: **www.hep.phys.soton.ac.uk/hycs/**

Many children do not have access to the internet at home, or have parents or carers who actively seek involvement or who, even if willing, know how to help their children learn at home.

- **How could you use the information provided at this site as homework tasks deliberately devised to involve parents or carers?**

Create a homework booklet that includes some practical activities that are not possible to undertake during the day at school. Bear in mind that for children living in towns and cities, their opportunities for looking at and recording directly changes in the night sky will be limited. Make sure that you include:

- **investigative skills;**
- **systematic recording;**
- **the use of secondary sources not exclusively based on ICT.**

Homework opportunities: To encourage parental involvement provide some points for researching at home and sharing with the class, perhaps linked to an oral literacy lesson. Although the internet can provide a wealth of information, books too can provide information at a level appropriate to your pupils.

Perhaps you could set up a 'loan system' for books or CD-ROMs or DVDs to be taken home. Build up a resource bank of information to be copied and used by your pupils. Encourage them to select points for them to explain to their peers.

PRACTICAL TASK PRACTICAL TASK PRACTICAL TASK PRACTICAL TASK PRACTICAL TASK

Look in daily newspapers to find out information about aspects of the Earth and beyond, e.g. the phases of the Moon.

Record the provided information over a period of time, e.g. in the case of plotting the phases of the Moon take one calendar month.

SATURDAY, JANUARY 13, 2007

Lighting up
London 4.17pm to 8.01am
Manchester 4.16pm to 8.18am
Sun rises 8.01am, sets 4.17pm.
Moon rises 2.36am, sets 11.21am.
High water Aberdeen 8:21am (3.3m), 8:42pm (3.4m); Bristol 1:00am (9.6m), 1:30pm (9.7m); Liverpool 5:44am (7.2m), 6:12pm (7.3m); London B'ge 8:12am (5.5m), 8:52pm (5.6m)

Lighting up
London 4.19pm to 8.00am
Manchester 4.18pm to 8.18am
Sun rises 8.01am, sets 4.19pm.
Moon rises 3.52am, sets 11.42am.
High water Aberdeen 9:29am (3.4m), 9:55pm (3.4m); Bristol 2:15am (9.5m), 2:45pm (9.7m); Liverpool 6:54am (7.2m), 7:25pm (7.3m); London B'ge 9:18am (5.4m), 9:51pm (5.7m)

Figure 15.6 Newspaper cuttings of Moon, times and tides

Subject knowledge that underpins the activities in this chapter

Twinkling stars

The apparent twinkling of the stars, particularly those low in the sky, is caused by the emitted light that is bent as it enters and passes through the layers of the Earth's atmosphere. When the layers of the air are affected by the wind the angle of refraction of the light from the star changes. This causes the apparent change of position of the star over very short periods of time and so the star seems to bounce up and down, causing the twinkling effect. The refraction of light as it enters the Earth's atmosphere also explains why light rays from the Sun can be seen both before sunrise and after sunset. Visit **www.enchantedlearning.com/subjects/astronomy/stars/twinkle.shtml** for more visual information on this topic.

Day and night

Many people find it difficult to understand that it is the Earth rather than the Sun that is in constant motion because our experience and observations show that the Sun rises every day in the east, moves across the sky during the day and sets every evening in the west. In reality, the Earth spins constantly on its axis, taking approximately 24 hours to make a full turn, whilst the Sun stays in the same place. During the day, one side of the Earth faces the Sun and receives sunlight. At the same time, the other side of the Earth faces outwards into the relative darkness of space and it is night. This explains why the Sun appears to move across the sky during the day and cannot be seen at night.

Imagining the Earth as a spinning top 8000 miles high and 25,000 miles around its middle and tilted slightly sometimes helps to explain the rotation of the Earth around its axis. In this model the Earth spins from west to east in an anticlockwise direction on its axis and completes a full turn in 24 hours. The Earth's axis is inclined at an angle of 23.5° from a perpendicular to the plane of its orbit so the Earth is not upright. This is called the inclination of the Earth's axis. The fact that the Earth is a solid sphere which receives its light from the Sun explains why there is night and day. Day and night alternate because the Earth rotates.

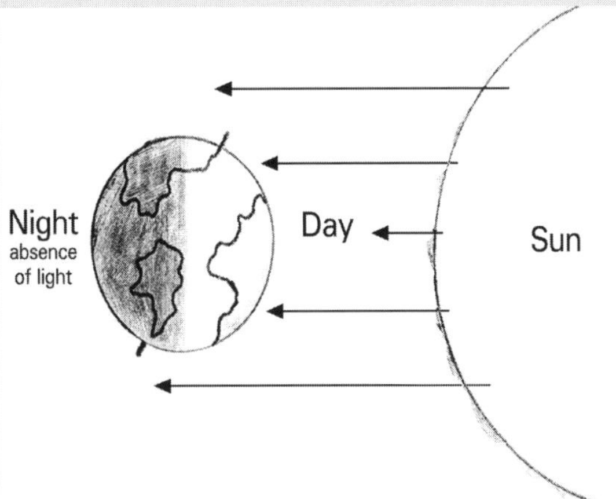

Figure 15.7 Day and night

The Earth is fatter at its equator so places on the equator turn 25,000 miles in 24 hours whereas elsewhere, points to the north and south of the equator travel fewer miles and there is less distance travelled at the north and south poles. This explains why day and night are not of equal length in most parts of the world except at the equator and why day length is longer in summer and shorter in winter. Each hemisphere has its longest day when the tilt of the Earth is in its full 23.5° towards the Sun and its shortest day when it is in its full 23.5° tilt away from the sun.

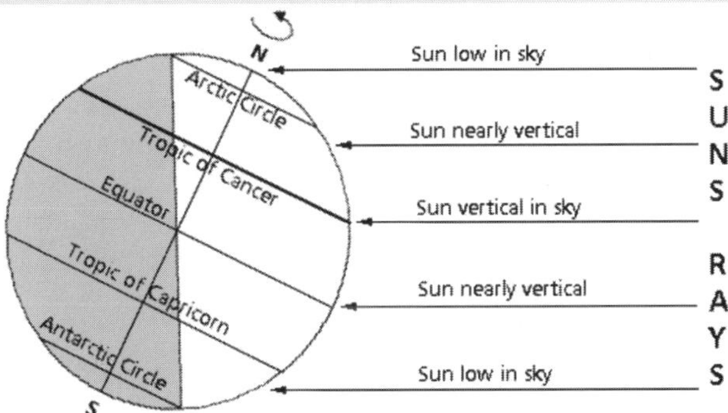

Figure 15.8 Summer in the Northern Hemisphere

The seasons

It takes approximately 365 days, one year, for the Earth to travel a complete circuit around the Sun. In winter, in the northern hemisphere, the Sun can be seen low down in the sky and therefore cover a larger surface area and not provide as much heat energy in any one place than at other times of the year. However, if we were to travel to the southern hemisphere, it would be summer, the Sun would be high in the sky and the Sun's rays would be very concentrated.

The Earth travels around the Sun in an orbit determined by the gravitational forces of attraction between the Sun and the Earth. The light energy from the Sun spreads out in all directions typically seen in children's drawings. However, because of the vast distance between the Sun and the Earth the light rays entering the Earth's atmosphere during the day are practically parallel to the plane of the Earth's orbit. However, the Earth's surface is curved so that the light hits different parts of the Earth at different angles from 0° to 90°. There is only one point at any one time where the light strikes the Earth vertically. In the northern hemisphere this occurs on 21 June at the Tropic of Cancer; this is known as the summer solstice. As the Earth revolves around the Sun, the vertical ray changes constantly, covering all parts of the world between the Tropic of Cancer and the Tropic of Capricorn every six months.

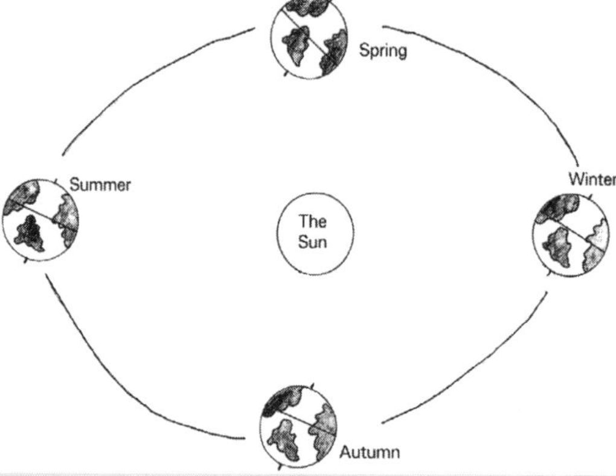

Figure 15.9 Seasons

There are two basic reasons why, normally, June days are warmer in the northern hemisphere than days in December. In June:

- **the Sun's rays are more concentrated because they fall on the Earth nearly vertically;**
- **the Sun shines longer than it does in December.**

So, June, July and August are normally our warmest months because the Sun's rays are more concentrated. Shorter days and weaker rays make December, January and February the coldest months.

However, seasonal changes do not only relate to the position of the Sun's rays on the Earth. Some places on the same latitude experience different conditions because of where they are in relation to large land or masses of sea. For example, the British Isles have a temperate climate with relatively small variations of temperature between the seasons. This is mainly due to their proximity to the Atlantic Ocean, from where the prevailing winds come, bringing warmer air masses in the winter than places like Canada on a similar latitude. Study of aspects of the climate and weather is located in the geography programme of study.

Every day the turning of the Earth around its axis and its gradual orbit around the Sun makes the Sun appear to make a curved path across the sky. In summer, it appears to be high in the sky and, in winter, low in the sky. This causes the length of shadows to vary during the day and according to the season (see Chapter 13) as well as the proportions of day and night to vary.

Task

Check your understanding of the seasons.

- **Where is the Earth in our spring and autumn?**
- **Explain why in the Arctic Circle there is no daylight at all on 21 December.**
- **Why in the Antarctic Circle at the same time is there constant daylight?**

Shadows

Light from the Sun travels in straight lines. Shadows are formed when an object stops some light rays from travelling whilst those all around the object continue to travel in straight lines. The Sun reaches its highest point in the sky in the middle of the day. This is when shadows are shortest because the angle at which light rays strike objects is directly from above. In the early morning and in the late evening, shadows are longest, but lie in opposite directions.

The Moon

The Moon is a natural satellite of the Earth and is also a spherical body. The Moon is held in a circular orbit around the Earth by the force of gravity acting between the Earth and the Moon and the Moon and the Earth caused by their huge mass: i.e. the Earth pulls on the Moon and the Moon pulls on the Earth. The Moon is smaller in mass than the Earth and as a result the gravity on the Moon is approximately one-sixth of that on Earth. Although the Moon appears large in the sky, sometimes larger than the Sun, this is because it is nearer to the Earth. In reality, the Moon is tiny compared with the Sun and about one-quarter the size of the Earth, having a diameter of 3476 km. It does not spin on its own axis so, surprising as it might seem, it always keeps the same face towards the Earth. It takes approximately 28 day for the Moon to revolve around the Earth. This is called the lunar month. The Moon is dry, dusty and has no atmosphere.

It is tempting to associate night with the appearance of the Moon and to think that the Moon in not visible in the day. This idea, however, is false. Although the Moon does not appear as bright in the sky when it is visible during the day, it is nevertheless sometimes visible at the same time as the Sun. Just as the times for sunrise and sunset are available, similar information is available for moonrise and moonset.

Saturday January 13 2007

Tides

Tidal predictions. All times GMT.
Heights in metres

Today	AM	Ht	PM	Ht
Aberdeen	08.21	3.3	20.42	3.4
Avonmouth	01.00	9.6	13.30	9.7
Belfast	05.53	2.8	18.11	2.9
Cardiff	00.46	9.1	13.16	9.1
Devonport	--.--	-.-	12.03	4.4
Dover	05.27	5.3	18.09	5.0
Dublin	06.43	3.2	19.04	3.3
Falmouth	11.53	4.0	--.--	-.-
Greenock	07.00	2.7	18.46	2.8
Harwich	06.03	3.2	18.34	3.1
Holyhead	05.06	4.3	17.27	4.4
Hull	00.18	6.0	13.03	5.7
Leith	09.23	4.3	21.54	4.3
Liverpool	05.44	7.2	18.12	7.3
London Bridge	08.12	5.5	20.52	5.6
Lowestoft	03.38	2.2	17.05	2.0
Milford Haven	00.23	5.1	12.51	5.2
Morecambe	05.54	7.2	18.22	7.3
Newhaven	05.28	5.2	18.01	4.8
Newquay	11.52	5.3	--.--	-.-
Oban	00.12	2.9	12.30	3.0
Penzance	11.22	4.2	--.--	-.-
Portland	00.18	1.4	12.28	1.4
Portsmouth	06.11	3.9	18.38	3.6
Shoreham	05.39	4.8	18.11	4.6
Southampton	05.36	3.7	18.04	3.5
Swansea	00.23	7.0	12.54	7.1
Tees	10.36	4.4	22.57	4.4
Weymouth	00.40	1.4	12.38	1.5

Hours of darkness
Sun rises: 08:01
Sun sets: 16:17
Moon rises: 02:36
Moon sets: 11:21
New moon: January 19

Lighting-up times
Aberdeen
15.55 - 08.40
Birmingham
16.19 - 08.12
Cardiff
16.29 - 08.13

JANUARY 14, 2007

High tides

	am	height	pm	height
Aberdeen	09.29	3.4m	21.55	3.4m
Belfast	06.55	2.8m	19.17	2.9m
Cork	-	-	12.37	3.3m
Dover	06.37	5.2m	19.24	5.1m
Dublin	07.45	3.3m	20.10	3.3m
Glasgow	08.34	4.1m	20.43	4.1m
Hull	01.35	5.8m	14.17	5.7m
Liverpool	06.54	7.2m	19.25	7.3m
London Bridge	09.18	5.4m	21.51	5.7m
Lowestoft	04.50	2.1m	18.02	2.1m
Milford Haven	01.37	5.0m	14.09	5.1m
Oban	01.52	2.9m	14.03	3.1m
Portsmouth	07.10	3.8m	19.49	3.6m
Rosslare	-	-	13.11	1.6m

Sun lights moon

	rises	sets/on	off	rises	sets
Aberdeen	08:40	15:57	08:39	04:41	11:10
Belfast	08:39	16:27	08:38	04:35	11:45
Birmingham	08:12	16:21	08:11	04:05	11:42
Bristol	08:10	16:29	08:09	04:02	11:52
Cork	08:36	16:51	08:35	04:30	12:13
Dublin	08:33	16:34	08:32	04:28	11:55
Glasgow	08:39	16:13	08:38	04:37	11:29
London	08:01	16:19	08:00	03:52	11:42
Manchester	08:18	16:18	08:18	04:13	11:38
Newcastle	08:23	16:08	08:22	04:20	11:25

Figure 15.10 Tide tables

You might find it difficult to understand why, unlike Earth, the Moon has no atmosphere. The reason for this relates to the Moon's mass and its reduced level of gravity that unlike the Earth's is not strong enough to hold the gas molecules that would otherwise create an atmosphere. Viewed from the Earth, the Moon exhibits phases at different times of the lunar month. The Moon's gravity also pulls on the seas and oceans as the Earth rotates.

The moon does not emit its own light. We can see it because the Sun's rays are reflected from the surface of the Moon. The changing face of the Moon is caused by the daily change in the position of the Moon in relation to the Sun and the Earth. Over the lunar month, different portions of the Moon's surface are lit by the Sun each night. These different shapes are termed phases.

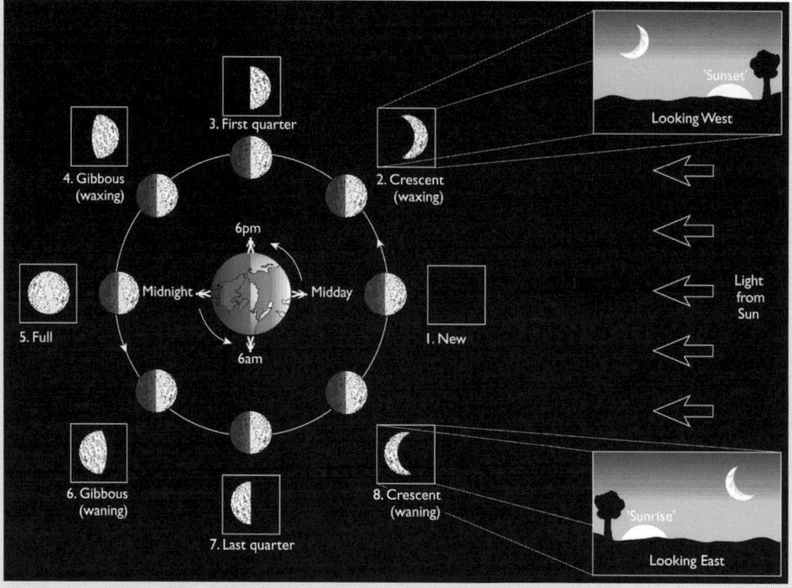

Figure 15.11 The changing face of the Moon

Pluto

On 24 August 2006, the BBC news reported that Pluto had lost its status as a planet. Researchers had demoted Pluto because it failed to dominate its orbit around the Sun in the same way as other planets. Scientists have now agreed that for a celestial body to qualify as a planet:

- **it must be in orbit around the sun;**
- **it must be large enough that it takes on nearly a round shape;**
- **it has cleared its orbit of other planets.**

Pluto was automatically disqualified because of its elliptical orbit overlaps with that of Neptune. It is now a dwarf planet. There are now three dwarf planets.

Task

Find out more about the night sky:

- **the planets and their properties and movement;**
- **star clusters, e.g. Leo, Taurus, Cygnus and Gemini;**
- **shooting stars.**

What is the evidence that shows that the Earth is not flat?

PRACTICAL TASK PRACTICAL TASK PRACTICAL TASK PRACTICAL TASK PRACTICAL TASK

Find out about the movement of the Moon around the Earth and the phases of the Moon. Using suitable props, how could you plan, organise and manage your pupils to act out the movement of the Moon around the Earth?

Find out about the special way the Moon moves in relation to the face of the Earth.

A SUMMARY OF **KEY POINTS**

In some ways the subject-based National Curriculum has divorced the factual, the 'mechanics' or objective aspects of this topic, from the understanding of its practical application. For example, a study of the weather closely associated with many ideas in this chapter is taught in geography and a study of how the stars have been used for navigation is covered in history. In doing so it has failed to help pupils to make the essential links between these ideas and therefore no matter how fascinating these ideas might be in themselves, they might be even more so set within a cross-curricular approach. In particular this chapter has:

- **presented a number of activities on the theme of Earth and beyond showing how learners' understanding of the basic ideas can be developed over the primary age range;**
- **indicated the close links between other subjects in particular history, geography and design technology;**
- **examined how parents can be involved in their children's learning in this topic and how their own scientific understanding might be enhanced as a result.**

Moving on

Given a little imagination, role play can be used within a variety of topics to help pupils to understand abstract concepts. Look back at the topics you have already studied and identify where role play might provide an alternative teaching strategy.

REFERENCES REFERENCES REFERENCES REFERENCES REFERENCES REFERENCES

Howe, A., Davies, D., McMahon, K., Towler, L. and Scott, T. (2005) Materials and their properties, Chapter 5 in *Science 5–11 A Guide for Teachers*. London: David Fulton

www.phys.soton.ac.uk University of Southampton School of Physics and Astronomy

FURTHER READING FURTHER READING FURTHER READING FURTHER READING

Burton, N. (2000) *Pocket Guides to the Primary Curriculum: Physical Processes*. Leamington Spa: Scholastic

Peacock, G., Sharp, J., Johnsey, R. and Wright, D., (2007) The Earth and beyond, Chapter 13 in *Primary Science: Knowledge and Understanding*, 3rd edition. Exeter: Learning Matters

Websites

http://seds.lpl.arizona.edu/nineplanets/nineplanets/

www.collinseducation.com/resources/ict%20activity/earth_FULL.swf simulation of Moon's journey around the Earth, etc.

www.nasa.gov/home/index.html massive resource bank

Glossary of terms

Absorb The take up of a gas by a solid or a liquid, or the take up of a liquid by a solid.

Absorption The process of absorbing or the action of being absorbed.

Acceleration The rate of increase of speed or velocity measured in m/s/s (or ms-2). When an object begins or is caused to move more quickly. (symbol a)

Active eye Model used by some learners to explain how they see objects. It requires light to go from their eye to the object (so they see because they are looking).

Adaptation Any change in structure/function of an organism that makes it better suited to its environment.

Amplitude The maximum difference of a vibration or oscillation from the point of equilibrium.

Animal cell See cell (1).

Asexual reproduction A form of reproduction in which new individuals are produced from a single parent without sexual reproduction.

Atom The smallest particle of an element that can exist. It consists of a positively charged nucleus surrounded by negatively charged electrons.

Axis An imaginary line through a body, about which it rotates.

Basic skills Activities that are commonly used to develop skills such as selecting or using equipment, drawing graphs, tables etc. as well as basic practical techniques such as measuring force or temperature.

Battery A number of electrical cells joined together.

Burn Flame or glow while consuming a fuel.

Burning Chemical combination with oxygen, involving the production of heat and light.

Camouflage The natural colouring or form of an animal which enables it to blend in with its surroundings thus evading predators.

Carbohydrate Any of a large group of organic compounds. The simplest are sugars, polysaccharides such as starch, and cellulose. They occur in foods and living tissues, and can be broken down to release energy.

Carnivore A carnivorous animal. An animal that eats meat.

Carnivorous plant Any plant that supplements the supply of nitrates by digesting small animals.

Carpel The female reproductive organ of a flower, consisting of an ovary, a stigma, and usually a style.

Cell (1) The structural and functional unit of most living organisms, consisting of cytoplasm and a nucleus enclosed in a membrane. (2) A device or unit in which electricity is generated using chemical energy or light, or in which electrolysis takes place.

Centrifugal force A force, arising from the body's inertia, which appears to act on a body moving in a circular path and is directed away from the centre around which the body is moving.

Change of state A change of matter in one physical phase (solid liquid or gas). The process of a substance changing from a solid to liquid to gas or vice versa.

Chart A sheet of information in the form of a table, graph, or diagram.

Chemical change (1) A change in which one or more new substances are produced with properties different from those of the starting substances. (2) A process in which reactants are changed into one or more different products. A chemical change occurs whenever compounds are formed or decomposed. During this reaction, there is a rearrangement of atoms that makes or breaks chemical bonds. This change is usually not reversible.

Chemical reaction When two chemicals react and a new compound forms.

Circuit A system of conductors and components forming a complete path for an electric current.

Classification The arrangements of organisms into a series of groups based on physical, anatomical or biochemical relationships.

Classify Arrange (a group) in classes according to shared characteristics.

Colloid Systems in which there are two or more phases where one is distributed in the other. Emulsions are colloidal systems where both substances are liquids. Gel, aerosols and foams are also other types of colloid.

Colour Sensation produced when light of different wavelengths enters the eye.

Combustion (1) The process of burning. (2) Chemical combination with oxygen, involving the production of heat and light.

Comet A small body that travels around the sun in an eccentric orbit.

Competition Interaction that occurs between two or more organisms, populations or species that share resources.

Compound A substance formed from two or more elements chemically united in fixed proportions. They cannot be separated by physical means.

Compress To force into less space.

Compression The action of compressing or being compressed.

Condensation The change of a vapour or gas into a liquid.

Control The part of an experiment used as a standard to compare experimental observations.

Corolla The petals of a flower, typically forming a whorl within the sepals.

Data logging The action of gathering data from an automatic device, control system, or sensor.

Denature Produce a structural change in a protein or a nucleic acid.

Density The mass of a substance per unit of volume.

Dependent variable A variable that cannot be arbitrarily selected and is determined by the independent variable.

Dependent variable This is the variable that is measured e.g. when investigating parachutes the dependent variable is the time taken to fall. Sometimes comparisons or rankings are used in place of standard units.

Diet The food needs of an organism.

Digestion The break down by a living organism of digested food material into chemically simpler substances that can be absorbed.

Dissolve (With reference to a solid) become or cause to become incorporated into a liquid so as to form a solution.

Dissolving The process whereby a solid is incorporated into a liquid so as to form a solution.

DNA Major constituent of the chromosome – deoxyribonucleic acid, a substance which is present in the cell nuclei of nearly all living organisms and is the carrier of genetic information.

Ductile 1. (of a metal) able to be drawn out into a thin wire.
2. able to be deformed without losing toughness.

Ductility The ability of certain metals to retain their strength when their shape is changed.

Durability Property of a substance to last.

Durable Hard-wearing.

Eclipse An obscuring of the light from one celestial body by the passage of another between it and the observer or between it and its source of illumination.

Ecosystem A biological community of interacting organisms and their physical environment.

Electric current A flow of electrons in an electrical conductor. The strength or rate of movement of the electricity is measured in amperes.

Electrical charge the quantity of unbalanced electricity in a body (either positive or negative) and construed as an excess or deficiency of electrons.

Electrical energy A form of energy related to the position of an electrical charge in an electrical field.

Electrical power Flow of current at a voltage, which is measured in watts (watts = amps x volts).

Electromagnet The centre consists of an iron core with a coil of insulated wire surrounding it. The core becomes magnetic only when an electric current is passed through the wire.

Electromagnetic spectrum The range of electromagnetic waves including: radio waves, infra red, visible light, ultraviolet and gamma rays.

Electromagnetic waves A wave that consists of an electric field in conjunction with a magnetic field oscillating with the same frequency.

Electron A stable negatively charged subatomic particle with a mass 1,836 times less than that of the proton, found in all atoms in groupings called shells around the nucleus.

Element A substance that cannot be decomposed into simpler substances e.g. gold, lead, oxygen, mercury etc.

Emulsion A colloid in which small particles of one liquid are dispersed in another liquid.

Endothermic reaction A chemical reaction in which energy has been taken in from the surroundings in the form of heat.

Energy Measure of a system's ability to do work.

Environment The physical, chemical and biological conditions of a region in which an organism lives.

Evaporate The change of state from a liquid into a vapour (gas) at a temperature below the boiling point of a liquid.

Evaporation The process of evaporating.

Evolution A gradual process by which the present diversity of plant and animal life arose from the simplest organisms.

Excrete The elimination of waste products that result from metabolic activity.

Exercise Muscular activity resulting in increased heart rate, oxygen uptake and metabolic rate. Important for health.

Exoskeleton Covering of the body of certain animals such as lobsters, crabs, tortoises, turtles, armadillos. It protects and supports the body. In some animals the exoskeleton needs to be shed to allow the animal to grow.

Exothermic reaction A chemical reaction in which energy is released into the surroundings in the form of heat.

Experiment A process or trial to test a scientific theory.

Exploration An important aspect of learning. The purpose of exploration is to allow time for observation and for pupils to become familiar with objects and to raise questions about the object.

Exploratory skills Skills developed during exploratory work including observation, questioning, pattern seeking, causal relationships (i.e. cause and effect), comparisons and use of vocabulary to describe and explain.

Fair test Experiment in which one condition (independent variable) affects another (dependent variable) by keeping all other conditions constant.

Fat A mixture of lipids that is solid at normal body temperature.

Feeding relationships One way in which living organisms in an ecosystem depend on each other for food and essential nutrients such as carbon and nitrogen, often takes the form of a feeding relationship.

Food Any nutritious substance that animals eat or drink or that plants absorb to maintain life and growth.

Food chain The transfer of energy from green plants through a sequence of organisms.

Food web A system of food chains that are linked to each other.

Force (symbol F) A force is a push or a pull. The SI unit of force is the newton (N). Forces always occur in equal and opposite action-reaction pairs.

Friction The force that resists the movement of one surface over another with which it is in contact.

Fruit The structure formed from the ovary of a flower usually after the ovules have been fertilised.

Galaxy A large collection of stars, together with gas and dust, held together by gravitational attraction.

Gametes A reproductive cell that fuses with another to form a zygote.

Genetic engineering The deliberate modification of an organism by manipulating its genetic material.

Graph A visual representation showing the relation between two variables.

Gravity A phenomenon associated with gravitational forces acting on any object that has mass and is situated within e.g. a planet or moon's gravitational field. The size of the gravitational force on a body's gravity depends on its mass.

Growth An increase in the dry weight of an organism through cell division and cell enlargement that can continue throughout the life of an organism. Woody plants growth continues throughout life whilst in mammals growth ceases at maturity.

Habitat The natural home or environment of an organism.

Hardness The property of being rigid and resistant to pressure not easily scratched; mineral hardness is measured on Mohs' scale.

Hazard A potential danger or an obstacle.

Herbivore An animal that feeds on vegetation.

Illustrative activity A practical activity that involves direction by the teacher at most stages of the process. These types of practical work are important because they provide the opportunity for pupils to learn important skills or procedures and also provide the opportunity for the practical work to illustrate some aspect of knowledge of science.

Image A representation of a physical object formed by a lens, mirror or other optical instruments.

Independent variable This is the variable that the tester chooses to change systematically.

Inertia A property of matter by which it continues in its existing state of rest or uniform motion in a straight line, unless changed by an external force.

Interdependence All organisms are affected by and depend on others. All animals ultimately depend on green plants for food and without microorganisms matter would not be re-cycled and reused. Some relationships are obvious as in food chains whilst others are more subtle e.g. symbiotic relationships.

Investigation Activities where ideas, predictions or hypotheses are tested and conclusions drawn in response to a question or problem.

Investigations These provide pupils with the opportunity to undertake complete or whole investigations where there are identifiable opportunities to:

- identify factors and change variables;
- identify factors or variables to measure or observe;
- allow choice by pupils.

Irreversible change A change in which one or more chemical elements or compound form new compounds. Whilst some reactions can to some extent react to give the original reactants in most cases this is negligible and so the reaction is said to be irreversible.

Kinetic energy Is energy of motion.

Kinetic theory A theory that explains the physical properties of matter in terms of the motions of its particles.

Latent heat A quality of heat absorbed or released when a substance changes its physical phase at a constant temperature.

Learning intention This is what the pupils are to learn. This should be the focus of the lesson. Learning intentions should focus upon knowledge, understanding, skills, procedures and attitudes in science over a period of time.

Learning outcome Specifically what pupils are expected to learn in a lesson. These are used for assessment purposes and are differentiated for different groups/individual pupils.

Light Form of electromagnetic radiation from about 390nm to 740 nm in wavelength to which the human eye is sensitive.

Loudness Amplitude of sound. Perception of sound intensity (the level of noise).

Luminescence The emission of light from a substance for any reason other than for a rise in its temperature (brightness).

Man-made material A manufactured material e.g. plastic. This term should not be used because it confuses learners. Non-naturally occurring is a more preferable term.

Mass The quantity of matter which a body contains, as measured by its resistance to acceleration or by the gravitational force it produces.

Material The matter from which something is or can be made.

Melt The change from a solid to liquid.

Melting The process of becoming a liquid.

Mineral A naturally occurring substance that has a characteristic chemical composition and crystalline structure.

Mixture A system of two or more distinct chemical substances. Homogenous atoms and molecules are interspersed e.g. mixtures of gases or in a solution. Heterogeneous mixtures have distinguishable phases unlike compounds mixtures can be separated by physical means.

Molecule One of the fundamental units forming a chemical compound. A group of atoms chemically bonded together, representing the smallest fundamental unit of a compound that can take part in a chemical reaction.

Mouth Opening of the alimentary canal. In most animals it is used for the ingestion of food.

Move Change or cause to change position.

Movement The process of change of position.

Muscle Tissue consisting of bundles of cells that can contract to cause movement or tension in the body. There are three types of muscles, voluntary e.g. joints, involuntary e.g. movement of intestine and bladder and cardiac muscle only in the heart.

Mutation Sudden random change in the genetic material of the cell that can cause it and the cells derived from it to differ in appearance or behaviour. Mutations occur naturally at a low rate and the majority of them are harmful. A small proportion may increase the organisms' ability to survive.

Natural selection The evolutionary process whereby organisms better adapted to their environment tend to survive and produce more offspring.

Naturally occurring material Exists naturally in nature.

Non-luminous Not bright or shining.

Nutrient A substance that provides nourishment essential for life and growth of an organism.

Nutrition The process by which organisms obtain energy for maintenance, growth and repair: heterotrophic used by animals fungi and some bacteria and autotrophic found in most plants and bacteria.

Octave Interval between two musical notes that have fundamental frequencies and describes the interval in terms of eight notes of a diatonic scale (low C to high c).

Ohm The SI unit of electrical resistance, transmitting a current of one ampere when subjected to a potential difference of one volt (Symbol: Ω)

Omnivore An animal that eats both plants and animal matter e.g. pigs.

Opaque Material that light cannot travel through.

Orbit (1) The regularly repeated elliptical course of a celestial object or spacecraft around a star or planet. (2) The path of an electron round an atomic nucleus. (3) Two sockets in the scull of vertebrates.

Organ A distinct part of an animal or plant adapted for a particular function, for example the heart or kidneys.

Organism An animal, plant or micro organism capable of reproduction, growth and maintenance.

Osmosis A process by which molecules of a solvent pass through a semi-permeable membrane from a less concentrated solution into a more concentrated one.

Ovary (1) Female reproduction organ in which eggs (ova) are produced. (2) Hollow base of a carpel of a flower containing one or more ovules.

Ovule Part of female reproduction organ of seed-bearing plants. After fertilisation the ovule becomes a seed.

Oxidation A chemical reaction with oxygen.

Ozone layer Layer of Earth's atmosphere where most of the ozone is concentrated 5–50 Km above the Earth's surface. It absorbs most of the solar ultra-violet radiation and protects living organisms on Earth.

Palate The roof of the mouth cavity of vertebrates.

Particle One of the fundamental components of matter.

Pasteurisation Treatment of milk to destroy disease-causing bacteria. Devised by Pasteur.

Periodic table Table of elements arranged in order of increasing proton number.

Permanent teeth Second and final set of teeth. Adult humans have 32. Consists of incisors, canines, molars and premolars.

Petal Each of the segments of the corolla of a flower.

Phases of the moon Shapes of the illuminated surface of the moon as seen from Earth.

Phloem Tissue that conducts food materials in vascular plants from leaves to where they are needed.

Phylum Category used in the classification of organisms.

Physical change (1) A change in which original substances remain unchanged and no new substances are produced. (2) A change in the form of matter but not in its chemical identity.

Pistil The female organs of a flower, comprising the stigma, style, and ovary.

Pitch The property of sound that indicates the highness or lowness in a sound or tone. Related to the rate of vibrations producing it.

Planet A celestial body moving in an elliptical orbit around a star.

Plant A living organism (such as a tree, grass, or fern) that absorbs water and inorganic substances through its roots and makes nutrients in its leaves by photosynthesis.

Plant cell Plant cells contain chloroplasts and a rigid cellulous cell wall.

Plaque Thin layer of organic material on the exposed surface of teeth containing dissolved food and bacteria. The bacteria metabolize sugar producing acid that can cause tooth decay.

Pluto Discovered in 1930 it is the outermost planet in the solar system that was downgraded to a dwarf planet in 2005.

Pollen Mass of grains containing the male gametes of seed plants.

Pollination Transfer of pollen from an anther to a stigma. Either of the same flower (self pollination) or different flower of same species (cross pollination).

Potential energy Energy possessed by a body by virtue of its position or state.

Practical work Opportunity to carry out 'hands on' practical experiences. These fall into a number of categories:

1. Investigations
2. Illustrative activities

3. Experiments
4. Basic skills
5. Observations

Predation Interaction between two animals in which one (predator) hunts, catches and kills the other (prey) for food.

Predator Animal that obtains its food from other animals.

Pressure (1) The continuous physical force exerted on or against an object by something in contact with it. (2) Measured in Pascals (SI unit symbol Pa).

Prey The source of food for a predator.

Primary consumer These feed primarily on plant material. They are herbivores – e.g. rabbits, caterpillars, cows, sheep and deer.

Primary producer Green plants capable of photosynthesis; the base of the food chain.

Protein Organic compounds found in all living things. These form structural components of body tissues and constitute an important part of the diet.

Proton Elementary particle with a positive charge and occurs in atomic nuclei.

Pulse Series of waves that pass along the arteries caused by pressure of blood pumped through the heart.

Pupil Central hole through which light enters the eye.

Quark Introduced in 1964. It is a sub atomic particle.

Radiant energy Energy transmitted as electromagnetic radiation (heat from the sun).

Radiation Energy travelling in the form of electromagnetic waves. A stream of particles from a radioactive source.

Rainbow Optical phenomena occurring when falling water droplets are illuminated by sunlight. Colours are produced by internal reflection of sunlight.

Rarefaction Is the reduction of a medium's density, the opposite of compression.

Rate of reaction The speed at which a chemical reaction takes place measured by a variety of means.

Reflect The return of heat, light, or sound without absorption.

Reflection The return of all or part of a beam of particles when it encounters a boundary. The angle of incidence equals the angle of reflection.

Refraction Change of direction as a ray of light passes from one medium to another. Caused by its change of speed.

Reliability How well a measured variable is consistent, stable, and uniform over repeated observations or measurements made under the same experimental conditions each time.

Reproduce Production of new individuals that are like the parent organisms.

Reproduction The action or process of reproducing.

Respiration A metabolic process in both animals and plants in which organic substances (sugar) are broken down into simpler products releasing energy. In most plants and animals the process requires oxygen and carbon dioxide is a waste product.

Reversible change (1) A change in which original substances remain unchanged and no new substances are produced. (2) A change in the form of matter, but not in its chemical identity.

Rhizome Horizontal underground stem such as strawberries.

Risk The likelihood of a hazard occurring.

Rust The oxide of iron.

Satellite A relatively small natural body that orbits a planet e.g. moon or an artificial body placed in orbit round the earth or another planet to collect information or for communication.

Scattering Light is deflected by the surface on which it falls.

Scheme of work Often termed 'medium-term plan'.

Scientific enquiry Is an umbrella term that encompasses many aspects of activity. National Curriculum (2000) denotes scientific enquiry as planning, obtaining and using evidence along with an understanding of the nature of scientific ideas. Exploration, illustrative and investigative activities would fall into this.

Scientific process Process and procedures used consistently when pupils are engaged in aspects of scientific enquiry.

Secondary consumer An organism that feeds on primary consumers: a carnivore.

Seed Developed from the ovule after fertilisation. The seed contains an embryo and food store to enable it to grow.

See-through Colloquial term for transparent. Should not be used as it encourages learners to use the active eye model.

Sensitive Quick to detect, respond to, or be affected by slight changes, signals, or influences.

Sensitivity One of the fundamental properties of all organisms that allows them to detect, interpret and respond to changes in the environment.

Sepal Each of the leaf-like parts of a flower that surround the petals, enclosing them when the flower is in bud.

Sexual reproduction A form of reproduction that involves the linking of two reproductive cells by a process called fertilisation.

Shadow The absence of light. An area of darkness formed on the surface when an object blocks the light from a source.

Shiny A surface that reflects light because it is smooth, clean, or polished.

Shoot Aerial part of a vascular plant consisting of stem supporting leaves buds and flowers.

Sight The ability to see.

Simulations An experiment that runs as a model of reality.

Skeleton Structure of an animal that allows for movement. It protects internal organs, is a framework for anchoring muscles and also production of blood cells in the bone marrow.

Skull Skeleton of the head that protects the brain.

Solar Of the sun.

Solar energy Electromagnetic energy from the sun.

Solar system (1) The sun together with the planets, asteroids, comets, etc. in orbit around it. (2) The name of the eight major planets, their natural satellites, asteroids, comets and meteoroids which move in an approximately circular orbit around the sun.

Solute The substance dissolved in a solvent forming a solution.

Solution A uniformly distributed mixture of a liquid with a gas or a solid.

Solvent The liquid in which another substance is dissolved to form a solution.

Sound A form of energy that causes vibration of particles at a frequency and intensity that can be heard.

Sound wave A wave of alternate compression and rarefaction by which sound travels through a medium.

Space (1) A three dimensional property of the Universe. (2) Part of the universe outside the Earth's atmosphere (outer space).

Spark (1) A small fiery particle thrown off from a fire, alight in ashes, or caused by friction. (2) A light produced by a sudden disrupted electrical discharge through the air.

Species A group of living organisms consisting of similar individuals capable of exchanging genes or interbreeding.

Spectrum A range of electromagnet energies arrayed in order of increasing wavelength.

Speed The ratio of the distance covered and the time taken for travel.

Speed of light The time taken for light to travel in a vacuum 2.99792458 x 10 (to the 8 ms-1)

Speed of sound The time taken for sound to travel in air at 20°C sound travels at 344ms-1. In water, at 20°C it travels at 1461 ms-1 and in steel at 20°C it travels at 5000 ms-1

Spore Spores are produced by plants fungi and bacteria. This is a reproductive cell that develops into a new individual without sexual reproduction.

Spring balance Also called a newtonmeter or forcemeter.

Stamen Male reproductive part of flower consists of anther on a filament.

Star A self luminous celestial body collected together in galaxies.

State of matter Name for three physical states in which matter exists i.e. solid, liquid or gas. Sometimes regarded as a fourth state of matter – plasma.

Stigma Tip of the carpel that receives pollen during pollination.

Stomach Part of the alimentary canal between the oesophagus and the small intestine. A muscular organ where ingested food is stored and the process of digestion begins. Some herbivorous animals have multi-chambered stomachs.

Strength The property of a material that enables it to withstand force.

Structured play Set up by the practitioner to meet previously planned learning outcomes, with a flexibility of approach.

Style A narrow extension of the ovary, bearing the stigma.

Survey A type of investigation that requires the collection of data e.g. counting the number of snails after it rains.

Suspension A mixture in which particles are suspended in a fluid.

Synthetic material Describes a material that has been artificially constructed and not from a natural source e.g. glass, concrete and plastics.

Table A set of facts or figures systematically displayed.

Tendon A flexible, but inelastic cord of strong fibrous tissue attaching a muscle to a bone.

Timbre The character or quality of a musical sound or voice as distinct from its pitch and intensity.

Tissue A collection of similar cells organized to carry out one or more functions.

Tooth Hard structures principally used for biting and chewing food.

Translucent Allowing light to pass through partially; semi-transparent.

Transparent Allowing light to pass through so that objects behind can be distinctly seen.

Tree A woody perennial plant, typically with a single stem or trunk growing to a considerable height and bearing lateral branches.

Tuber A swollen underground stem or root. It enables plants to survive through the winter or a drought and is also a method of propagation. A potato is a stem tuber and dahlia is an example of a root tuber.

Tuning fork A two pronged metal fork that produces a predetermined frequency when hit.

Universe All the matter, energy and space that exists.

Unstructured play Where the practitioner provides equipment, but there is no clear outcome intended. The role of the teacher here is to stand back from the activity and watch for more informal opportunities to take learning on from a child-initiated starting point. Learning is assessed on an individual basis.

Upthrust The upthust is the upward force exerted on the body by a liquid. The upthrust is equal to the weight of the water displaced.

Variation Differences between individuals of a species. Can result from environmental conditions or genetic change.

Vegetable The part of a edible plant not containing seeds.

Velocity The speed of something in a given direction. (symbol v).

Vertebrate Large group of animals with backbones includes birds, fish, reptiles, amphibians and mammals.

Vibrate Move with small movements rapidly to and fro.

Vibration A mechanical backwards and forwards movement about a fixed point e.g. the motion of a tuning fork or the movement of a reed in a clarinet.

Viscosity The resistance to flow of a liquid.

Vitamin One of a group of organic compounds essential for normal nutrition. They are important in the diet because they cannot be synthesized by the body.

Volt The unit of electromotive force in the SI system, the difference of potential that would carry one ampere of current against a resistance of one ohm. (symbol V SI unit of electrical potential)

Voltage The electromotive force or potential difference expressed in volts. (symbol V)

Volume The amount of space occupied by a body or mass of fluid. It should not be used to describe the degree of loudness of a sound.

Weed A wild plant growing where it is not wanted and in competition with cultivated plants.

Weight The force exerted on the mass of a body by a gravitational field.

Xylem A tissue that transports water and dissolved mineral nutrients in vascular plants. The walls can be thicker and the xylem contributes to the strength of a plant.

Zygote A cell resulting from the fusion of two gametes.

Appendix 1: ASKIS Research summary: The fair test

Table 3: 'Fair Test' has a special meaning in school science investigations. Below are some examples of how pupils have used these words. Please consider whether you think the use of these words is scientifically acceptable.

Statements made	Not acc. KS2 (%)	Not sure KS2 (%)	Acc. KS2 (%)	Not acc. KS3 (%)	Not sure KS3 (%)	Acc. KS3 (%)
To make it a **fair test**, I will make sure the force meter is in working order	63.6	17.4	19.0	83.3	10.7	6.2
To make a **fair test** of how good our pressure-pads are at detecting burglars, we must make the same person tread on each pad that we test	13.7	5.6	80.7	15.7	6.9	77.4
When we were testing whether light affected germination of seeds we made it **fair** by watering the seeds equally and putting them all on blotting paper to grow	15.0	8.9	75.7	7.7	11.2	81.1
We rolled a toy car down a ramp from different heights. We made it a **fair test** by always measuring from the bottom of the ramp to the nearest point of the car	16.8	15.4	65.7	21.9	18.8	59.2
We repeated the measures three times to make it more fair	34.0	24.0	42.0	72.0	10.6	17.2

A definition of a fair test, from Improving Science Education 5–14 (**www.ise5–14.org.uk**) says that a fair test is: Experiment in which one condition (independent variable) affects another (dependent variable) by keeping all other conditions constant.

Appendix 2: Health and safety

The following answers to the questions on page 23 are based on the idea that there is no greater risk of using them in school than in everyday life given from recognised practice, and are taken from guidance provided by either CLEAPSS or the ASE. However, your school policy may or may not agree with the view presented here, so it is imperative to check out all activities with your school before putting them into practice

1. **Fireworks: False**, this is highly dangerous. Both the risk and the hazard would be judged as high. The risk (the likelihood) would be high that the hazard (explosion with a spark from an electrical appliance) would occur. If it did and the children were gathered around the firework, blinding, and loss of limbs could result.
2. **Rechargeable batteries: Generally false**. This will depend on the school policy, which will be governed by the local authority. Many local authorities prevent schools from using rechargeable batteries, as they can get hot and as a result may cause burns. The risk of this happening is a medium one, but the child might receive an uncomfortable burn. Here there is a safe alternative. In this case non-rechargeable batteries would be the option every time as children are not being put in any risk of danger, however slight the alternative risk might be.
3. **Copper sulphate: True, but under supervision**. Copper sulphate is poisonous if ingested. So it should not be left around the classroom or school. Making crystals will help children to see that a dissolved material has not disappeared. This provides a very valuable experience. The amount of the chemical used should be small and the copper sulphate should be labelled and stored in a locked cupboard at all times when not in use. Other chemicals that make crystals such as alum or borax might be used instead, but again small quantities should be kept and any solution should be disposed of safely after the activity is completed.
4. **Keeping animals in school: False** – The type of animal and the care of the animal will determine whether it is safe to keep in a school. Children with allergies to fur or feather may have an impact upon what can be kept in individual classrooms. What happens to the animal at the weekend and the holiday time is also important. Animals have the right to be treated with care and consideration and it may be more sensible to have days when pets come in to school, or to 'adopt' an animal, e.g. from Chester zoo, rather than having a class pet that is ignored at night and left behind at weekends. If, however, all the issues related to care can be arranged in a way that is caring for the animal, a class pet can be a good way of learning about aspects of science. However, it is wise to fully research the needs of the animal and to identify any potential problems before an animal lives in your classroom, e.g. hamsters and gerbils are very popular, but when handled by excited pupils can issue a nasty bite. It is also important to think about the potential cost if the animal becomes sick and what might happen to any offspring if you keep a number of animals together. Hand washing and care with feeding and food is vital. You may wish to seek guidance from the RSPCA on the keeping of animals in school (**www rspsa.org.uk**).
5. **Plants: False**. Again this depends on the type of plants. Some plants will cause skin rashes when brushed against. Cacti are great to show the adaptation of leaves, but it is important to remind children that spikes hurt and may cause infections. It is important not to provide the experience, but to make children aware of the hazards. Some bulbs

e.g. daffodils are harmful if eaten, but the likelihood of most children eating one instead of planting one is low. However, while the general risk may be low in most classrooms, you must assess the risks within your classroom whilst not using this as an excuse not to undertake the activity. Looking in a publication like *Be Safe* helps, as it will give you the plants that cause most problems and those which are much more suited to use in the classroom.

6. **Blood: False** – there are many problems associated with blood and other bodily fluids in the classroom. Such activities are not recommended as the risks of transmitting diseases in the blood are too great and the consequences (the hazard), including HIV and Hepatitis are life-threatening (high). Carrying out such activities in most local authorities would constitute serious professional misconduct. You do not know what infections children may carry and you should not make assumptions. Children should be protected from each other and yourself, whenever blood and bodily fluids are present by wearing plastic gloves and behaving in a safe and sensible way. In most local authorities it is also not expected that children will be exposed to blood or spinal materials of animals. So many dissections are now not recommended in primary schools. If you feel you would like to carry one of these out, then it is vital that you first consult your school, the local authority and/or Cleapss (**http://www.cleapss.org.uk/**).
7. **Bacteria: False** – although this activity was recommend in the 'Horrible Science Series' by Nick Arnold where even a growing medium and instructions were provided this activity is not recommended. Indeed, bacteria should **never** be cultured (grown), as this again could result in life-threatening action, a high hazard, and the risk or likelihood of it happening, is also high. If you want children to see some negative effect of bacteria then simulation using ICT would be much more effective.
8. **Kettle: False** – the hazard here is the risk of scalding by boiling water or steam. The risk of this happening depends on supervision, the type of children and any unplanned-for distractions. The reason for the use of a kettle is a more pertinent issue. If you want to show that solutes dissolve more quickly in hot water, then children should not be given water hotter than 50° C. Water of this temperature should be provided for pupils in pump action containers that keep the temperature hot without the need for extra supply or heat. If you want to show insulation again 50° C is hot enough to show changes in the classroom and a ready supply of hot tap water would probably work well enough. However, you may wish to consider an alternative model if the kettle is to be used to represent the water cycle. An alternative model might even be more representative and meaningful. When, for example, would you see the sea or a puddle boil? When would either need a source of electricity? How does all that we see link to what the children see and understand about the water cycle in real life?
9. **Animals under the school building: it depends** – the hazard would be from the droppings and other animals that would be attracted by the left over food. Generally foxes would not come near the children, and are unlikely to attack, but you have to ask whether you would want to have the equivalent of dog mess near to where the children were working. Decisions in this case would depend on how many foxes there were and the cleaning facilities available. Again the answer requires a risk assessment.
10. **African Land Snails: False** – African land snails, like most animals can carry salmonella, so the hazards (at the extreme, vomiting and diarrhoea and occasionally death in the very young or very old), are all associated with non-hand washing. The risks will relate to whether the animals are handled and what supervision is available to ensure hand washing. The snails do not carry any other diseases and even if they themselves have meningitis, in order to catch this, children would have to eat the snail. Again, you need to risk assess as in the case of the keeping of animals, but those bred in England do not

carry meningitis, will not require heat, but will mate rapidly once more than one snail is kept together. You need to be prepared to keep and look after them on a long-term basis as they cannot be released into the local environment.

Appendix 3: Practical task: electricity

Be safe!

Never use rechargeable batteries for investigative work

Any electrical appliance used in school must comply with safety regulations.

Stress to children that investigations must only be carried out using low voltage batteries and **never** mains electricity.

Watch for misuse and waste of resources, always ensure a match between components and appropriate battery voltage.

Do not allow circuits to be left connected indefinitely.

Watch for children making 'short' circuits – this is dangerous as wires and batteries become very hot and run down quickly.

Trouble-shooting

If a circuit is not working check for:

Loose connections.

Buzzers connected to wrong terminals.

Short circuits.

Faulty components.

Incomplete circuits.

Wire insufficiently stripped.

Mismatch of battery/component voltage.

'Dud' batteries.

Appendix 4: Spinner activity

The type of material, size of spinner, adding weight (make paperclips of different sizes available), height of drop, holes in wing, number of holes, length of wing, width of wing, structure of blade, way it is dropped, height of drop, etc.]

Index

Added to the page number 'f' denotes a figure.